Soviet–Vietnam Relations and the Role of China, 1949–64

This book analyses Chinese influence on Soviet policies towards Vietnam and shows how China, beginning in the late 1940s, was assigned the role as the main link between Moscow and Hanoi.

Drawing on new information on the Sino-Soviet-Vietnamese relationship in the early 1960s, this volume offers a fascinating insight into communication within the Communist camp. As long as this functioned well, Beijing's role as Moscow's major partner in Vietnam was a success. Moscow could focus on other, more pressing, issues while Beijing took care of Vietnam. With the Sino-Soviet split in the open, especially from 1963 onwards, Moscow was forced to make the vital decision on whether to support the Vietnamese communists. This book shows how the Soviet failure to understand the Vietnamese commitment to reunification, combined with the growing tensions between Moscow and Beijing, reduced Soviet influence in Hanoi in a significant period leading up to the US intervention in Vietnam.

The author has used two particular approaches, the leverage of smaller states on superpower politics and the validity of ideology in foreign policy analysis, to explain the dynamics of Soviet perceptions of the Chinese role in Vietnam, as well as to determine from what point Moscow began to perceive Beijing as a liability rather than an asset in their dealings with Vietnam.

This book will be of great interest to students of Cold War history, International History and Asian politics in general.

Dr Olsen received her doctoral degree in History from the University of Oslo in 2005 and has worked within the field of New Cold War History since 1993. Her main research interests include Soviet foreign policy towards Vietnam and China and the role of ideology in foreign policy. Dr Olsen now works in the Norwegian Ministry of Defence.

Cass Series: Cold War History
Series Editors: Odd Arne Westad and Michael Cox
ISSN: 1471–3829

In the new history of the Cold War that has been forming since 1989, many of the established truths about the international conflict that shaped the latter half of the twentieth century have come up for revision. The present series is an attempt to make available interpretations and materials that will help further the development of this new history, and it will concentrate in particular on publishing expositions of key historical issues and critical surveys of newly available sources.

1. **Reviewing the Cold War: Approaches, Interpretations, and Theory**
   Odd Arne Westad (ed.)

2. **Rethinking Theory and History in the Cold War**
   Richard Saull

3. **British and American Anticommunism before the Cold War**
   Marrku Ruotsila

4. **Europe, Cold War and Co-existence, 1953–1965**
   Wilfred Loth (ed.)

5. **The Last Decade of the Cold War: From Conflict Escalation to Conflict Transformation**
   Olav Njølstad (ed.)

6. **Reinterpreting the End of the Cold War: Issues, Interpretations, Periodizations**
   Silvo Pons and Federico Romero (eds)

7. **Across the Blocs: Cold War Cultural and Social History**
   Rana Mitter and Patrick Major (eds)

8. **US Paramilitary Assistance to South Vietnam: Insurgency, Subversion and Public Order**
   William Rosenau

9. **The European Community and the Crises of the 1960s: Negotiating the Gaullist Challenge**
   N. Piers Ludlow

10. **Soviet–Vietnam Relations and the Role of China, 1949–64: Changing Alliances**
    Mari Olsen

Soviet–Vietnam Relations and the Role of China, 1949–64

Changing alliances

Mari Olsen

Routledge
Taylor & Francis Group

LONDON AND NEW YORK

First published 2006
by Routledge
2 Park Square, Milton Park, Abingdon, Oxon OX14 4 RN

Simultaneously published in the USA and Canada
by Routledge
270 Madison Ave, New York, NY 10016

Routledge is an imprint of the Taylor & Francis Group

© 2006 Mari Olsen

Typeset in Times by
Integra Software Services Pvt. Ltd, Pondicherry, India
Printed and bound in Great Britain by
Biddles Ltd, King's Lynn

British Library Cataloguing in Publication Data
A catalogue record for this book is available from the British Library

Library of Congress Cataloging in Publication Data
Olsen, Mari.
   Soviet–Vietnam relations and the role of China, 1949–64 : changing
alliances / Mari Olsen.—1st ed.
      p.   cm.—(Cass series—Cold War history ; 10)
   Includes bibliographical references and index.
   ISBN 0–415–38474–5 (hardback)
   1. Vietnam (Democratic Republic)—Foreign relations—Soviet Union.
   2. Soviet Union—Foreign relations—Vietnam (Democratic Republic)
   3. Vietnam (Democratic Republic)—Foreign relations—China.
   4. China—Foreign relations—Vietnam (Democratic)   5. Vietnam—
History—1945–1975.   I. Title.   II. Series.
   DS560.69.S65057 2006
   327.597047′09′045—dc22

ISBN10: 0–415–38474–5
ISBN13: 978–0–415–38474–2

Contents

Acknowledgements   ix
List of Abbreviations   xi
Introduction   xiii

1   **Choosing sides: The Democratic Republic of Vietnam and the World, 1945–1949**   1

The DRV's search for allies 1
Soviet strategies in Southeast Asia 4
Vietnamese diplomatic initiatives in Bangkok and Moscow 5
Renewed Soviet interest in Asia 11

2   **Setting the stage: The Soviet Union, China and the First Indochina War, 1949–1953**   13

Moscow and the Communist victory in China 14
Recognition 16
The Franco-Vietnamese War 21
Recognition and new challenges 26

3   **The end of the war and the Geneva conference, 1953–1954**   28

Preparing for the conference 29
The final offensive 36
Negotiating in Geneva 38
Geneva and the future of Soviet–Vietnamese relations 44

4   **Together for Communism? Sino-Soviet cooperation and the rebuilding of North Vietnam, 1954–1957**   48

Reconstruction and consolidation in Vietnam 49
Military cooperation and Chinese withdrawal 53

Sino-Soviet relations and the Geneva agreement 55
Hanoi and the Twentieth Congress 59
Land reform and its critics 62
Moscow, Beijing and Hanoi's new Southern strategy 66
A balancing act 70

**5   Reunification by revolution? The Soviet and Chinese
role in Vietnamese reunification plans, 1957–1961**   72

Accepting two Vietnams 73
Renewed interest in the Geneva agreement 76
Sino-Soviet cooperation 77
The Lao Dong debates its policy on reunification 79
Embarking on a new Southern strategy 84
Mediating the emerging Sino-Soviet conflict 88
Moscow and the new Southern strategy 90
The end of diplomacy? 92

6   The fight over Laos, 1961–1962   94

The civil war in Laos 95
Calls for a Geneva conference on Laos 97
Negotiations begin in Geneva 100
A temporary setback 105
Assistance to Laos 108
Geneva: A power struggle? 111

7   From disinterest to active support, 1962–1965   113

Soviet perceptions of China in Vietnam 114
Tougher frontlines within the Communist camp 118
Attempts to improve Soviet–Vietnamese relations 121
Hanoi's turn to China 125
*Moscow and the result of the 9th Plenum
   of the Lao Dong 129*
The tide is turning 132
From disinterest to active support 133

Conclusions: Changing alliances   136
*Appendix 1: Politburo and Secretariat of the Lao Dong
   Central Committee*   151

Appendix 2: Economic assistance and specialists from the
    Socialist camp to the DRV, 1955–1962   155
Appendix 3: Soviet ambassadors to Vietnam, 1954–1965   157
Archives in Moscow, Russia   159
Notes   161
Bibliography   193
Index   199

Acknowledgements

This study would never have been completed without encouragement and good advice from a large number of people. I am indebted to my main supervisor, Odd Arne Westad at LSE. He has played an important role in my academic work since 1993.

This book is based on my doctoral dissertation written while I was a doctoral student at the International Peace Research Institute, Oslo (PRIO). My supervisor at PRIO, Hilde Henriksen Waage, has been an important source of inspiration. PRIO director and Vietnam specialist, Stein Tønnesson, has shared with me his indepth knowledge of Vietnam and Indochina and contributed with numerous comments and good advice. I would also like to thank Pavel Baev, librarian Odvar Leine, and his assistant Olga Baeva for their assistance and support over the years.

I owe my knowledge of the Russian archives to senior researcher Sven G. Holtsmark at the Norwegian Institute for Defence Studies (IFS) in Oslo. Sven has been my guide to the archives since my first working trip to Moscow in the spring of 1994. I could surely not have done this without his support, encouragement and advice. I am also grateful to IFS for publishing my Cand. Philol. thesis and providing me with a working place while writing my doctoral proposal.

Working in the Moscow archives has not always been easy and has taught me a lot about patience. However, that is not the fault of the excellent staff, especially in my main archive, the Archive of the Foreign Ministry of the Russian Federation (AVP RF). The AVP RF reading room staff all deserve special thanks for their kind assistance during my frequent stays since the mid-1990s: Sergei Vitalevich Pavlov, Larissa Ivanovna Semichastova, Galina Alekseevna Chuliga, Natalija Revazovna Chekerija, and not least the archivist in charge of the Vietnam and China collections, Elisabeta Igorevna Guseva. Over the years I have also enjoyed the assistance of many other reading room staff and archivists. Thank you all. I am also greatly indebted to the assistance of the staff at both Central Committee archives: the pre-1953 archives, Russian State Archive of Socio-Political History (RGASPI), and the post-1953 archive, the Russian State Archive of Contemporary History (RGANI).

A number of people have contributed with valuable support, comments and encouragement to this project from the start. Among these are colleagues and fellow doctoral students at PRIO, doctoral students at the University of Oslo and abroad, fellow historians working in the Moscow archives, and friends. Some of the people I would like to thank are: Ragna Boden, Lorenz M. Luthi, Sophie Quinn-Judge, Galina Murasheva, Nguyen Vu Tung, Luu Doan Huynh, Ranveig Gausdal, Arne Røksund, Inger Skjelsbæk, Elise F. Barth and Åshild Kolås for their support and encouragement during the course of this project – and to the rest of my friends – thank you!

Last, but not least, I would like to thank those who have remained my main inspiration during these years – my husband, Stig Rune, and our daughter, Aurora – for their love and support.

All the people mentioned here are of course without blame for this study's many insufficiencies – I am solely responsible for all conclusions.

Oslo, 27 April 2005
Mari Olsen

Abbreviations

ARVN	Army of the Republic of Vietnam (South Vietnamese)
CC	Central Committee
CCP	Chinese Communist Party
CMAG	Chinese Military Assistance Group
CPAG	Chinese Political Assistance Group
CPSU	Communist Party of the Soviet Union
DPRK	Democratic People's Republic of Korea (North Korea)
DRV	Democratic Republic of Vietnam
GRU	Main Intelligence Directorate (*Soviet foreign and domestic military intelligence*)
ICC	International Control Commission
KGB	Committee on State Security
Lao Dong	Dang Lao Dong Viet Nam (Vietnamese title of the VWP)
MAAG	Military Assistance Advisory Group
MID	Soviet Ministry of Foreign Affairs
NLF	National Liberation Front of South Vietnam (also NLF(SV))
PAVN	People's Army of Vietnam (North Vietnamese)
PLA	People's Liberation Army
PRC	People's Republic of China
RVN	Republic of Vietnam (from 23 October 1955)
SEAD	Southeast Asia Department (*sub-department in MID*)
SEATO	Southeast Asia Treaty Organization
SVN	State of Vietnam (to 22 October 1955)
USSR	Union of Soviet Socialist Republics
VNFF	Vietnam Fatherland Front
VWP	Vietnam Worker's Party

Introduction

In July 1949, shortly before the Communist victory in China, Liu Shaoqi, one of Mao Zedong's chief lieutenants, made a secret visit to Moscow. During the meetings in Moscow, Liu and Josef Stalin discussed China's future role in the world, as well as the future relationship between Moscow and Beijing. As part of the discussions, Stalin proposed an arrangement which had the character of a division of labour, in which China should take on responsibility for helping what he called 'national and democratic revolutionary movements in colonial, semi-colonial, and subordinate countries [...].'[1] He emphasized that China was in a much better position than the Soviet Union to play such a role in Asia.

Stalin's vision of the future labour division between the Soviets and the Chinese soon became visible in Soviet policies towards the Democratic Republic of Vietnam (DRV). On 18 January 1950, when the Chinese Communists, less than three months after the declaration of the People's Republic of China (PRC), recognized the DRV, Moscow followed, announcing its recognition on 30 January. The decision to establish diplomatic relations marked the start of the official Soviet–DRV relationship. Both the Soviet and Chinese recognitions were of vital importance to the Vietnamese leaders, who, at the time, were in the middle of a war against the French. But in a short-term practical perspective, it was the victory of the Chinese Communist Party (CCP) in 1949–50 that had the strongest impact on the Vietnamese situation, as the CCP immediately began to support the Vietnamese in their struggle.

The Soviets, on the other hand, seemed from the early days content with leaving the practical responsibility to Beijing. The change of power in China strongly influenced Moscow's view on the region and, as a result, forced the Soviet leadership to pay more attention to the Asian continent. Thus, for the decades following 1950, the Communist victory in China and, with it, the dominant role of the new Communist state in Asia would have a profound influence on the future direction of Soviet policies towards Vietnam.

The aim of this study is twofold. On the one hand, it is an analysis of Soviet policies towards Vietnam from the establishment of the PRC in October 1949 until the late autumn of 1964. A part of this is a discussion of how the Soviet leadership evaluated developments in Soviet–Vietnamese relations taking place during this period and what they expected to achieve with regard to the relationship. On the other hand, it is an analysis of how Soviet leaders from Josef Stalin to Nikita Khrushchev perceived China's role in Vietnam relative to the Soviet role, and how these perceptions influenced the Soviet–Vietnamese relationship. The main emphasis will be on explaining how and when Moscow's enthusiasm for the active Chinese role in Vietnam came to an end – or, in other words, from what point was Beijing's involvement in Vietnam perceived as a liability, rather than an asset, in the strategies of Soviet policy makers.

Previous accounts

Both classical and recent works on Soviet foreign policy and on Soviet–Vietnamese, Sino-Soviet and Sino-Vietnamese relations have inspired this study. While completing my Candidata philologiae[2] thesis on relations between the Soviet Union and the Vietnamese Communists in the latter half of the 1950s, I became increasingly interested in the influence China exercised on this relationship.[3] The specific question of how the Chinese role in Vietnam was perceived by the leadership in Moscow, by the relevant departments in the Soviet foreign ministry and by Soviet diplomats in both Hanoi and Beijing remains to be the main topic of an analysis based on available Soviet documents and literature. This study aims to fill that gap and to expand our knowledge of Soviet perceptions of their prime ally, and rival-to-be, in Southeast Asia.

In classical works on Soviet foreign policy, Moscow's role in Vietnam is characterized as passive in the early years, dictated by its relations with China, but not to the extent that Soviet policy makers would allow Vietnam to 'lapse exclusively into the Chinese sphere'.[4] A common conclusion is that, in spite of the low Soviet interest in the area, Moscow had a high degree of leverage on the Vietnamese Communists and that Hanoi would not make a decision to resume armed struggle to reunify Vietnam unless it had been sanctioned by the Soviets in advance.[5] These conclusions were made at a time when access to primary sources on the Soviet side was a far-fetched fantasy at best. During the 1980s, most scholars working on Soviet–Vietnamese relations subscribed to the theory that the Vietnamese Communists were loyal clients of the Soviet Union, unable to pursue policies that would gain their cause and reduced to a pawn in a Great Power puzzle.[6]

The current work falls within the field of new Cold War history and is an attempt to complement the already existing works on Soviet–Vietnamese relations by adding a new perspective. So far three larger studies and several articles based on Soviet documents have become central in the new history of Soviet foreign relations with Indochina.[7] These new works have further expanded our views on the Soviet–Vietnamese relationship and contest previous assumptions of Moscow's leverage in Hanoi, especially in important questions such as the means and methods used to achieve Vietnamese unification. Access to fresh sources has shown that the DRV's decision to launch armed struggle in order to supplement the diplomatic struggle for reunification was made in spite of Soviet disapproval.[8]

In his two works on Soviet–Vietnamese relations, Russian scholar Ilya V. Gaiduk sees Vietnam as a problem that should be eliminated from the Soviet foreign policy agenda to prevent it from becoming a disturbing element for other, more important issues, such as Soviet relations with the United States and détente with the West. In the years from 1954 to 1963, Gaiduk views Vietnam first and foremost as a 'thorny issue' in Moscow's relations with the West. He claims that the Soviet wish for peace in Southeast Asia was dictated by this attitude, and not so much by a peaceful disposition on the part of the Soviet leaders. Moscow's main problem was, according to Gaiduk, its failure to dictate orders to the Vietnamese, and also a lack of allies that could help the Soviets discourage the Vietnamese from their military plans, combined with the escalating Sino-Soviet dispute, which finally made Moscow decide in favour of a disengagement from Indochina in the early 1960s.[9]

Similar arguments prevail in his account of the relationship in the period from 1964 to 1973.[10] In this work, emphasis is on how the growing Sino-Soviet split accelerated the rapprochement in Soviet–DRV relations, while at the same time forcing Moscow to be very careful in handling its Vietnamese allies in the new situation. He underlines that, although Moscow did prevail as the main provider of assistance to the Vietnamese, Chinese influence remained strong. According to his findings, the Vietnamese skilfully manoeuvred between Moscow and Beijing and thus preserved their independence, formulating their political aims while at the same time becoming more and more dependent on material assistance from their allies. He claims that the Soviet Union never obtained monopoly on such assistance because its influence was wrecked by that of China throughout the war. Gaiduk further argues that the Soviet Union was the only winner in the Vietnam War because it was able to promote itself as an ardent supporter of the principles of proletarian internationalism, leading to a position of status within the world Communist movement. Unfortunately, Moscow was not able to use the devastating experience of the American involvement in Vietnam to avoid similar failures of its own later.[11]

In view of Gaiduk's good access to sources from the Russian archives, his work on the latter part of the 1950s adds surprisingly little new information to the history of Soviet–Vietnamese relations in the period. The major problem seems to be a preoccupation with the American side of the story, combined with a predisposed view of the Soviets as interest-driven only. As a result, he fails to properly grasp both the climate in the bilateral relations, and the possible impact of factors such as ideology on the relations between Moscow and Hanoi. Additional problems are the gap of time between the two studies and his failure to properly explain why the Soviet Union took over from China as Hanoi's major beneficiary from late 1964.

French historian Benoit de Tréglodé has undertaken research in several Russian archives, focusing on the early formative years of the Soviet–Vietnamese relationship. He shows how Soviet–Vietnamese relations were re-established after the Second World War largely due to Vietnamese efforts out of their representative office in Bangkok in 1947 and 1948. From a Vietnamese point of view, however, these attempts were unsuccessful, and the Vietnamese were obliged to wait for the success of the Chinese Communists before they could receive substantial assistance in their war against the French.[12]

The many new books and articles released on Sino-Vietnamese relations based on Chinese sources have been of undeniable value and a great inspiration for this study. Qiang Zhai's *China and the Vietnam Wars, 1950–1975*, is a detailed analysis on the development of the Sino-Vietnamese relationship, starting with the Chinese recognition of the DVR in January 1950. Zhai's analysis of Mao's preoccupation with the Soviet factor in the making of China's foreign policy forms a particularly interesting background for my work on Chinese influence on Soviet policies. Chen Jian's *Mao's China and the Cold War* includes several articles on China's involvement in the two Vietnam Wars as well as articles on the Sino-Soviet relationship, and Ang Cheng Guan's *Vietnamese Communists' Relations with China and the Second Indochina Conflict, 1956–1962* aims to show the gradual change in Beijing's attitude towards the Vietnamese Communists' intensification of the reunification battle, taking into account domestic policies in both countries, the role of individual leaders and the changing international conditions, especially within the Communist bloc. Without these and similar works on Chinese foreign policy the completion of the current study would have been impossible.[13]

Another topic which has benefited from the release of sources from both Soviet and Chinese archives is, of course, the history of Sino-Soviet relations. Several works on the topic, both classical and recent, have helped define ideas for the present study.[14] Among the more recent works shedding light on this conflict are Vladislav Zubok and Constantine Pleshakov's *Inside the Kremlin's Cold War*, and O.A. Westad (ed.) *Brothers in Arms: The Rise and Fall of the Sino-Soviet Alliance, 1945–1963*, a collection of articles by former Soviet, Chinese and American historians.[15] In addition to the works mentioned above, a significant effort to publish documents and articles on the Sino-Soviet-Vietnamese relationship has been made by the Cold War International History Project (CWIHP) at the Woodrow Wilson Center in Washington D.C.[16]

Over the last few years a number of new studies have appeared that further explain the Vietnamese side of the story. Of particular interest to the present study are the works by American historians Mark Philip Bradley and Robert K. Brigham. Bradley's work *Imagining Vietnam and America* analyses the failure to establish relations between the United States and the DRV and shows how predetermined perceptions of the other disturbed the US–DRV relationship in the pre-Cold War years.[17] Brigham's study of the foreign policy of the National Liberation Front of South Vietnam (NLF(SV)) is the first of its kind looking at the complex relationship between the NLF in the south and the Vietnamese Communist leadership in the north. Brigham argues in this study that the Front was neither a puppet of Hanoi nor an autonomous organization.[18]

Sources and methods

This is a study of Soviet policies towards Vietnam in the light of the triangular relationship between Moscow, Hanoi and Beijing. It is written from a Soviet point of view, and the primary sources used come from several former Soviet archives. However, this is not only a bilateral study nor a complete triangular study, but rather a study of how the bilateral relationship between two countries (the Soviet Union and the DRV) was influenced by the policies of a third country that has close relations with both, namely the PRC.

These distinctions are important because they determine the sources and perspectives of this study and challenge the author to define the possible pitfalls inherent in choosing such an approach. The exclusive use of Soviet primary sources is not unproblematic, and as an author one faces several methodological problems. I would like to single out four: The first is related to the problem of studying a triangle from only one side. I have compensated for the problem of one-sidedness inherent in using only Soviet sources through extensive use of scholarly works written by experts on Chinese and Vietnamese foreign policy. A second critical problem has been gaps in the source material. A full coverage will never be possible, but by using several archives and a wider interpretation of existing sources, a satisfactory account should still be possible. The last two problems circle around the question of sources and how they are used: first, to what extent they reflect what I am looking for, and second, how key issues and approaches will influence the choice of sources. These four problems are considerable, and with these in mind I hope to have reduced the possibility of a bias that would seriously undermine the project's main purpose – namely to describe and analyse how the Soviet view of China influenced Moscow's perceptions of and actions towards Vietnam.

The main bulk of documents for this study has been retrieved from the Foreign Policy Archives of the Russian Federation (Arkhiv Vneshnei Politiki Rossiyskoy Federatsii (AVP RF)) and from the two Central Committee archives: the pre-1953 archive, Russian State Archive of Socio-Political History (Rossiiskii Gosudarstvennyi Arkhiv Sotsial'no-Politicheskoi Istorii (RGASPI))[19], and the post-1953 archive, the Russian State Archive of Contemporary History (Rossiiskii Gosudarstvennyi Arkhiv Noveishei Istorii (RGANI))[20].

Of these three archives, the Foreign Policy archive contains the largest available holdings on Soviet–Chinese and Soviet–Vietnamese relations and contains documents for the entire period covered in this study. In addition, it also contains materials on Soviet relations with Laos and Cambodia, as well as collections from the work of the two conferences in Geneva: the 1954 conference on Korea and Indochina, and the 1962 conference on Laos. For the period after 1953, relevant documents are stored in the RGANI. Two parts of this archive have been of particular interest: the international department responsible for relations with ruling parties in Socialist countries, and the propaganda department.[21] While working in this study I have had good access to files in the AVP RF and have gone through all available relevant materials from the Vietnam fund from 1947 to 1965, the China fund for the same period, the Geneva conference fund (1954/1961–62), and to a lesser extent the Laos fund, as well as several Foreign Minister and Deputy Foreign Minister funds for the relevant years.[22]

The Soviet archives contain documents in several different categories such as memorandums, analytic and merely descriptive reports of events, instructions to ambassadors, suggestions to, and resolutions by, the Central Committee and the Politburo, and a large amount of records of conversations. All conversations between Soviet representatives and local officials, as well as Soviet ministers and deputy ministers' conversations with foreign officials at home and abroad are recorded and filed in chronological order in the archives. Documents that account for direct meetings, confrontations between Soviet officials and locals and in particular the Soviet ambassadors' conversations are particularly useful to understand the cultural conceptions that influenced how they saw the Vietnamese and Chinese.

Approaches and theoretical framework

In this study, two particular approaches, the leverage of smaller states on superpower politics and the validity of ideology as a useful concept for analysis of international politics, will be used in an attempt to better explain the dynamics of Soviet perceptions of the Chinese role in Vietnam. With access to more and more materials from both sides of the conflict, new possible frameworks for the study of the Cold War have emerged. And with the new materials a need for new approaches has developed contending that the complex relations between states during this period cannot be fully understood on the basis of the classical schools of interpretation of the Cold War.[23] Nor can these schools explain all aspects of the dynamics in the triangular relationship between Moscow, Hanoi and Beijing. Thus, to fully comprehend the history of Soviet–Vietnamese relations from the late 1940s until the mid-1960s, it is necessary to complement classical theories of the Cold War with new approaches and theoretical explanations.

New sources and new research have highlighted the fact that during the Cold War the policies of many smaller, and more peripheral, states had a much more significant impact on the decision-making of the superpowers than was previously thought. But what can Soviet sources reveal about the leverage of a smaller client state on the formation of Great Power policy decisions? This study will examine whether this applied to the Soviet–Vietnamese relationship. To what extent did Hanoi, rather than listening to its larger allies, first and foremost follow its own independent policies, at times regardless of whether these were approved by its allies? And did this behaviour impact Soviet policy towards Vietnam? Recent studies based on fresh sources point to a more complex relationship between Moscow and Hanoi than what was previously assumed and also refute some of the earlier arguments on the relationship of strength between the two countries.[24] Both Soviet and Chinese sources seem to support the picture of a much more independent and strong-minded Vietnamese leadership than previously assumed by historians in the field.[25]

A second approach is to examine more closely the role of ideology. Ideas, pre-existing systems of beliefs and values – all these are names that attempt to explain the very content of the category more commonly named ideology. But is it usable – can it be applied to the history of the Cold War and constitute a useful framework for analysis? During the Cold War, ideology was seen as a tool of limited relevance in helping us understand Soviet policies. Access to new sources have modified that view, and the impact of ideology now seems to be the major new finding after more than ten years with at least limited access to archives in the former Soviet Union, Eastern Europe and China.[26]

There is yet no universally, or even generally, accepted understanding of the term 'ideology' and its role in politics. Thus one of the main problems in the use of 'ideology' within an interpretative framework is how to define it. What is, within a Soviet policy framework, Soviet 'real politik'? Could it be that what we define as 'ideological' was considered to be 'real politik' and interest-driven in the eyes of Soviet policy makers? In the sources now available the evidence that ideology was taken seriously, especially by Soviet officials and leaders, is overwhelming. In forums never intended for public scrutiny, both Soviet leaders and officials articulated ideological principles and at times even cited the classics of Marxism–Leninism to support specific positions. According to Vojtech Mastny there was no double book-keeping.[27] Others have described the reading of declassified Soviet communist documents as entering into 'a conceptual world whose basic assumptions and categories are fundamentally different from our own'.[28]

With these reflections on the concept of ideology we have to ask ourselves to what extent the new sources can help us define whether ideology played an important role and, if it did, in what way? How important was it in Soviet foreign policy-making during the Cold War, and to what extent may it help us to better understand the complex relationships within the Socialist camp? According to William C. Wohlforth, a stronger emphasis on the role of ideology might help to explain why the relatively weak Soviet Union often seemed so keen to compete with the wealthy West. And also why Moscow took actions that only fostered cooperation between its adversaries, and why, when realizing the cost of such behaviour, the Soviet Union did not stand back from these overextended commitments.[29]

The main aim of this study is to evaluate the influence of the PRC on Soviet policy-making towards Vietnam, and thus fill a gap in the already existing literature on Soviet–Vietnamese relations. Whereas the general international situation did, of course, play an important part in Soviet policy makers' considerations when planning policies towards Vietnam, the situation with China was special, in relation both to Vietnam and to the Soviet Union. Moscow depended on Chinese practical assistance, Chinese knowledge of Vietnam, and in several cases the Chinese ability to put pressure on or restrain the Vietnamese. As long as the Sino-Soviet relationship functioned well, Beijing's role as Moscow's major partner in Vietnam was a success because it enabled the Soviet leaders to focus on other issues while ensuring that the Chinese took care of the situation in Vietnam. However, once Sino-Soviet relations began to deteriorate, the more aggressive Chinese stance with regard to developments in Vietnam, especially from 1963 onwards, forced the Soviets to engage themselves more actively and make the vital decision on whether to support the Vietnamese Communists or not.

One of the major shortcomings of earlier studies of Soviet–Vietnamese relations has been the exaggerated focus on Moscow's power in Hanoi. New sources available today highlight the fact that during the Cold War many smaller actors had a stronger position in their relationship with larger powers than previously thought. Such was also the case in Vietnam. Neither the Soviets nor the Chinese expected the Vietnamese to act as independently as they sometimes did. This study will show that in the early phases of the Soviet–Vietnamese relationship, and especially in the years up to 1949, it was the Vietnamese, and not the Soviets, who played the most active role in seeking and establishing contact with the other. During the later part of the 1950s, and especially with regard to the shift from diplomatic to military struggle to achieve a unified Vietnam made during the 15th Plenum of the Lao Dong in January 1959, the Vietnamese made their own decisions regardless of, and even at times in opposition to, the Soviets (and also the Chinese).

In spite of the many new sources indicating that ideology played an important role as part of Soviet foreign policy thinking, existing studies of the Soviet–Vietnamese relationship have paid surprisingly little attention to this side of the story. Thus, another argument of this study is that ideological considerations did play a part in Soviet foreign policy planning towards Vietnam. The Soviet leaders were convinced that the Vietnamese should learn from the Soviet experience, and in many areas Soviet advisors attempted to transmit Soviet ideas and plans to the DRV leadership. At the same time there was a strong conviction among the DRV leaders that the Soviet Union and China possessed the models necessary to rebuild and re-strengthen Vietnamese society. These mechanisms explain why practical cooperation between the Soviets and the Chinese with regard to Vietnam lasted longer than suggested by the existing literature and the growing ideological differences at the time. Even during the very early years of the 1960s, when the polemics were rather strong, and the Soviets had withdrawn their advisors from China, Moscow and Beijing were able to cooperate in Vietnam and Indochina.

1   Choosing sides

The Democratic Republic of Vietnam and the World, 1945–1949

The Democratic Republic of Vietnam (DRV) was established in August–September 1945, in the immediate aftermath of the Japanese surrender in the Second World War. In the so-called August Revolution, revolutionary committees paying allegiance to the Communist-led Vietminh[1] seized power in all main parts of Vietnam and established the new Democratic Republic, with Ho Chi Minh as president. The insurrection was brought about on local initiative, with no significant involvement by either the Chinese Communist Party (CCP) or the Communist Party of the Soviet Union (CPSU). Indeed, the successful August Revolution seems to have taken Communists worldwide by surprise, and there was virtually no reporting of the events in Indochina in the international Communist press.[2]

After the August Revolution, the DRV leaders, in particular President Ho Chi Minh, initiated an active search for allies. In the latter part of the 1940s, he and his envoys actively sought support from both the United States and the Soviet Union, but without any significant effect. The purpose of this chapter is first and foremost to analyse the role of these initial contacts between the Vietnamese and the Soviets in the period leading up to Soviet recognition of the DRV in January 1950, while at the same time evaluating Soviet views of the early years of the Franco-Vietnamese war, and also the first Chinese Communist Party (CCP) attempts to support the Vietnamese Communists.

The DRV's search for allies

One author has argued that 'Vietnam's post war diplomatic contacts with the region and the world began in Thailand in 1945, and not in China in 1950'.[3] In the years before Soviet and Chinese recognition of the DRV in January 1950, while the Vietminh was waging a guerrilla war against French colonial forces, there was little contact between Soviet and Vietnamese leaders. However, during these years several attempts were made by the Vietnamese side to build a relationship. Although the attempts at securing Soviet support for the struggle against the French failed, they form an important background for the establishment of a Soviet–Vietnamese relationship in the years following Soviet recognition of the DRV. They also highlight the important fact that the Vietnamese Communists were able to conduct foreign affairs independently before the victory of the Chinese

Communists in 1949–50 and may help to explain why the China factor became the single most important denominator in Soviet policies towards Vietnam in the following two decades.

Between the August Revolution and the outbreak of war in December 1946, Ho Chi Minh and his government searched for allies who would both secure him support against the French reconquest of southern Vietnam and contribute to the construction of the DRV in the north. While searching for allies, the DRV government tried to build alliances or solicit support for their new state within Southeast Asia, with the United States, the Soviet Union and the Chinese (Chiang Kai-Shek government/the Guomindang). The very first efforts of this kind were made in the immediate aftermath of the August Revolution when Ho Chi Minh sent parallel series of cables to both Stalin and Truman asking for recognition and support.[4] Nothing came out of either. Cooperation with Chiang Kai-Shek also broke down when he agreed with France to withdraw the Chinese occupation troops from northern Indochina.[5] After the outbreak of full-scale war from 1947, the DRV government used Bangkok as its main diplomatic outlet.[6]

Although the Thai government did not recognize the DRV, it allowed the opening of a 'Representational Office of the Democratic Republic of Vietnam' in Bangkok in the late summer of 1946. The office was set up with the help of Vietnamese nationals in Thailand and began to operate fully from 14 April 1947. The office was tolerated by the progressive national government of Pridi Banomyong. According to one Vietnamese author, the Bangkok office received money and funds from Pridi, who also allowed the Vietnamese to set up a war base at the frontier where soldiers could receive training before being sent back through Laos and Cambodia into Vietnam. Bangkok was a very important liaison point for the Vietnamese because the DRV's diplomatic mission there could initiate and maintain contacts with other Southeast Asian countries and world powers through their Thai embassies. The office was not recognized as a legitimate legation or embassy but played a significant role in the DRV's foreign affairs. Bangkok would function as the DRV's main opening to the world until the conservative coup in Thailand in 1948, after which Rangoon took over some of Bangkok's role. Thailand's new ruler from 1948 deprived the DRV representative office of its diplomatic status, and it was forced to reduce its activity.[7]

During 1947, Bangkok was the scene of encounters between Vietnamese and American officials, as well as Vietnamese and Soviet officials. Ho Chi Minh's encounters with American officials in France and Vietnam during 1946 had been characterized by a friendly and respectful atmosphere. The American attitude towards colonialism and the independence of the Philippines may have provided some of the Vietnamese leaders with hope that the United States could support them against France or at least put a moderating pressure on France.[8] During early 1947, shortly after the outbreak of full-scale war between the Vietnamese and the French, the DRV launched a four-month diplomatic initiative to secure the support of the Truman administration. The initiative was led by Dr Pham Ngoc Thach, deputy minister in the Office of the President and one of Ho Chi Minh's closest advisors. From April to June, Thach approached the Americans in

Bangkok with several proposals. Among these were calls for recognition, requests for assistance in mediating the conflict with the French, for loans for Vietnamese rehabilitation, for economic concessions to US businesses in Vietnam, and appeals for technical assistance and cultural exchange. However, just like Ho Chi Minh's attempt to secure American support immediately after the August Revolution, Pham Ngoc Thach's initiatives in the first half of 1947 failed.[9]

The DRV began constructing their fragile new state in a period of international turmoil. On the eve of the Cold War a growing fear of Communism was slowly spreading among American policy makers. Despite many favourable assessments from American officials in both Vietnam and other Southeast Asian countries, Ho Chi Minh's government received no support for its case from the Truman administration and began to realize that it was necessary to turn to other countries for support. The DRV's approaches to the United States must be evaluated within the context of the Vietnamese relationship with the French. In the aftermath of the war anti-colonial sentiments prevailed in the international arena with one distinct exception – the French attitude towards its former colony Indochina. In order to prevent a French re-colonialization of the area, the Vietnamese needed a strong and independent ally for support.

Parallel to the approaches to the Americans, the DRV leaders also sought support from the Soviet Union. As in the case with the Americans, in the latter half of the 1940s, contact with Moscow was initiated and maintained largely through the DRV delegation in Bangkok. Ho Chi Minh had strong links with the Communist world from his prewar work with the Comintern, his role within the French Communist Party, and, not least, his long-term stays in Moscow. Still, in the immediate period after the August Revolution, the DRV government was not successful in securing material support from any of its future Communist allies.[10] At that point Mao Zedong did not yet hold power in China and was far away. So was the Soviet Union.

Soviet sources describe how the first encounters between Soviet and Vietnamese officials took place in early spring 1947.[11] From 23 March to 2 April, a Soviet delegation led by comrades Zhukov and Plishevskii participated at the Asian Relations Conference in New Delhi.[12] During the conference the Soviets met with Tran Van Giau, former leader of the August Revolution in Saigon and southern Vietnam, who led the Vietnamese delegation to the conference. Tran Van Giau described the situation in Vietnam as a disaster and appealed, on behalf of Ho Chi Minh, for assistance from Moscow. According to Giau, 'the French were gradually tightening the rope around the virtually unarmed Vietnamese units,'[. . .] 'and would crush the Democratic Republic completely within 4 to 5 months'.[13] That would happen regardless of the fact that Ho Chi Minh and the Communist party had the full support and respect of the Vietnamese people. 'Vietnam needs immediate assistance', he continued and emphasized that the major problem was the lack of weapons. The Vietnamese government primarily needed money in order to purchase weapons through China. In addition, Tran Van Giau reminded the Soviet delegates that diplomatic support through the United Nations would also be very much appreciated.[14]

The meetings between Tran Van Giau, Zhukov and Plishevskii took place around the same time as Pham Ngoc Thach began his approaches to the Americans in Bangkok. However, in the first years after Second World War the Soviet Union was primarily concerned with developments in Europe. In postcolonial Asia, Moscow first and foremost paid attention to Indonesia,[15] and of course China and Korea, but showed little interest in the national liberation struggle in Indochina before 1950.

Soviet strategies in Southeast Asia

Previous accounts of Soviet relations with Southeast Asia in general, and the Democratic Republic of Vietnam in particular, suggest that during the early years of the DRV's existence the Soviet Union appeared to have been appropriately sympathetic to the Vietminh cause, although non-committal concerning any specific assistance the Vietnamese might expect.[16] In the early post-war years the Soviet Union did not want to disturb its relations with Paris, where the Communists were part of the government until March 1947. This fact undermines the suggestions that the Soviet Union, as early as 1947, played the role as moderator for the Southeast Asian Communist parties.

In his work *Soviet Strategies in Southeast Asia*, Charles B. Mclane distinguishes between two separate developments when characterizing Moscow's colonial strategies in the period from 1947 to 1950. From 1945 to 1947 Moscow seemed to follow a relatively moderate strategy. A change came, according to Mclane, towards the end of 1947, when Zhdanov presented a more militant line in Soviet foreign policies. This was further enhanced with the acceptance of Chinese views (Liu Shaoqi) through 1949 and early 1950 – views that were clearly more aggressive in terms of assisting Communist revolutions than the initial Soviet stand. Another equally important development according to Mclane was the shift of focus from Europe to Asia. This shift apparently began with the Calcutta Conference in 1948, and continued with the CCP's establishment of the PRC in the fall of 1949.[17]

In the first years following the Second World War, Stalin's attention was focused on Europe. Naturally enough, the Soviet leaders were much more concerned about their relationship with France, Great Britain and the United States than with the events in Indochina. There are no records of worldwide appeals on Vietnam's behalf from the Soviet side. When negotiations between Ho Chi Minh and the French broke down in December 1946, and the Franco-Vietminh War broke out, the Soviet Union apparently never even considered intervening. Ignoring the fact that the Franco-Vietminh war was the first case of conflict between a colonial subject and an imperialist power in an Asian country, Moscow underestimated a war that would seriously affect the course of events throughout the East.[18] The Soviet reluctance to get directly involved in the Vietnamese situation underlines how much importance Moscow attached to a reasonable relationship with the West European states, especially France, and the United States.

In a speech at the founding of the Communist Information Bureau (Cominform) in September 1947 in Poland, Soviet Politburo member Andrei Zhdanov presented the so-called 'two-camp' thesis. He divided the world into two distinct camps, an imperialist one led by the United States and the other that of anti-imperialism, socialism and peace.[19] Within that context the DRV was described as 'associated' with the anti-imperialist camp, and the Vietminh war was termed 'a powerful movement for national liberation in the colonies and dependencies'.[20] The speech marked a watershed in Soviet post-war strategies. It affirmed a policy already decided upon by Stalin and the CPSU Central Committee and was an event that set the tone of international relations during the Cold War.[21]

In his speech Zhdanov encouraged Communists abroad to be more energetic in their ways of advancing the common goal. He underlined that through economic power the Americans aimed at organizing Western Europe and countries politically and economically dependent on the United States such as Near Eastern and South American countries and Chiang Kai-Shek's China into an anti-Communist bloc. The Russians, on the other hand, were in the process of forming another bloc together with the so-called new democracies in Eastern Europe, Finland, Indonesia and Vietnam and with the sympathy of India, Egypt and Syria. With this division into blocs, Zhdanov announced what may be seen as the rebirth of the 'two-camp' view of the world that was characteristic of Soviet foreign policy in the late 1920s and early 1930s.[22]

Although the message inherent in Zhdanov's speech was aimed at all Communist parties in the world, only the European Communist parties were present during the founding meeting of the Cominform. There were no representatives from any colonial or previously colonial country. To convey the message to these parties the Cominform decided to hold an Asian conference in mid-November the same year. But the message at this conference only partly reflected the new line in Communist policy. The key note address to the participants at the conference was delivered by Asia expert and historian Evgenii Michalovich Zhukov. He acknowledged the need for a more vigorous role for Communist parties in the colonies, an attitude that to a much larger degree reflected a way of thinking that was more characteristic of pre- than post-Zhdanov attitudes towards the Eastern question. At the same time, records from the conference did not confirm the idea of a more active Soviet policy towards the colonial world, but rather added more confusion to the state of Moscow's intent in these countries.[23] The same Zhukov who gave the opening speech at the Asian conference was the one who met with Tran Van Giau in New Delhi in late March or early April 1947 to discuss the situation in Vietnam. As an academic his role was more as an advisor than a policy maker, but his views on Soviet policies towards the colonies were influential in the post-war years.

Vietnamese diplomatic initiatives in Bangkok and Moscow

We have seen how the attempts made by Tran Van Giau to solicit support from the Soviet Union in the spring of 1947 were unsuccessful. Judging by previous accounts on the Soviet–Vietnamese relationship, the Soviet attitude towards the revolutionary struggle in Vietnam was more sympathetic after the Zhdanov speech. Thus the picture ought to change after September 1947, but Soviet archival sources do not support this view. In the period after the Cominform meeting Moscow was equally hesitant once the issue of practical economic or military assistance was raised. At this time there was also considerable suspicion of Ho Chi Minh as a rightist deviator who had dissolved the Indochinese Communist Party.[24]

Pham Ngoc Thach, who during spring and summer had been in charge of approaches to the US government, met with the Soviet envoy to Switzerland, Anatolii Georgevich Kulazhenkov, in Bern in early September of 1947.[25] Pham Ngoc Thach, then described as deputy state secretary of the Presidium of the Council of Ministers of the Republic of Vietnam, was in Switzerland under the pretext of being treated for tuberculosis. His main aim was to make an illegal trip to France, where he was supposed to present his credentials to the leading French Communists Maurice Thorez and Jacques Duclos. He came to the Soviet mission in Bern to provide information about the current situation in Vietnam. Describing how the DRV government organized the fight against the French army, he emphasized the lack of weapons in the Vietnamese army. Military units did not have the necessary equipment, and the government did not have enough foreign currency to buy what they needed. There was also a lack of senior cadres to take the command. Owing to the situation the CCP decided to assist Vietnam and send in a group of military advisors.[26]

On the current situation in Southeast Asia, Pham Ngoc Thach underlined that during the fight for independence Communist parties had been founded in most countries and had an important influence among the populations. He emphasized Vietnam's role as the proliferation centre of Communist influence in Southeast Asia. On his way to Europe Pham Ngoc Thach had met with Communist leaders in other Southeast Asian countries such as Malaysia and Burma. He also told them that the Vietnamese Communist Party ('Kompartii Vietnama')[27] had planned a congress of all Southeast Asian Communist parties in 1947, but that this had proved impossible due to the ongoing war between Vietnam and France. With regard to the French Communist Party (PCF) Thach reported that they had so far not discussed the question of Vietnam and had done nothing substantial to hinder the French imperialist war against the republic.[28]

Within the PCF the attitude towards support for the Vietminh changed in 1947. They offered only very prudent political and diplomatic support to the DRV in 1946 while the PCF was a member of the French government coalition and war had not yet broken out in Indochina. In the spring of 1947, however, the war had become a highly debated issue in France, and the PCF was evicted from the coalition. They now became gradually more sympathetic to the Vietminh but had neither any real power in France nor any influence over Ho Chi Minh. After the PCF left the French government coalition, the Soviet Union also started to voice some support for the DRV and blamed the civil war in Indochina on French reactionary circles and British imperialist manoeuvres. According to Moscow, the French government should bear full responsibility for the situation.[29] Pham Ngoc

Thach also underlined the importance of the many different factions within the Vietnamese Communist Party and the fact that this party was not an entity as it is perceived in Europe. According to him, the two PCF leaders he had been in touch with had expressed the view that Vietnam should focus all its energy on the fight for independence and not give any concessions to the French imperialists.[30]

Describing the attitudes towards the United States and Great Britain, Pham Ngoc Thach claimed that they were hated in all Southeast Asian countries; however, in spite of this the US position was becoming increasingly solid. Countries were flooded with American goods, and the Americans pretended not to be against the fight for national liberation. They even encouraged it, assuming that as soon as the countries were free from English, French and Dutch influence, they would automatically fall into the hands of the Americans. According to the US military attaché in Siam, who proclaimed his sympathy with the Vietnamese people, the Americans could not interfere with the war and had no plans to assist the French. Pham Ngoc Thach also expressed his wish to visit the Soviet Union and personally inform them about the situation in Southeast Asia. However, he did not want a Soviet visa in his passport since that could create problems once he tried to return to Thailand (Siam).[31]

There are no records of direct support from the Soviet Union to the Vietnamese in 1948. However, the Southeast Asian Youth Conference that took place in Calcutta in February 1948 has been regarded as a turning point, and there has been much discussion on the role of the Calcutta conference in Soviet strategies towards Southeast Asia. According to one scholar, Ho Chi Minh's Vietnam received more Soviet attention after the Calcutta conference and full Soviet approval from the spring of that same year.[32] The conference took place between 19 and 25 February, and 39 organisations from both Communist and non-Communist countries sent their delegations to participate in, or observe, its work. Many of the discussions at the conference circled around the 'two-camp' doctrine presented by Zhdanov in September 1947, and the general atmosphere revealed the spreading of militancy in the world Communist movement.[33]

Because of the outbreak of numerous Communist-led uprisings shortly after the conference, there have been allegations that Moscow used the conference to pass on instructions to the Southeast Asian parties. Two specific arguments stand in the way of such a possibility. The first is that the composition of the conference did not make it a suitable vehicle for revolutionary instructions. Most participants were non-Communists, and Moscow did not view meetings such as the Southeast Asian Youth Conference as a revolutionary tool, but more as an arena to project Moscow's ideas on world affairs to Communist sympathizers and leftists. Secondly, there was the question of who would have been in charge of passing on these instructions. The Soviet delegation to the conference consisted of a group of Central Asians, none of whom held high-ranking positions in the CPSU. It is unlikely that any of these were trusted to pass on such instructions, and, in addition, there were few other Communist representatives to receive such instructions. The only known Southeast Asian Communist who attended the conference was the Burmese party leader Than Tun.[34]

The absence of materials on the Calcutta conference in Soviet diplomatic and Communist party records reduces the likelihood that this conference played an important role in distributing instructions from the Soviet Union to the Southeast Asian Communist parties. However, there are still unexplored sources that might reveal more about the conference, such as those of the Soviet Youth Organization Komsomol.[35] But even if the conference was not used to pass on instructions, it has been argued that it served a useful purpose within Soviet strategy. The reason for that was the emphasis put on discussing the Zhdanov theories and the fact that one participant after another spoke out in favour of militant anti-imperialism. Whether Moscow approved of the more militant course taken by the Southeast Asian Communists after Calcutta is difficult to establish through available materials. There was no fixed pattern in the Soviet response to the upcoming rebellions in Southeast Asia. Nor was there any to draw significant conclusions from Communist experiences there which might be applied to the rest of the colonial world. As such the overall conclusion must be that, to find explanations for the uprisings in the Southeast Asian countries in those years, it will be more fruitful to look at conditions within the countries themselves.[36]

Whether it was due to the Calcutta conference or not, from 1948 on meetings between Soviet and Vietnamese representatives took place on a more regular basis. The recurring theme at these meetings was the question of Soviet assistance to the Vietnamese, both economic and military. At a meeting in Moscow in late August 1948 between the deputy head of the Vietnamese information bureau in Bangkok, Le Hy, and M. Sh. Bakhitov, deputy head of the Southeast Asia Department (SEAD) in the Soviet foreign ministry, these issues were raised. The purpose of the meeting was, according to Le Hy, to report on the situation in Vietnam. Le Hy informed Bakhitov that at that point the Republic of Vietnam[37] ('Respublika Viet-Nam') had already for three years fought against the French military intervention, supported by the British and the Americans and with the tacit approval of the Guomindang clique in China. Due to its geographic location (China in the north and French forces in the south) and the developing international political situation, Vietnam fought without any help or support – except moral – from the outside. For tactical reasons, the leaders of the Vietnamese Communist Party had decided to disperse the party into different democratic and mass organisations to preclude it from officially standing forth as the leading force in the government and among the masses.[38] Le Hy's emphasis on the division of the party might have been his way of defending the official dissolution of the ICP in November 1945, which had caused suspicion in Moscow.

During the meeting with Bakhitov, Le Hy also talked about the original purpose of his trip. He was on his way to Prague to open a Vietnamese information agency. The purpose of the office would be to strengthen the ties and improve contacts with progressive and democratic states. Le Hy would be in charge of the agency, and the staff would consist of three people – among them Australian Communist Alexander Brotherton. He also reported that he was forced to wait in Moscow for further instructions from his government. The purpose of his visit to Moscow was among other things to present an unofficial inquiry on behalf of the

Communist party circles in Vietnam whether the Soviet government and the party could help the Vietnamese Republic with weapons, ammunition and other kinds of equipment and present this as a loan. In case of a positive answer to the inquiry, Le Hy wondered whether the Soviet Union could send a plenipotentiary delegation to Vietnam for proper negotiations.[39]

Le Hy also had another request. He wondered whether the Soviet government would allow some Vietnamese students to come to the Soviet Union to study. He underlined the respect of the Vietnamese people for the Soviet Union and emphasized the fact that Ho Chi Minh had lived for nine years in the Soviet Union. He also added that the Vietnamese government reckoned that for the moment it would be inconvenient to address an official request for assistance from the Soviet Union. Because of this he had to present this request on behalf of the Communist circles in Vietnam and ask whether the Soviet Union could give any kind of assistance to Vietnam in any form that would be convenient for the Soviet Union. If it should prove impossible to get such support from the Soviet government, he would do it through the Soviet Communist Party. Bakhitov did not give any promises, but answered that some action would be taken to clear this up.[40]

Apparently the Soviets found the organization of Vietnamese representation in Thailand somewhat confusing. The role of Le Hy was the most prominent example. His claim to be an official representative of the DRV, and his approaches to the Soviets for support, seemed to be a source of concern to other Vietnamese officials. That also caught the attention of the Soviets in Bangkok. Sergei Nemtchin confronted Nguyen Duc Quy on the issue of Le Hy and was told that Le Hy had a limited task – to organize propaganda about Vietnam in Europe and that he was not an official representative of the Vietnamese government and took all decisions on his work independently.[41] The confusion around the role of Le Hy could be part of the reason why Soviet envoy Nemtchin characterized the behaviour of Vietnamese diplomats in Bangkok as disorganized and amateurish.[42]

The August meeting with Le Hy was followed up in late September 1948 when the Soviet envoy in Thailand, Sergei Sergeevitch Nemtschin, met with the head of the Vietnamese delegation in Southeast Asia, Nguyen Duc Quy – who was a proper representative for the DRV. In 1948 the Soviet legation in Bangkok was the only Soviet representation in Southeast Asia. At that time Thailand and, from 1948, Burma were the only independent countries in the region, and thus the only possibilities for setting up representation. Thailand gave Moscow permission to set up the legation in exchange for the Soviet Union's vote at the United Nations on Thailand's bid to join. Thailand was accepted as a UN member, and Moscow formed its first formal diplomatic post in Southeast Asia by March–April 1948.[43]

The purpose of Nguyen Duc Quy's visit to the Soviet envoy was to establish contacts with the representative of the Soviet Communist Party in Thailand. He assumed that the envoy, Nemtchin, was also the CPSU representative. Nemtchin, however, explained that that was not the case and that he only represented the Soviet state as such. While talking to Nemtchin, Nguyen Duc Quy also referred to the September 1947 meeting that had taken place in Switzerland between

Pham Ngoc Thach and Anatolii Kylashenkov. The lack of reference to Le Hy's mission in this context further confirmed his unofficial status and accentuated Nguyen Duc Quy's distrust of Hy. From the records of this meeting we have already seen how Pham Ngoc Thach presented a request from the Vietnamese government for assistance from the Soviet Union. In addition, according to Nguyen Duc Quy, Pham Ngoc Thach had also used the opportunity to deliver a direct request to the Soviet government from Ho Chi Minh, in which the latter sought support for a proposal that the United Nations intervene in the Franco-Vietnamese conflict.[44]

In addition to Nguyen Duc Quy, another Vietnamese official, referred to as Chuong, was involved in the discussions.[45] He is referred to in Nemtchin's reply as a member of the Vietnamese government and a secretary of the Central Committee of the Vietnamese Communist Party. His mission was to establish contact with the Soviet Communist Party, and he needed a visa to go to Moscow. Due to the situation, Nguyen Duc Quy wondered whether the Soviet mission in Thailand could act as a liaison between the Vietnamese and the Soviet Communist parties and assist Chuong in getting a visa to the Soviet Union. According to Nguyen Duc Quy, Chuong had two tasks to perform: one was to inform Moscow of the situation in Vietnam, and the second was to discuss assistance to Vietnam. Returning to conditions in Vietnam, Nguyen Duc Quy reported that the struggle was in such a phase that it was necessary to receive assistance from abroad since the Vietminh's heavy weapons were insufficient.[46]

On a direct question of how to implement this assistance, Nguyen Duc Quy answered that the Vietnamese wanted the Soviets to help them raise money that was needed to buy necessary weapons from American smugglers. Vietnam would need about 2–5 million US dollars. However, with the ongoing French blockade it was too difficult to transfer money out of Vietnam. Nguyen Duc Quy explained that they did have an opportunity to buy weapons from American smugglers, overcome the blockade and transport these into Vietnam. On numerous occasions during the conversation Nguyen Duc Quy referred to 'our party' as if to assure Nemtchin that the Vietnamese Communist Party was in charge of everything in Vietnam.[47]

Throughout 1948 Vietnamese diplomats in Bangkok continued to approach the Soviets with requests for assistance, but without any apparent success. Toward the end of September 1948 Nguyen Duc Quy informed the Soviet attaché in Siam, Igor Grigorevich Ysatchov, that the Vietnamese Communist Party was about to send a request to the CCP for military aid – and as a part of that they would also ask for two senior officers to lead military operations. To solve the most immediate problems related to supplies of weapons, they had made a deal with Burma on intermediate landing of Vietnamese aircraft on Burmese territory for loading. The Vietnamese were also ready to buy Burmese weapons (US surplus weapons) and let aircraft drop them over Vietnam with parachutes. That would help overcome the French blockade.[48]

In the years before the establishment of the PRC contact between the Chinese and Vietnamese Communists remained limited, even though Ho Chi Minh, as well as several of the other leaders in Hanoi, previously had entertained close connections with the Chinese Communists in the 1920s and 1930s. During his time as an active member of the PCF in Paris, Ho met several of the men who would become central within the CCP, such as Zhou Enlai, Wang Ruofei, Xiao San and Li Fuchun. Ho had also worked in China for a long period in the mid-1920s when the Communist International sent him from Moscow to Guangzhou, where he assisted Mikhail Borodin, the Comintern representative to the new Chinese revolutionary government led by the Guomindang.[49]

According to Chinese sources, from 1945 to 1949 assistance from the Chinese Communists to the Vietminh was mostly in the category of mutual assistance. One example was the incident in March 1946, when a unit from the CCP's People's Liberation Army (PLA) sought refuge in North Vietnam and was welcomed by the Vietnamese Communists. The unit had withdrawn into Vietnam to avoid a Guomindang attack, and Ho Chi Minh asked if they could help train his troops so they would be better prepared for a war against the French. That encounter was important for the future of Sino-Vietnamese relations. Although no evidence suggests that the CCP provided regular contributions to the Vietminh until 1949, the CCP sub-bureau in British Hong Kong seems to have provided them with some funds on a more irregular basis from 1947. Even the lines of communication between the Chinese and Vietnamese Communists were not very strong before 1950. The first direct line of telegraphic communications between the two parties was set up in the spring of 1947.[50]

Chinese aid was a welcome support, but the Vietnamese strongly emphasized that they were not interested in receiving aid only from the CCP. The requests for Soviet support continued. In early October 1948 Nguyen Duc Quy requested both military and economic assistance. At the time there was no military academy in Vietnam, and this had resulted in a general lack of officers to lead the fight against the French. Duc Quy therefore asked about the possibility of educating 50 officers – captains and lieutenants – in higher military academies in the Soviet Union. In addition he asked for stipends and educational opportunities within the area of economy, so that in turn the Vietnamese would be better equipped to run their own national economy.[51]

The immediate Soviet reaction was negative. Nemtchin explained that since the end of the Second World War Soviet educational facilities has been filled up with those who had interrupted their studies due to the war, and hence there was very little space for foreign students. Nguyen Duc Quy once again asked Nemtchin to pass a request for money and weapons to conduct the war to the Soviet Communist Party, upon which Nemtchin once again replied that since he was not a Communist party official, he could not pass on such a request.[52]

Renewed Soviet interest in Asia

The Vietnamese Communists' first attempts to establish relations with the outside world have the characteristic of a classic history of rejections. Their attempts to establish relations with the United States and the Soviet Union went on more or less parallel tracks. A second wave of attempts to secure assistance from the United States or the Soviet Union was made through the DRV representative office in Bangkok during 1947. First, the Vietnamese representatives flirted with the Americans in the spring, hoping that the US stand on colonialism could secure support against the French. That attempt failed because those who favoured support to Ho Chi Minh did not have enough influence within the Truman administration, and the final lid on the possibility of American support came with the start of the Cold War, when the Americans already believed that the DRV was part of the Communist world. The unsuccessful attempts at establishing relations with the Americans were followed by an attempt to secure assistance from the Soviet Union in the fall of 1947. But Moscow was no more eager than Washington to assist the Vietnamese, and the DRV was rejected once again.

Even after the French Communists were expelled from the government, Moscow remained reluctant to support the Vietminh in their struggle against the French forces. Thus, by the end of 1948 the Vietnamese Communists had to realize that their attempts to secure Soviet support in their war against the French had failed. Repeated requests and pleas to the Soviets both in Bangkok and Moscow had led to moral support at most. Europe was still the major target of Soviet foreign policy, and Stalin was not willing to risk that over support for the Vietnamese.

In the late 1940s Vietnam was too far away and too insignificant to become the main focus of Moscow's foreign policy. Thus, as one historian has put it, from 1948 onwards, the Vietnamese had to accept that in the coming years the success of the CCP and Mao Zedong represented their best chance to break the isolation in their war for independence.[53] So, in short, one could argue that while the DRV's relations with the world began in Thailand in 1945, and from 1947 were represented by Bangkok as the only diplomatic outlet for the DRV, the *successful* Vietnamese relations with the world began with the Communist victory in China in 1949, and the subsequent Chinese recognition of the DRV in January 1950.

However, in 1949 the situation in Asia changed dramatically, and in 1950 the success of the Chinese Communists forced Stalin to pay more attention not only to China but also to Vietnam. In May 1949 Soviet analysts concluded that 'the success of the People's Liberation Army of China undoubtedly has a strong influence on the outcome of the Vietnamese people's fight for national independence'.[54] The role of both Moscow and Beijing in Asia was discussed during Liu Shaoqi's visit to Moscow in the summer of 1949, when Stalin suggested that China take on the main responsibility for supporting revolutionary movements in the former Asian colonies once the People's Republic was in place.[55]

2 Setting the stage

The Soviet Union, China and the First Indochina War, 1949–1953

After the proclamation of the PRC on 1 October 1949, Stalin met with Mao in Moscow in December. When they discussed Vietnam, the Soviet leader underlined that the practical part of assisting Ho Chi Minh and the Vietnamese Communists was primarily a Chinese responsibility.[1] The victory of the Chinese revolution had radically transformed international relations in East Asia. Not only did it destroy the existing international order based on the Yalta agreements and the 1945 Sino-Soviet treaty, it also forced the established powers to face a new revolutionary state that had arisen from a civil war. When dealing with this new state, previous rules no longer applied, neither for the United States nor for the Soviet Union. Moreover, especially for Moscow this new order would seriously influence its policies towards East Asia.

Earlier the Soviet Union had, by coordinating its policy with that of the United States, the potential to obtain economic and security advantages in East Asia. However, when the Chinese revolution finally succeeded, the Soviet Union was forced to adjust its policy to the objectives of the Chinese Communists.[2] As a result, Stalin's attitude in 1949 would prove to have serious consequences for the future relationship between Moscow and Hanoi. By resting its policy towards Vietnam on the role of China, Moscow limited its responsibilities as well as its opportunities, laying parts of the foundation for future frustration over the situation in Southeast Asia. In sum, the Communist victory in China contributed to increased attention to developments in the Far East both from the United States and the Soviet Union. To Moscow, this also meant that its attention was drawn more specifically to the situation in Vietnam.

The aim of this chapter is to discuss the relationship between the Soviet Union and Vietnam in the first three years after the Communist victory in China. Focus will be on the impact of the Communist victory in China on Soviet–Vietnamese relations, the events surrounding Chinese and Soviet recognition of the DRV, the discussions on how and when to establish Soviet–Vietnamese diplomatic missions, and, finally, the Soviet, as well as the Chinese, economic, military and ideological role in the Franco-Vietnamese War.

Moscow and the Communist victory in China

When Mao Zedong announced the establishment of the PRC on 1 October 1949, Beijing had already been in Communist hands since January that year, and the PLA was in control of most of Northern China but not yet the regions bordering Indochina. Mao's announcement on 1 October was the result of a long civil war. The CCP came to power in 1949 with only 4.5 million members, but by the end of 1950 it had increased to approximately 5.8 million. The first major task for the new government was to stabilize the economy and consolidate the regime and to take control of the rest of the country. The PRC aimed to build a new society based on the development of agriculture and industry. The Guomindang was declared reactionary, and in principle all citizens were guaranteed rights such as free speech and free religion. The PRC planned land reforms, collectivization and heavy industrial development after the Soviet model.[3]

Mao Zedong's first official visit abroad was to the Soviet Union. He stayed for roughly two months, from 16 December 1949 to 17 February 1950, and during his stay he discussed two items of particular interest with the Soviet leader. The first was the degree and form of Soviet assistance to the PRC, and the second was the new role of China in Asia and, in particular, Southeast Asia. Parallel to Mao's visit to the Soviet Union, the DRV government sent out a declaration encouraging all states to recognize the DRV as the only legitimate government of Vietnam. As such, Chinese, Soviet and other countries' recognition of the DRV came at about the same time as the Sino-Soviet agreement was signed in Moscow.[4]

Once Mao was in power in China, Stalin, surprised but still pleased with the successes of the Chinese Communists, had no other option than to support the CCP. This support was primarily announced through the Sino-Soviet Treaty of Friendship, Alliance and Mutual Assistance, signed on 14 February 1950. The treaty was not the first of its kind between the two countries. A Sino-Soviet treaty was signed as early as during the Yalta Conference in 1945 between the Soviet Union and the Guomindang-led Republic of China. However, with the Communist victory the leaders of the new China were eager to renegotiate or abolish the existing treaty and establish a new one. The discussions around the treaty took place during Mao's visit to the Soviet Union. Talks between Stalin and Mao in the latter part of December did not lead to an agreement, and it was only after the arrival of Zhou Enlai in Moscow on 20 January 1950 that a new treaty came within reach.[5] The signing of the treaty was, of course, important to the newly founded Communist state, and in the end it was achieved after concessions from both sides.

While in Moscow, Mao was joined by Ho Chi Minh. Ho had left Beijing for the Soviet Union together with Zhou Enlai in early February and arrived in Moscow just in time for the signing of the Sino-Soviet Agreement. During the meetings in Moscow with Ho and Mao, Stalin once again encouraged China to take the lead in promoting revolution in Asia, while at the same time emphasizing that the Soviet Union would provide the necessary assistance.[6] A Vietnamese account of Ho's trip to the Soviet Union fixes his arrival to 3 February[7] and further tells that

Ho Chi Minh's trip to China and the Soviet Union was kept secret because Guomindang forces still controlled most of the border regions to Indochina, and Ho feared for his security. During the trip through the Soviet Union Ho disguised himself as 'an old man in indigo clothes, a white towel covering his beard, a knapsack on his shoulder, like other members of the delegation'.[8]

We do know that Ho and Stalin met at least once while Ho was in Moscow. According to the memoirs of the Chinese ambassador to Moscow, Ho Chi Minh attended the banquet held in honour of the signing of the Sino-Soviet Treaty. President Ho used that occasion to explain the situation of the Vietnamese revolution to Stalin, who apparently had little previous knowledge of what went on in that country. After listening to Ho's account, Stalin apparently agreed to the strategy and tactics of the Vietnamese Communist Party. He advised Ho to pay attention to the whole western mountainous region of Vietnam, because control of that region would allow the Vietnamese Communists to control the whole country. Stalin also agreed to provide some aid to the Vietminh troops, more specifically a regiment of 37-mm anti-aircraft guns, several Molotova trucks and some medicine. In addition, China would arm one infantry division and an artillery unit. The Soviet aid would be conveyed through China to Vietnam.[9]

Stalin's comment on how Soviet aid to the Vietnamese Communists would be facilitated by the Chinese shows how the Communist victory in China had an immediate practical impact on the Vietnamese situation. In more general terms, this victory meant the end of Vietnam's 'dark days' and the beginning of a new era in Sino-Vietnamese relations. The most important change was the fact that northern Vietnam no longer faced the prospect of being surrounded by enemies. Communist China was about to become North Vietnam's major ally and provider in the war against France. In addition, the new situation also implied, as we have already seen, the possibility of assistance, both economic and military, not only from China but hopefully also from the Communist bloc in general. In several ways, the establishment of the PRC functioned as a door opener to the Vietnamese Communists, who, since the outbreak of the Franco-Vietnamese war, found themselves increasingly isolated from the outside world. The Chinese Communist victory enabled the DRV to establish successful relations with, and obtain recognition from, the Communist world. However, on the other hand, the DRV's inclusion in the Communist world meant a higher degree of isolation from the rest of the world and in particular, the West. But from a Vietnamese point of view, in early 1950 the most important task was to establish lasting relations with the Communist world and first and foremost with the Soviet Union.

In Beijing, Soviet analysts argued that the victory of the Chinese revolution and the formation of the PRC was of immense importance to people all over the world but first and foremost to the people of the Far East and Southeast Asia. They emphasized that the formation of a friendly state such as the PRC at the northern border of Vietnam significantly eased the difficulties the Vietnamese were enduring. It facilitated the ongoing war of resistance and broke the blockade that so far had restrained the DRV's contact with the outside world. Not least, it provided Hanoi with the opportunity to establish direct contact with the other people's democracies. In sum, Soviet analysts in Beijing concluded, the PRC victory was a vital factor that increased the DRV's success both in the war of resistance and in the upsurge of the country's national economy.[10]

Recognition

On 14 January 1950, while Mao was in Moscow, but before Zhou Enlai and Ho Chi Minh arrived there, the DRV government sent out, in response to a Chinese suggestion, a declaration inviting all countries to recognize the DRV as the only legitimate government in Vietnam. The DRV also recognized the PRC. Because of the war between the DRV and France and the international atmosphere in 1950, recognition of the DRV by China and the Soviet Union would have consequences beyond the Sino-Vietnamese and Soviet–Vietnamese relationships. This had to be considered before such steps were taken. Obtaining recognition of the two major Communist powers was of vital importance especially as an opportunity to obtain assistance in the struggle against France. Both Moscow and Beijing concluded that the advantages of recognizing the DRV outweighed the disadvantages. Beijing's response came on 16 January, and Moscow replied two weeks later, on 30 January.[11] However, it was first of all Beijing who wanted the recognition. Mao encouraged Ho Chi Minh to send out the declaration and then advised Moscow to follow the Chinese lead in this matter.

The events surrounding Chinese recognition of the DRV is a story illustrating how Mao's victory in China prompted closer relations between Hanoi and Beijing. In December 1949, about two months after Mao's proclamation of the founding of the PRC, Ho Chi Minh sent two envoys to Beijing to seek advice on how to win the battle against the French. As a result of Ho's request, the CCP Politburo held a meeting on 24 December to discuss whether the PRC should recognize the DRV. The overall conclusion at the meeting was that it would be more beneficial than harmful for China to form diplomatic ties with the DRV before an expected French recognition of the PRC. On 28 December 1949, therefore, the CCP Central Committee sent a cable to Ho Chi Minh and told him that they were ready to enter into diplomatic relations with his government.[12]

Once the issue of recognition was clarified with China, the Vietnamese went forward with their official announcement. On 15 January the first direct and formal request was sent to China. Mao, who at the time was in Moscow negotiating the Sino-Soviet Alliance treaty, soon stated that the PRC agreed to establish formal ties. He also instructed the Chinese Foreign Ministry on 17 January to forward Ho Chi Minh's request to both the Soviet Union and the other members of the Socialist camp.[13]

Chinese sources tell the story of how Mao and Stalin discussed diplomatic recognition of the DRV. The Chinese leader told Stalin that China was ready to support the Indochinese people in their struggle for national independence. The Soviet leader, however, seemed slightly more reluctant to support the Indochinese struggle but agreed to recognize the DRV after the PRC had done so. Chinese sources also reveal that Stalin told Mao that Moscow too was willing to supply the necessary aid to Ho Chi Minh.[14] Unfortunately, Soviet documents from these meetings remain unavailable, and thus Stalin's statements cannot be verified.

A plausible explanation of Stalin's hesitation could be the Soviet reluctance to alienate the French.[15] As in the case of China, two different factors should be taken into account when discussing its readiness to assist the DRV. First, the fact that its position as an Asian power made it less dependent on the European powers and thus more free to conduct its own policy in its surroundings. Second, it is vital to take into account that China's past influence in Vietnam played a decisive role in how the Chinese looked upon this neighbouring country. From a Chinese perspective, Vietnam was, without doubt, within its 'sphere of interest' – and just as the Chinese devoted themselves to the revolution in Vietnam, Beijing expected the Vietnamese to submit to Chinese advice. After the Communist victory in China, the Soviet press also paid more attention to Indochina, and often referred to Chinese influence within the Vietminh. Parallel to this there was also an increase in Soviet scholarly work on East and Southeast Asia with a particular focus on the victory of the CCP and its effect on the power balance in Asia.[16]

Soviet recognition followed 12 days after the Chinese, on 30 January, and the official statement was printed in the Soviet press on 31 January. Since the decision to recognize Ho's government had been thoroughly discussed with Mao in December, the actual Soviet recognition of the DRV did not cause much discussion. From Moscow's point of view, it was rather the slow routine of the DRV bureaucracy and discussions about diplomatic representation that caused trouble. On 14 February, two weeks after the official announcement in Pravda, the Soviets had still not received a confirmation from the Vietnamese, which is rather strange, since Ho Chi Minh was in Moscow at the time.

Nevertheless, the lack of response from Hanoi was a source of concern in Moscow. Their reply to Ho's request was delivered to the DRV representative in Bangkok, Nguyen Duc Quy, on 1 February, to be passed on to the DRV Foreign Minister, Hoang Minh Giam.[17] Shortly after, on 3 February, Ho Chi Minh arrived in Moscow to discuss future assistance with Stalin himself. These discussions took place, as we have already seen, during the banquet that followed the signing of the Sino-Soviet treaty. According to Chinese sources, Stalin told Ho that he would have to depend mainly on Chinese assistance and that the Soviet Union would not sign an agreement with the DRV similar to the one the latter had signed with China. Ho Chi Minh returned with Mao to Beijing on 17 February.[18]

There are no descriptions of these meetings in available Soviet documents or any comments on Ho's visit. The lack of written material, and a slow flow of information, could be why the foreign ministry officials were concerned with the lack of answers from the DRV leadership. During his stay in Moscow, Ho most probably conveyed his answer to the Soviet recognition of Vietnam to Stalin personally, and thus there would be no trace of this in the files. Given the fact that at the time the DRV had no permanent resident capital it would also be difficult for it to coordinate and convey a swift formal answer to Moscow.[19] They might also have chosen to trust that their leader would take care of this business while in

Moscow. Thus, in the end this was just the worry of some petty bureaucrat in the Soviet foreign ministry and had no particular importance to the overall Soviet–Vietnamese relationship.

Since the issue of recognition had already been settled, the parties started to discuss the exchange of representatives. Due to the situation in Vietnam, neither the Chinese nor the Soviets wanted to send diplomatic officials. The Chinese did, however, send Luo Guibo, at the time the director of the General Office of the CCP Central Military Commission, to serve as the CCP Central Committee's liaison representative to Ho's party. Luo's instructions were to establish contact with the ICP,[20] investigate the general situation in Vietnam and report his findings to Beijing so that the Chinese party leadership could make their decisions on assistance to the Vietnamese Communists. The plan for Luo was to stay in Vietnam for three months, but he stayed for seven years, until 1957. His first assignment was as the head of the Chinese Political Advisory Group (CPAG) in the DRV from 1951 to 1954, and the following three years until 1957 he served as China's ambassador to the DRV.[21]

As seen above, the Chinese almost immediately established formal contact with the leadership in northern Vietnam. Moscow, however, did not establish such channels of information. Although Ho Chi Minh announced his desire to receive a Soviet ambassador in Vietnam, Moscow declined the offer and underlined that they saw the appointment of a Soviet ambassador to DRV as undesirable as long as the Vietnamese government had not yet established a permanent residence. Soviet attitudes indicate that the most important issue was the organization of Vietnamese representation in Moscow. This corresponded well with the main wish of the DRV – namely to have an embassy in Moscow. Available foreign ministry files in Moscow pay surprisingly little attention to the question of Soviet representation in the DRV. There might be a single reason for this attitude – namely the overall situation in Vietnam. According to both Soviet and Chinese sources, Moscow and Beijing chose to postpone the installation of ambassadors in Hanoi due to the unstable situation in the country.[22]

However, in the meantime, the question of representation had to be solved one way or another. In February 1950 the Chinese ambassador to the Soviet Union, Wang Jiaxiang, informed Andrei Gromyko that Ho Chi Minh had already asked Mao Zedong and Zhou Enlai whether the Chinese ambassador could represent Vietnamese interests in the Soviet Union until the arrival of the Vietnamese ambassador. The solution proposed by the Vietnamese and the Chinese was accepted by the Soviets on the terms that the Chinese embassy will be allowed to represent the interests of the DRV.[23] However, the Soviets clearly explained that the Chinese ambassador could not take on the position of envoy (ambassador) for Vietnam since the principle of substitute officials was not an accepted diplomatic practice and could create an unwanted precedence.[24] To the Vietnamese it was so important to be represented in the Soviet Union that they were willing to compromise their wish for their own embassy for a limited period of time and let the Chinese handle contacts with the Soviets on the DRV's behalf because they had no other options at the time. The decision to appoint Nguyen Long Bang ambassador to Moscow was already made, and the DRV was determinded to get its own diplomatic representation in order as soon as possible.

While the arrangement with the Chinese secured Vietnamese representation in the Soviet Union, there was still the question of Soviet representation in Vietnam. In spite of the Soviet recognition of the DRV in late January 1950, information on Vietnam continued to come to Moscow mainly through unofficial DRV representatives in southern China[25] and the Soviet embassy in Beijing. Instead of setting up an embassy in Hanoi under the present circumstances, the Soviets chose to keep in touch with Vietnamese officials through their consulate in Canton. The Vietnamese had set up an official delegation in the city, and information about conditions in Vietnam went via the consulate in Canton to the Soviet embassy in Beijing. So, in fact, the Soviet consul in Canton functioned as the Soviet representative in the DRV. However, this arrangement meant that the information about Vietnamese conditions that was sent to the Far East department in the Soviet foreign ministry was second- and third-hand information. Soviet foreign ministry officials did not gather first-hand information, at least not on a regular basis.[26]

Once the question of recognition and provisional representation was settled, it was time to sort out the future rank of representatives to the opposite country. This task should have been easy but turned out to be rather complicated. The PRC and DRV governments had already decided to exchange ambassadors. The Soviet foreign minister expected that the Soviet Union and DRV would do the same; consequently, this was the first intention of both countries. A week before the recognition took place on 23 January 1950, this was outlined in a letter from Vietnam to the Soviet Union and other people's democracies. However, in a second letter sent in February that year, the DRV foreign minister referred to the exchange of diplomatic representatives without specifying their exact rank. Because of the special situation of the PRC ambassador acting as DRV envoy in Moscow, the Vietnamese found it natural to exchange envoys and not ambassadors with the Soviet Union. According to Soviet representatives at the embassy in Beijing, it was after a statement made by Soviet Foreign Minister Vyshinski on 30 January 1950, in which he referred to the Soviet decision to exchange envoys with the DRV, that the Vietnamese went back on their earlier express wish to exchange ambassadors.[27] The outcome was the exchange of ambassadors, and the first Vietnamese ambassador to the Soviet Union, Nguyen Long Bang, arrived in Moscow in April 1952, more than two years after the recognition. It took two and a half years more, and a Geneva agreement, before the Soviet Union was properly represented in Hanoi.

The discussions and misunderstandings over the exchange of representatives might at a glance seem like a small, and quite trivial, issue. However, at the same time it illustrates the need of the Hanoi government to secure some kind of direct contact with both of its primary allies. That the Chinese ambassador would represent the DRV in Moscow clearly reflected the Stalin–Mao agreement that China would take main responsibility for colonial liberation struggles in Asia. At the same time, the discussion around the level of diplomatic exchange between

Moscow and Hanoi showed that the Vietnamese were anxious to establish high-level contacts with Moscow and thus probably avoid dependence only on China, but not on such a high level that it would irritate the Chinese. The exchange of envoys would be a way to avoid that problem and at the same time secure the Vietnamese direct and independent contact with Moscow. However, it is unlikely that the Vietnamese considered it an advantage to be represented through the PRC; it was rather seen as the only available option at the time.

There is no doubt that recognition from China and the Soviet Union was of vital importance to the DRV leaders. The Western powers did, of course, see the situation from a different perspective. In Washington the main concern was the reports of an ever-growing Chinese assistance to the Vietminh. China's new strength increased American fears of Communist expansion in the area. In Paris and London the Communist victory in China was seen primarily as a threat to European colonial possessions in Southeast Asia. From a French point of view this was reflected in an immediate concern for a possible direct Chinese intervention in the Franco-Vietminh War.[28]

The Soviet leadership was rather satisfied with the impact recognition had on the Western powers and especially on the French government. During the spring of 1950 the Soviet foreign ministry reports referred to French newspapers that characterized the carefully constructed recognition of the Bao Dai government as a 'bursting soap-bubble' threatening not only the American reactionary policies in Asia but also the pro-American government in France. The French government was characterized as confused and impotent due to the fact that 'when Ho Chi Minh's government was recognized by the Democratic Republics the French government preferred not to react at all, in order to avoid further complications and not find themselves forced to once again attract public attention to the Indochinese question that thanks to the PCF has become critical to the French'.[29]

Yet another comment spoke of how Franco-American plans to include Indochina in their sphere of influence and their efforts to strengthen the international position of the state of Vietnam was upset by the Soviet recognition of the DRV. Contrary to the predictions in the French bourgeois press, the French government would not dare to break off diplomatic relations with the Soviet Union or renounce the Franco-Soviet treaty of 10 December 1944. With reference to earlier comments made by former Soviet Foreign Minister Molotov, the Southeast Asia department in the Soviet Ministry of Foreign Affairs (MID) emphasized the significance of Socialist education in the DRV. In addition, they argued that the DRV's strengthened connections with the camp of peace and democracy would promote the further development of the anti-imperialistic, national liberation movements in the countries of Southeast Asia.[30]

Recognition formalized the relationships between the Soviet Union and the DRV, but did it alter the relationship between Moscow and Hanoi? The effects of recognition and its impact on relations should be evaluated both in terms of immediate and long-term results. The immediate result would first of all be a possible boost of self-confidence among the DRV leaders, as they were now accepted within the Communist camp. In addition, recognition implied promises of future support, morally and financially. Since neither the Soviet Union nor the DRV installed permanent representatives in each other's countries immediately, recognition in itself did not contribute to a more steady flow of information between them. In spite of this situation, recognition both increased the interest in the situation in Vietnam among Soviet leaders and also led to an increase in information about Vietnam arriving through other sources such as the Soviet consulate in Canton and the Soviet embassy in Beijing.

During the first years after recognition the Soviet Union had no permanent mission in the DRV and relied mainly on reports sent by the Soviet consulate in Canton. During the early 1950s most of the information was, naturally enough, related to the war with the French. According to reports from Vietnam, the situation of the DRV was difficult. The larger cities and the most important lines of communication, as well as airspace and important ports, were controlled by the French. However, from the Soviet side, the Americans were seen as the most important aggressor as they financed the war on behalf of the French.[31] To plan a policy towards Vietnam, the Soviet leadership needed information about the situation in both the northern and southern parts of the country, as well as information on the French and American positions in Vietnam.

Recognition of the DRV by China, the Soviet Union and other Socialist governments was vital to the Hanoi government. The Soviet Union had been at full liberty to offer recognition to the DRV also at an earlier stage, but until the victory of the Chinese Communists Stalin had not been willing to offer the Vietnamese more than moral support at the most. With the changed situation on the Chinese mainland, Moscow was forced to devote more attention to Vietnam, and although Stalin granted Mao the practical responsibility for dealing with the situation in Vietnam, Soviet recognition and the possibility of future support made a huge difference to Hanoi. The fact that this happened only after the proclamation of the People's Republic further underscores China's important role with regard to Vietnam.

The Franco-Vietnamese War

When the Soviet Union and China recognized the DRV, the Franco-Vietminh war had lasted for more than three years. Not unexpectedly, the war and ways of assisting the Vietminh was one of the major topics in Soviet–DRV–China relations during the early 1950s. Developments in this period show that Beijing was much more involved in the affairs of the Vietminh than Moscow. As we have seen in the immediate postwar period, Stalin's foreign policy attention in the latter part of the 1940s was directed primarily towards Europe, to the degree that Stalin's focus on Asia up to 1950 was on developments within China. His first priority was the relationships with the United States, France and Great Britain, and all of these states were much more important to Kremlin than events in Indochina. When negotiations between Ho Chi Minh and the French failed to produce more than a modus vivendi agreement in September 1946 and full-scale war broke out in November–December, the Soviet Union apparently never even considered speaking up on behalf of the newly founded DRV.

The Soviet foreign ministry was regularly updated on developments in the war by Canton and through conversations with Vietnamese representatives in Southern China. Many of the details that came through the consulate were probably also available to Moscow through other, and quicker, sources. And both the Main Intelligence Directorate (GRU)[32] and the CPSU probably had other channels of information.[33] Still, the documents not only contained practical information on the progress of the war and the development of the economy, they also passed on the general sentiment existing among the Vietnamese people. The Vietnamese were eager to show the enthusiasm of the people, and the Soviet representatives willingly reported back to Moscow, even when the information presented had a clear character of propaganda. One such occasion was in April 1951, when a report presented to the Soviet consulate in Canton by DRV representatives described the mood amongst the people of Vietnam by saying that the repeated victories of the National Liberation Army had strengthened people's belief in the final victory in the resistance war against the French and American imperialists. It added further that the population had begun to participate more actively in the mobilization of forces that would assist the Vietminh front and that when they met trouble such as destruction causing floods or sudden attacks by French forces, this did not decrease the enthusiasm of the population in their effort to support the front.[34] No doubt, the Vietnamese hoped that their will to fight and overcome all obstacles could lead to more substantial Soviet support in the future.

Parallel to information on developments in the war, Moscow was also updated on internal developments in Vietnam. In spite of the war economy, the Vietminh leaders wanted to start building a society in accordance with Socialist principles. During the latter part of 1950 and the spring of 1951, several conferences were held to strengthen the foundation of the government, and, according to the Vietnamese report, those attending the conferences had all been very excited about the outcome. It was also underlined how this was an opportunity to build a society that 'draws on the multi-faceted experience of the people's democracies also in a situation when the state in question is established in an occupied zone, and the opposite party, the marionette regime, is on the way to breakdown without any opportunities to strengthen its position'.[35] This report shows some of the channels through which the Soviets received their information about Vietnam, but more importantly it gives an indication as to how the Vietnamese themselves wished to present the current development in their country. It is not unlikely that they hoped such an insight into the current situation would prompt some kind of Soviet assistance.

The autumn border campaign in 1950 was the first example of active Chinese assistance to the Vietminh army. Shortly after recognition, Ho asked the Chinese for military experts to train and advise the Vietminh army before and during battles. The Chinese agreed to send advisors but refused to send field commanders, and on 17 April 1950 the Chinese Military Advisory Group (CMAG) was formed. The CMAG consisted of advisors to the People's Army of Vietnam

(PAVN)[36] headquarters, three full divisions, and finally, an officers' training school. Altogether the CMAG would count 281 people – of which 79 were advisors and their assistants.[37]

The first major task for the CMAG was assisting the PAVN while planning and conducting the autumn border campaign in the summer/fall of 1950. Ho Chi Minh presented the idea of such an offensive in June 1950. The aim of the campaign was to clear out the French forces that occupied the northern part of Vietnam bordering China. With the French expelled from the area, the lines of communication with China would be open, and it would become much easier for the PAVN to receive both supplies and manpower from China. In spite of heavy losses on the Vietnamese side and the fact that the campaign exposed severe deficiencies within the PAVN with regard to both planning and command structure, the campaign was considered a success.[38]

In the early months of 1951 the optimistic mood after the success in their autumn border campaign, in which Chinese material and practical assistance had played a significant role, inspired the Vietminh to launch a large-scale regular-unit assault on the French positions around Hanoi in the Red River delta and the border region to China. The attack was a major setback, and the Vietminh lost around 6,000 soldiers.[39] Because this second campaign turned out to be rather catastrophic, the military situation in the DRV continued to be difficult throughout the latter part of 1951. Although several civilian tasks such as strengthening of government positions and, not least, the formal establishment of the Vietnamese Workers Party (VWP) had been successfully completed during 1951, the army had not been able to gain control over more vital territory. The larger cities and most important lines of communication remained in the hands of the French, who also had control over the airspace and the sea. This situation was, according to the Soviet embassy in Beijing, primarily a result of the increased American interest in Indochina. Whereas they earlier only assisted the French, the Soviets now claimed that Americans had become the 'principal aggressor' in the Indochinese war.[40]

The difficult military situation was not the only concern of the Soviets in Vietnam. The country's economic base remained extremely weak, and there was no industry to speak of. Once again the Soviet embassy pointed to the role of China and underlined that in the current situation it would be very difficult for the DRV government to continue the war on its own and therefore needed outside assistance, in particular from its closest neighbour – the PRC.[41]

In addition to the CMAG, the Chinese also participated in a campaign initiated by Ho Chi Minh to consolidate and strengthen the DRV government in 1951. Early that year the Chinese set up a civilian counterpart to the CMAG, the CPAG. The group was led by Luo Guibo, future ambassador to the DRV, and was set up to handle different sections within the North Vietnamese bureaucracy. It had sections for military affairs, finance and economy, public security, culture and education, united front, party consolidation and land reform. Altogether it consisted of over 100 advisors, who during that first year helped Ho Chi Minh set up laws and policies on matters ranging from finance to treatment of minorities.[42]

The two advisory groups, CMAG and CPAG, both played vital roles in consolidating the areas under Vietminh occupation and its military forces. They were both part of a larger programme initiated by Ho Chi Minh and were made possible by generous Chinese military and manpower assistance. In addition, they both showed China's interest in and willingness to contribute to the cause of the Vietnamese Communists even during a time when they were deeply committed to another Asian war – in Korea.

During 1952–53 the French turned to a more defensive strategy in the war against the Vietminh. This change was mainly due to a lack of manpower that constrained their military effectiveness. The French attitude opened up new possibilities to the Vietnamese, and in early 1952, this time initiated by the CMAG, the PAVN began planning a large campaign in the northwest territory of Vietnam. There were two main reasons for targeting this region in particular: First, the French defences there were considered to be rather weak and the odds for a Vietminh victory were good. Second, if the Vietminh could secure this area under its control, the chances of an attack from its rear would be very unlikely. The whole plan for the northwest campaign was followed closely in Beijing, and Luo Guibo's strategies were approved by CCP Central Military Commission before the Vietnamese went into action.[43]

In contrast to the Chinese, the Soviets apparently were not involved in the planning and financing of the PAVN campaigns during the Franco-Vietnamese War. However, the Chinese had asked Moscow for advice and approval before the autumn 1950 campaign started. While visiting the Soviet Union between 17 August and 22 September 1951, Zhou Enlai mentioned the plan for a Northwest campaign to Stalin. Zhou was then in Moscow to seek Soviet economic aid. According to one scholar, Stalin approved of the campaign and suggested that if the Vietminh could succeed in surrounding Hanoi, Ho Chi Minh could bring up the issue of peace talks with France. Stalin further added that if Paris rejected any form of negotiations, the Vietminh could move southwards after taking control over Hanoi.[44]

In April 1952 the DRV sent its first ambassador to the Soviet Union. Nguyen Long Bang was born in 1904 and had been an active revolutionary in Vietnam in the mid-1920s.[45] With Nguyen Long Bang's arrival, the Soviet leaders now had a direct source of information from Vietnam. Due to the war the Soviets had yet to set up representation in Vietnam, and when the DRV ambassador came to Moscow, he was met with questions on whether the DRV had been able to decide on a capital in the liberated areas of Vietnam. In response to this, Nguyen Long Bang informed them that although the liberation army had control over several towns, the DRV did not yet have a permanent capital. Until a decision was made, the central governmental and party establishments would have to periodically move from one place to another, principally within the limits of the three provinces Thai Nguyen, Bac Kan and Tuyen Quang. The ambassador also added that the towns within this area were almost completely in ruins.[46]

The Soviets were already familiar with the Chinese military assistance to the DRV, but Nguyen Long Bang could add more details to the tale. In his report to the Soviet foreign ministry handed over on 14 May 1952, he stated that 80 per cent of the weapons used by the PAVN were supplied by the Chinese. Parts of the Vietnamese army in the northern regions of the country were rather well equipped with light infantry weapons.[47] What they did need were machine guns and automatic weapons. He also emphasized the vital role of the Chinese advisors in planning attacks and teaching soldiers and officers. The DRV army's military operations had gained a much higher standard since the Chinese came to help.[48] The facts presented by the DRV ambassador were well received in Moscow, and the Soviet leaders seemed rather pleased with the Chinese taking on all the practical and economic issues related to Vietnam.

Although Stalin assured Zhou Enlai that he approved of the forthcoming campaign, Ho Chi Minh found it best to talk to the Soviet leader himself. He went on a secret trip from Beijing to Moscow in October 1952 to attend the Nineteenth Congress of the CPSU. Before the meetings took place Ho and Stalin corresponded about the circumstances surrounding Ho's visit. Because of the situation in Vietnam, Ho was very reluctant to publicly announce his arrival in Moscow, as he explains in his letters to the Soviet leader. Throughout the exchange of letters the tone between the two leaders was extremely polite, and even to a certain degree loving, this in spite of accusations that Stalin distrusted Ho Chi Minh.[49] In a letter of 30 September 1952, Ho first informed Stalin about his plans to travel to Moscow and attend the 19th Party congress incognito. He underlined that he did not want attention drawn to his visit, because he feared that the enemy (French) could use the opportunity to attack the Vietminh forces. However, if he would be unable to make it to the Party congress himself, he would like to send Nguyen Long Bang as his representative. Nevertheless, he intended to visit Moscow to inform them about the situation in Vietnam and discuss questions related to the struggle and the work within the Vietnamese Communist Party with Stalin. Stalin replied with a cable on 2 October 1952, in which he welcomed Ho to Moscow and said that he approved of the idea of travelling incognito. In his reply on 17 October, Ho informed Stalin that he wanted Liu Shaoqi to participate in the discussion about Vietnam.[50] During his stay in Moscow, Ho Chi Minh met with Stalin and Liu Shaoqi on 28 October to discuss the current policies of the Vietminh.[51] On 19 November Ho wrote in his farewell letter to Stalin that he would work hard on the implementation of land reform and the war. Since the details of these discussions remain unavailable on the Soviet, Chinese and Vietnamese side, the actual details of the talks remain unknown; however, taking into account Ho's words in his letter of 19 November the Vietnamese leader most probably sought Stalin's support.[52]

By the summer of 1953 the practice of Chinese military assistance to the DRV was well established. The current state of China's role in Vietnam was discussed during a meeting between the Soviet ambassador to Beijing, Vasilii Vasilievich Kuznetsov, and Zhou Enlai in June 1953.[53] At the time, the army under Ho Chi Minh's control was continuously gaining strength and manpower. These forces had Chinese advisors, and DRV officers were educated in China. From a Chinese point of view, the main problem was the lack of people to join the armed forces.

As in Korea, most of the population lived in the southern part of the country. However, Zhou Enlai underlined, 'we are not going to send our forces to Indochina'.[54] The Chinese attitude showed that in 1953 the Chinese were as involved as they wanted to be in Vietnam. They had no intentions of participating in the battles along the same lines as they recently did in Korea.

Available sources suggest that the Soviet Union's involvement in the Franco-Vietnamese War was minimal and that the interest did not increase even with the conclusion of the Korean War. Throughout 1953, the DRV government was preoccupied with the conduct of land reform – a campaign that was fully supported by the Chinese contingent in Vietnam and that to a large degree was formed after the Chinese model. One has, however, to keep in mind that the North Vietnamese campaign took on a less rigid form than the Chinese reform. Through the land reform campaign, the DRV leaders showed how much they depended on the Chinese experience to form their future state. Although Vietnamese nationalists/Communists had talked about land reform since the 1920s, it was only with Chinese guidance they had gotten so far.[55]

Recognition and new challenges

With the proclamation of the PRC in 1949, Stalin emphasized China's important role as the leading Communist power in Asia by indicating a division of labour between Moscow and Beijing. The Soviet Union would deal with Europe, and China would take charge of developments in Asia. However, Stalin's division of labour proposal should be viewed with some suspicion. Even if the Sino-Soviet relationship functioned well at the time, Stalin's previous experience with independent Communist leaders, more precisely Tito, suggests that he would not allow Mao any independence in the region. It is equally unlikely that he would regard positively the rise of a strong and independent Vietnamese leader such as Ho Chi Minh. And as a result, during the last years of his life, Stalin did not want to put the Soviet Union at risk by directly sustaining revolutions in Asia. He left this burden to China, with regard to both Korea and Indochina.

The major change in Moscow's view on the Vietnamese situation came with the victory of the CCP. Events surrounding the recognition show how both China and the Soviet Union were considered important partners by the Vietnamese. During the first few years of the 1950s the triangular relationship between Moscow, Hanoi and Beijing seems to have functioned satisfactorily in the view of all three countries. The DRV received large amounts of assistance from China, and to a lesser extent from the Soviet Union through China, in the form of equipment, officers and advice. The Soviet Union could follow the situation in Vietnam from a distance, content with the fact that the aid it provided through China was well applied, and did nothing to harm Moscow's relations with more important countries in the West. The PRC secured its own strong position in the Communist world, and especially within Asia, acting as provider of equipment and advice to a struggle that would prevent French or even American domination in Vietnam. While the PRC was important because it secured Vietnam's northern border, the

DRV served as a buffer between the PRC and possible takeover of South Vietnam by imperialist states.

From a Soviet point of view, this form of cooperation was indeed very advantageous, and it was possible to pursue it because in the first few years of the 1950s Moscow was clearly superior to Beijing within the Socialist camp. The approach relieved the Soviets of heavy burdens in countries far away, and it allowed the Chinese a certain amount of liberty in the foreign policy conduct towards Indochina. The one party that suffered most from this arrangement must have been the DRV and its leaders; however, even to them the picture was not entirely grim. They had managed to establish an important link to the Soviet Union and awakened at least marginal interest in their cause among the Soviet leaders even though it was through Chinese channels. Later on, the Vietnamese leaders would regret that they had been unable to forge close relations with Moscow in this period and hence had became too dependent on China. In retrospective, Moscow might have shared these regrets wishing that it had not made its own relationship with the Vietnamese so dependent on Beijing.

3 The end of the war and the Geneva conference, 1953–1954

While both 1951 and 1952 had been bad years for the Vietminh, by 1953 the situation was about to change. With the end of the Korean War that summer, the Chinese could now be more attentive to the needs of the Vietnamese Communists in their struggle with the French. In 1953 and early 1954, in response to French military changes, the Vietminh made significant changes in its military strategy; the implementation of these changes eventually led to the battle at Dien Bien Phu in the spring of 1954, and subsequent negotiations at Geneva during that summer.[1] Parallel to the changes in military fortunes, the governments of France, the Soviet Union, China and the DRV became gradually more positive to seeking a diplomatic solution to the conflict.[2]

The main aim of this chapter is to evaluate the Soviet role in the period leading up to the conference and during the negotiations in Geneva, primarily with focus on its position vis-à-vis its Chinese and Vietnamese allies. Providing advice to the Vietnamese Communists was an important task for both the Soviets and the Chinese, and while Moscow was in charge of the stage directions, the Chinese dealt with all the practicalities. The active role assigned to Beijing also meant that, on certain occasions, the Soviet leadership allowed its Chinese comrades to make at least some vital decisions, although only within certain predefined frameworks discussed with the Soviets in advance.[3] By taking on the role as the active party, Beijing's policy considerations would exerted a significant influence on Soviet policies and therefore became one of the most important Soviet tools during the conference.

Another central focus in this chapter is Moscow's overall agenda, which was not only about the future situation in Indochina. An equally important driving force behind Soviet strategies and diplomacy during the Geneva conference was the need to secure Moscow's foreign policy interests, both in Indochina and in other parts of the world. To what extent was this position compatible with its commitments to its Chinese and Vietnamese allies? Together with the PRC, the Soviet Union shared a common desire to end the wars in the region, and during the conference the two countries followed a line of consultations and close cooperation. Moscow was the more moderate partner of the two and expected less from the final outcome than the Chinese and much less than the DRV.[4]

In the aftermath of the conference, strategists in Moscow and Beijing were accused of restraining the DRV while at the same time letting international strategic considerations take precedence over their ideological commitment to support the struggle of a fellow Communist party.[5] Without doubt, issues other than the future interest of the Vietnamese Communists played a significant role as part of Moscow's plan in Geneva; notwithstanding this, Soviet policy makers also worked out their plans based on what they considered to be the best possible solution for Vietnam and the future strategy of the VWP. Is it possible that partition in itself did not trouble the Soviets, simply because they viewed the final outcome of the conference as advantageous to Hanoi based on the notion that the North now would be able to consolidate and rebuild its strength before taking further steps to achieve reunification? This chapter attempts to further elaborate this question.

Preparing for the conference

After the end of the Korean War in the summer of 1953 the Communist powers launched what has been labelled a 'peace offensive'. The beginning of this initiative was the proposal of 26 September from the Soviet Union to the governments of France, Great Britain and the United States to organize a five-power conference, with the participation of China, to discuss ways of easing international tensions. On 8 October the Chinese endorsed the Soviet suggestion. Three months later, Beijing followed up with another proposal in which they emphasized that the problems in Asia needed to be resolved through direct discussions among the big powers. The final endorsement of the Soviet proposal came at a four-power conference in Berlin at the end of January 1954, at which it was decided to convene an international conference at Geneva to discuss the restoration of peace in Korea and Indochina during the summer of that year.[6]

On 8 May the Indochina phase of the conference opened, and more than two months later, on 20 July 1954, the Geneva agreements were signed. The signing of the agreements marked the end of the Franco-Vietminh war and the beginning of French withdrawal from Indochina (Vietnam, Laos and Cambodia). During the conference, Vietnam was divided into two zones, with separate administrations. The southern zone, the State of Vietnam (SVN) was ruled by the American-supported Ngo Dinh Diem, and the northern zone, the DRV, by Ho Chi Minh and the Communist party.[7]

One of Moscow's main aims before and during the conference was to actively integrate the PRC into the club of the Four Great Powers – the United States, Great Britain, France and the Soviet Union. That was an acknowledgement of the role China was playing both in Korea and, more recently, in Vietnam. Moscow's emphasis on the Chinese role was not only displayed through Sino-Soviet cooperation in preparations for the conference but also in Soviet–American encounters. The Soviet insistence on bringing China into the conference as an equal partner, even in spite of American protests, indicates the degree of importance the Soviets were willing to attach to the role of China in reducing international tensions in Asia.[8]

Soviet Foreign Minister Vyacheslav Molotov, who was in charge of Soviet preparations for the conference, argued in a meeting with the US Secretary of State, John Foster Dulles, during the Berlin conference that the Soviets would not agree to any accusations against China on the question of Indochina. He pointed to the fact that the war in Indochina began several years before the establishment of the PRC and thus was a result of the unsatisfactory policies pursued by the French, and not the fault of the Chinese. Molotov reminded Dulles that at the beginning of the Berlin conference he had told French Foreign Minister Georges Bidault that the Soviet Union and the PRC could assist with mediation in the Indochinese question. However, he remarked, since then the French had not said anything except on general issues.[9]

Thus, the status of the PRC and their role during the conference became a major issue alongside the more practical question of how to organize day-to-day work during the conference. In March, several conversations took place between Charles Bohlen, the US ambassador to the Soviet Union, and Soviet Deputy Foreign Minister Vasilii Vasiljevich Kuznetsov on the subject of China's role in Geneva. Bohlen insisted on keeping all discussions within the sphere of the four Great Powers, whereas the Soviet Union wanted the leaders of the PRC to be consulted on several issues. In 1954 the United States had not yet recognized the PRC government and considered Chiang Kai-Shek's Republic of China in Taiwan to be the legitimate representative of China.

Moscow's insistence on keeping the Chinese informed soon led to trouble. A Soviet comment regarding the organizational aspects of the conference stating that 'the Soviet Union had been discussing organizational questions regarding the conference with Beijing', and that 'the People's Republic of China agreed with the Soviet position', seriously provoked the Americans.[10] Ambassador Bohlen made it clear to the Soviet Union that they might well consult China if they wanted to but should keep in mind that the it was the four Great Powers which were responsible for the conference and that the PRC only had participant status. Replying to this, Soviet Deputy Foreign Minister Kuznetsov underlined that the Soviet Union had no intention of ruining the agreement made in Berlin and further argued that discussing these practical questions with China would make organization of the conference easier.[11] The Berlin communiqué, the official announcement following the Berlin conference published on 19 February 1954, declared that during the Geneva conference the PRC should have a position equal to that of the four Great Powers.[12] In spite of these Soviet arguments, Washington kept insisting that the four powers, not five, would remain responsible for organizing the conference and added that once the conference began, all participating countries would have an equal status.[13]

Once the Berlin conference was over, Soviet officials began preparations for the conference in Geneva, which was scheduled to open on 26 April. Korea was the first item, and the session devoted to the Indochina problem was scheduled to begin on 8 May. In Moscow, the Southeast Asia department in the Soviet foreign ministry was in charge of compiling preparatory materials for the Soviet delegation to the conference.[14] While Moscow was discussing organizational questions with the Americans, the Chinese began preparing for the trip to Geneva. The new leaders in Beijing were about to participate in their first international conference; and in meetings with the Soviets during preparations for the conference, Prime Minister Zhou Enlai assured the leaders in Moscow that China would do its best to cooperate with the Soviets.[15]

The Chinese were excited by the prospects of participating at the Geneva conference and not least the acknowledgement of the 'new' China that was inherent in this event. Since its foundation, the PRC had been excluded from many activities of the international community, and the fact that it would now participate at an international conference alongside the Great Powers signalled that it had emerged as a major power.[16] It was in this atmosphere that the Chinese began their preparations for the conference. The main architect behind the Chinese preparations was Zhou Enlai. In several speeches to his associates Zhou analysed the prospects, indicating that while it would probably be difficult to achieve a peaceful settlement in Korea, the chances of reaching agreement on the Indochina issue were much better. Zhou further argued that the main reason why it could be possible to reach consensus on the Indochina issue was the differences that existed between France and the United States. Based on this, Zhou wanted to create a Communist strategy that would appeal to the French while at the same time alienating the Americans. The idea that France was the key to an agreement was followed by the Chinese throughout.[17]

In early March, China's preparations for the conference had already come quite far, and by 2 March the Chinese had already worked out a preliminary document on how to proceed during the conference. The document, entitled 'Preliminary Paper on the Estimation of and the Preparation for the Geneva Conference', maintained that the Chinese should primarily attempt to exploit the differences between the Western countries. They should try to reach an agreement even if only a temporary one and should continue to strive for the restoration of peace in Indochina even if it might be a long-term struggle. The most important task was to avoid a fruitless conference. The Chinese were also prepared to negotiate even if fighting was still going on, and such a situation should be exploited to increase the differences between the United States and France, as well as to increase internal pressure in France. From a Chinese point of view, that could prove to become very valuable for the success of the national liberation struggles in Indochina.[18]

During the Geneva preparations China left nothing to chance. The best example was the case of Huang Hua, who was appointed spokesman for the Chinese delegation. In early March, Huang was recalled from the Chinese negotiation team at Panmunjon, where negotiations for the Korean conflict took place, to Beijing, to contribute his knowledge and expertise in international negotiations to the Geneva team. To make sure that he would be able to handle the different questions that were likely to be posed in Geneva, a mock meeting with the press was organized to test his ability to answer properly.[19]

Alongside national planning procedures, coordination of policies and strategies between the Soviet, Chinese and North Vietnamese leaders was the most important part of the preparations. The Chinese played an active part in pushing preparations forward, not least with regard to the Vietnamese. In mid-March, Zhou Enlai told Ho Chi Minh to hurry up and start preparations. The Chinese premier emphasized to the Vietnamese Communists that the current international situation and military developments in Vietnam were advantageous for the DRV to conduct a diplomatic struggle. Furthermore, no matter what came of the Geneva conference it would serve the cause of the Vietnamese struggle to actively participate. Zhou also encouraged the Vietnamese to make up their mind on where a demarcation line should go in case a ceasefire was within reach. At the end of March, Ho left for Beijing and flew on to Moscow. The three parties had their first meeting to discuss strategies for the conference on 1 April 1954, when Zhou Enlai, Ho Chi Minh and Pham Van Dong met with Premier Nikita Khrushchev and Foreign Minister Molotov in Moscow.[20]

Soviet proposals for the restoration of peace in Indochina were on the table by mid-March. Although no Soviet records of these meetings are currently available, it is safe to assume that the memorandum served as a basis for negotiations between the three parties. The document consisted if three parts and the first part outlined the basis on which the Soviet delegation would negotiate. The Soviet delegation must establish the right of the representatives of the DRV to participate at the conference. If the Western powers agreed to this, the Soviet delegation should leave it to the Vietnamese and Chinese delegations to show initiative in putting forth suggestions on the conditions for establishing a ceasefire or the restoration of peace in Indochina. Finally, the Soviet delegation should strive for the establishment of ceasefire conditions in Indochina that would be acceptable to the Ho Chi Minh government, as well as strive for the opening of negotiations between the DRV and France on further steps to establish peace. Thus, Soviet policy makers concluded that, while supporting and standing up for the legitimate interests of the DRV, the Soviet delegation should at the same time pursue the goal of strengthening the relations between the Soviet Union and France.[21] These statements from Moscow underlined how the Soviet Union intended to assign the difficult task of dealing with the Vietnamese Communists to the Chinese delegation. At the same time Soviet policy priorities were quite clear: the goal of improving relations with France and, as a part of that, preventing German rearmament by undermining the establishment of the European Defence Community (EDC) should not be sacrificed to secure gains for the DRV.

The Soviet plans were further divided into three separate positions. The first part was labelled the maximum programme. As indicated by its name, this was the preferred solution seen from a Soviet point of view. Its first condition was a full ceasefire in the whole territory of Vietnam. In the sphere of Franco–Vietnamese relations it required French recognition of the full sovereignty and independence of the DRV, withdrawal of all French forces from the territory of Vietnam within six months, the establishment of a French–Vietnamese commission to discuss all questions of the restoration of peace in Indochina and to supervise the fulfilment of the conditions of the ceasefire, including mutual exchange of prisoners of war. From the Vietnamese side it would be expected that the DRV recognize the presence of French economic and cultural interests in Vietnam (use of the French merchant fleet, trade/commerce, etc.) on conditions subject to the agreement between the governments of France and the DRV. The DRV government must present a declaration saying that they would not prosecute persons who had worked for the French expeditionary corps in the war against the DRV. The final point in the first position was directed towards the United States, demanding that their interference in the matters of Indochina must come to a stop.[22]

The second Soviet position was more moderate than the first, and therefore a much more likely basis for negotiations. The section demanding a full ceasefire had been replaced with a demand for a full stop in military actions on the whole territory of Indochina, and full French withdrawal was limited to the territory north of the 16th parallel. In this position, Moscow also put forth the first mention of a referendum to reunite Vietnam as soon as all French forces had been withdrawn. However, just as in the first position, the second position contained a clause that the 'U.S. interference in the matters of Indochina must come to a stop'.[23]

Finally, the document contended, the Soviet delegation should resort to the third, and final, position emphasizing that in case it turns out to be impossible to reach agreement on the basis of the suggestions of the second position, go for a solution that military actions should stop on the condition that the French forces are drawn back to specific places in Vietnam which had already been decided upon by the two parties involved. After reaching a ceasefire, they should decide on a commission composed of representatives from France and the DRV which would work out conditions that would secure a peaceful regulation of the Vietnamese problem. The commission would also be responsible for observing the conditions of the ceasefire. In the last point of the third position, the Soviets underlined that one should provide recommendations for both parties to resolve difficult questions and to prevent a resurrection of military actions.[24] In the very last comment on the prospects for successful negotiations, the Soviet memorandum concluded that 'in case we reach no agreement on the Indochinese problem, we should submit for consideration to the conference the suggestion recommending that France and the DRV begin direct negotiations on how to re-establish peace in Indochina'.[25]

From mid-March 1954, when these instructions were on the drafting table, and until the conference began, issues might have been added or removed. Still, this draft does give several clues as to how the Soviet delegation intended to pursue peace in Indochina during the conference. The most noticeable difference between the first position and the final outcome of the conference is the absence of suggestions regarding the three most important features of the Final Declaration, namely the partition of Vietnam at the 17th parallel, the all-Vietnamese elections to be held within two years and, finally, the establishment of the International Control Commission (ICC).[26]

In the second position, which was the closest to the actual Final Declaration of the conference, the Soviets took a more moderate stand. Most important in this position was, of course, the very first mention of possible partition at the 16th parallel. However, there were several elements in this position that were difficult to negotiate with the Western powers. The most difficult aspects of the second position were probably the tough stand on US interference and the uncertainties around the future of the non-Communist part of Vietnam after the proposed elections. And although a partition at the 16th parallel was indicated in the suggestion on how and when the French forces would withdraw from Vietnam, an actual division of the country into two distinctly separate parts was not mentioned directly in either of the three negotiation positions in the Soviet memorandum.

While preparing for the conference, Soviet policy makers safeguarded their positions by introducing several alternative options for negotiations. Such a strategy was reflected in the three-stage instructions from mid-March. The strategy document also reveals that to Moscow the most important aspects of the negotiations were to establish contact between the Vietnamese Communists and the French government and to make sure that in case none of the other suggestions were accepted by the Western powers, it would at least be possible to reach an agreement between these two parties. It is also worth noticing that in the third and final position the Soviets had abandoned the clause prohibiting US interference. That further indicates how far Moscow was willing to go to reach consensus with the Western powers over the Indochina issue. On a more general level the thorough planning in the spring of 1954 also shows that the Soviet leaders were determined to achieve a solution before the closure of the conference, even if it meant going back on some of their initial wishes laid out in the so-called 'maximum programme'.[27]

During the spring of 1954, Soviet analysts continued to work on ideas similar to the three 'positions' outlined above. The continued emphasis on several of the main aspects of these positions indicate their importance in the discussion of Soviet strategies for the conference. This was primarily reflected during plans for discussions with the Chinese, and also the Vietnamese, during the next few months.[28]

By early April, the Soviet position seemed clearer and more articulated. One reason could be information obtained by the Soviet ambassador in Paris on French ideas for possible solutions to the Indochina problem at the end of March. However, these solutions were presented not by the government in power but by a foreign policy advisor to the coming French Prime Minister, Pierre Mendés-France. According to this advisor, France would agree to the following conditions: a ceasefire in Vietnam, Laos and Cambodia, free elections controlled by neutral countries in Vietnam, and introduction in Vietnam, for a limited period of time, of forces from neutral countries to control the implementation of these free elections; in addition, France wanted to secure its economic and cultural interests in Vietnam after an election. Further, the French acknowledged that a new regime was necessary in Vietnam based on the election results, and that it was necessary to prevent repressions against those who had collaborated with the other side during the war. One should, however, note that during this conversation emphasis was on regulation of the situation in Vietnam, and for Laos and Cambodia it was only a question of obtaining a ceasefire. France wanted to keep the monarchy in Laos and Cambodia and underlined that the political regime in these countries was not a topic for discussion with regard to the restoration of peace in Indochina.[29]

The meetings between the Soviets, Chinese, Vietnamese and North Koreans took place in Moscow between 1 and 3 April, but the participants were not able to reach any final decisions on strategies for the Indochina phase of the conference. Thus, the Soviets planned more specific questions that would be raised in future talks with Zhou Enlai and Ho Chi Minh. Among these were the question of whether Laos and Cambodia would participate with their own delegations and, if not, whether representatives from these countries could be included in the DRV delegation. If the conditions were acceptable to the DRV, the Soviet Union suggested that the Communist side not initiate a proposal for ceasefire, but support France if she suggested that. Likewise, a settlement was dependent upon French support for the DRV's independence and non-alignment, the withdrawal of all French forces, the DRV's recognition of French economic and cultural interests in Vietnam, and a guarantee that the DRV abstain from prosecution of those who had collaborated with France.[30] These conditions were all very similar to those proposed by Mendés-France's foreign policy advisor – thus a policy that at least with time would be acceptable to the French.

The Soviet leaders were also eager to determine Zhou Enlai and Ho Chi Minh's attitude to all-Vietnamese free elections. In the Soviet plans for negotiations in Geneva, the only mention of elections was the possibility of a referendum in the part of Vietnam south of the 16th parallel, and no suggestions of common elections for the whole country. Another issue that would have to be sorted out was the Chinese and North Vietnamese attitude to partition of Vietnam at the 16th parallel as suggested in the Soviet plans. In case the Western powers suddenly should suggest a coalition government in Vietnam the Soviet leaders saw a need for a unified strategy. And finally, Moscow also wanted to discuss whether the Communist bloc should develop their own strategy for the partition of Vietnam which would grant advantages to the DRV, such as recognition of the country's independence and sovereignty, the withdrawal of French forces, etc.[31]

All the issues mentioned above were, to some degree, open to discussion, but on the question of the United States' presence in Vietnam, the Communist bloc had made up their minds: 'any agreement on Indochina, also a ceasefire, shall contain a clause on the end of U.S. interference in Indochinese affairs'.[32] And as a part of the strategy to avoid a deeper American involvement in the affairs of Indochina in general and Vietnam in particular, the Communist side attached great importance to how to present their case in Geneva. Under no circumstances should it be possible to interpret Communist actions and statements 'as if the People's Republic at present is providing assistance to the DRV'.[33] The Soviet Union feared that an acknowledgement of Chinese assistance to the DRV could complicate the negotiations.

The final offensive

Information on developments in the Franco-Vietnamese war was a vital part of Soviet planning. In 1954, Moscow had no official representative in Vietnam, but there are indications that Soviet officers visited the southern part of China bordering Vietnam, or even Vietnam itself, to gather intelligence on the military situation. At the end of March, Soviet Lieutenant General Petroschevskii, who worked as military attaché at the Soviet embassy in China and military advisor to the PLA, reported to the Soviet ambassador in China, Pavel Fjodorovich Iudin, on his conversations with Chinese officials regarding the situation in Indochina. He informed Pavel on the status of the Vietminh and French forces at Dien Bien Phu, as well as more details on Vietminh strategies for April. Highlighting the importance of Chinese assistance and support, Petroschevskii quoted the Chinese point view on the current and future situation in Indochina. According to Petroschevskii, the Chinese emphasized how

> the people of Vietnam had expressed their wish to see Chinese volunteer units fight together with the Vietnamese People's Army in order to liberate Indochinese territory, just like we did in Korea. That would be impossible. To bring Chinese armed forces into the territory of Indo-China could complicate the international situation, and would be unfavourable for the national-liberation movements in Thailand and Burma.[34]

Petruschevskii added what seems to have been a Chinese opinion on how to solve the Indochinese problem. His Chinese conversation partner outlined three different ways to resolve the situation; the first option was to hold free elections for a government among the whole population of Vietnam, after the withdrawal of occupational troops, in which case most votes would be secured for the Democratic Republic. The second option would be a Korean solution with the partition of the country into two separate parts, and the third option would be to leave the situation in its current position.[35] Lieutenant General Petruschevskii gathered this information just before the Moscow meeting between the Soviets, Chinese and Vietnamese in early April.

Parallel to the preparations for the Geneva conference the Vietminh began attacking the French garrison at Dien Bien Phu. We have already seen how Chinese military advisors played a crucial role in the planning of Vietminh strategies in this period. In the period from 1950 to 1953 the Chinese had invested much money and manpower in strengthening the Vietnamese Communist forces. The Chinese attitude stood in stark contrast to what we have seen from Moscow. While the Chinese concluded that a victorious Vietnamese army would help secure success at Geneva, Moscow was reluctant to provide overt assistance to the Vietnamese in this crucial period leading up to the conference, even when confronted with rather small requests from the Vietnamese.

One example of Moscow's reluctance can be traced to January 1954, when the Vietnamese sent a request for trucks and regular cars to be used during the spring.

Reviewing the request, Deputy Foreign Minister Valerian Aleksandrovich Zorin came to the conclusion that, since it was not a question of weapons but about means of transport, 'it should be possible to satisfy the request of the Central Committee of the Vietnamese Workers Party, and supply these trucks with the help of the Chinese'.[36] There had earlier been requests for weapons such as the overt hints in the May 1952 report from the Vietnamese ambassador, Nguyen Long Bang, in which he underlined what kind of weapons the Vietminh lacked.[37] However, judging by Zorin's comment regarding the trucks, no weapons had been delivered or would be delivered from the Soviet Union to the Vietnamese Communists.

The decision to set up a strongly fortified garrison at Dien Bien Phu had been made by the French General Henri Navarre. Navarre was assigned to the post as commander of the French forces in Indochina in May 1953 and immediately began to work out a new three-year strategy aimed at winning back the advantage on the battle field. The plan was supported by the United States, who was now free from the burden of Korea and concentrated all its worries on the consequences of a French loss in Indochina. With a dramatic increase in US military and financial support to France, the French began to send additional forces to Indochina. General Navarre's plan consisted of a three-stage strategy intended to reverse the balance of forces and strengthen the French military position. During the fall and winter of 1953–54 he aimed to secure the strategically crucial Red River delta, and during the spring of 1954 he wanted to pacify the Communist-controlled areas in central and south Vietnam, in order to finally launch a general offensive to pursue, and destroy, the Vietminh main forces in the north.[38]

The first Vietminh attack on Dien Bien Phu came in January 1954. The attack, planned by the CMAG, came before the French had firmly established themselves in their positions. The Vietminh suffered heavy losses during this 'human wave' attack both because they had trouble moving artillery pieces fast enough and because the French troops moved much faster than expected. But because of the problems during this first attack, the CMAG and Vietminh decided to change tactics. Rather than searching for 'a quick solution' they would go for a strategy of 'steady progresses'. As a part of this steady progress strategy, the Chinese supplied the Vietminh with anti-aircraft guns that would enable the Vietnamese to break French air superiority and incapacitate the Dien Bien Phu airstrip. In addition to providing the anti-aircraft guns, the Chinese taught the Vietminh soldiers how to use snipers to disrupt French troop activity and to undermine the French morale. The Chinese also sent engineering experts who had served in Korea to assist in the construction of trenches in the areas surrounding the French garrison. The Vietnamese used these trenches to approach the French positions without the risk of being exposed to French firepower.[39]

The success of the Vietnamese Communists during the Dien Bien Phu campaign was to a large degree a result of the enormous practical and logistical support from the PRC. However, one should not disregard the enormous effort made by the thousands of Vietnamese men and women who carried out the battle and, not least, provided the necessary support for the front lines.[40] The victory at

Dien Bien Phu was regarded as imminent both by the Vietnamese and the Chinese. Beijing explains the Chinese support, emphazising how 'Mao wanted a victory at Dien Bien Phu in order to strengthen the Communist position at the negotiating table'.[41] And in that regard the timing was perfect. The Vietminh launched its final offensive on 1 May 1954, and six days later, on 7 May, the French capitulated. The Indochina phase of the Geneva Conference was scheduled to open the day after – 8 May.[42]

Negotiating in Geneva

On several occasions, Chinese sources underline the close cooperation between the Soviet Union and China before and during the conference and add significant information on the topic currently unavailable in Russian archives. Both Soviet and Chinese sources emphasize the mutual understanding between Moscow and Beijing on the importance of China's role during the conference. Still, the Soviet Union was clearly the 'older brother' in Geneva, and during the conference sessions Zhou Enlai always sought advice, and received approval, from Molotov before presenting the parties with new suggestions. The reason for this good cooperation was that the Soviet and the Chinese views were consistent; they both wanted to end the war in Indochina. However, their expectations from the conference were different. Whereas the Soviet Union was pessimistic and did not expect too much, China, on the other hand, wanted to strive to achieve results. The Chinese underlined that just the very fact that the PRC, the DRV, and North Korea were allowed to participate was in itself a victory.[43] To Moscow, however, the participation of China, North Korea and the DRV at the conference was among the prerequisites for the negotiations.[44]

In the spring of 1953 General Vo Nguyen Giap, Commander-in-Chief of the PAVN, had moved his troops into Laos but withdrew after a few months. In October 1953 his troops once again entered Laos, and by January 1954, units of PAVN controlled more than half of Laos and small areas of northern Cambodia. Giap's offensives were meant to support the liberation movements in these countries.[45]

While in pre-conference consultation with both Beijing and Moscow, the Vietnamese Communists apparently agreed that a settlement following the principle of temporarily dividing Vietnam into two zones was acceptable. However, the victory at Dien Bien Phu made the Vietnamese believe that they were in a position to squeeze more concessions from their adversaries at the conference table. According to Chinese sources, the head of the Vietnamese delegation, Pham Van Dong, announced at the conference that in order to settle the Indochina problem, 'the Vietminh would ask for establishing its virtual control of most parts of Vietnam (through an on-the-spot truce, followed by a national plebiscite, which they knew that they could win), and, while denying the existence of Vietminh troops in Laos, pursuing positions for the "resistance forces" in Laos and Cambodia by treating the settlement of the Laos and Cambodian problems as part of a general settlement of the Indochina problem'.[46] The statements from

Pham Van Dong caused considerable trouble among the Communist delegations at the conference. On several occasions, the Chinese had to use considerable pressure to stop the DRV foreign minister from undermining the possibility of a settlement.[47]

On 24 June 1954, while in Moscow during a three-week recess of the Geneva conference, Foreign Minister Molotov gave a preliminary report on the work of the conference to the CPSU Central Committee Plenum. The conference had now finished its first phase. During this phase it had mainly discussed the Korean question, on which it had not been able to find common ground, but the participants had also begun discussion of the Indochina issue. Underlining that the discussion on Indochina was still at a very early stage, Molotov remarked that the political negotiations had yet to begin. Until now the parties had concentrated on discussing the terms of a ceasefire.[48]

However, one of the major problems with regard to establishing a ceasefire was the Vietnamese refusal to admit that their troops had taken active part in fighting in both Laos and Cambodia.[49] According to Foreign Minister Molotov,

> the delegation of the Democratic Republic of Vietnam had during the Geneva conference, acknowledged that on the territory of Laos and Cambodia there had previously been a certain number of Vietnamese volunteers, that participated in the national-liberation movements of these countries, but that these volunteers had at one time been withdrawn. They had also admitted: if we find out that also today there are any Vietnamese volunteers in these countries, also these remaining volunteers will be called back. On this point one cannot but see the aspiration of the Democratic Republic of Vietnam to cooperate with all means in order to re-establish peace in all of Indo-China.[50]

Molotov's report to the CPSU Plenum was not entirely truthful. What he did not say in the report was that Vietnam was cooperating with regard to the volunteers not only because they wanted to withdraw their forces in the neighbouring countries but rather due to very strong pressure from both their allies, in particular the Chinese.

While Soviet documentation on negotiations during the conference remains scarce, the Chinese have released more detailed information on the day-to-day negotiations in China. One feature that stands out from the Chinese materials, and that is further reinforced by the lack of materials on the Soviet side, is the immense task of restraining the Vietnamese. Available materials show that this task was to a very large degree managed by the Chinese. In Molotov's report above, cooperation with the DRV is portrayed as uncomplicated, whereas the actual situation was somewhat different.

When the three delegations from the Soviet Union, the PRC and the DRV met on 5 May to finalize the Communist stand on the peace settlement in Indochina, they agreed to pursue an overall settlement including all three Indochinese countries. But the Vietnamese reluctance to withdraw, or even admit to the fact that they had troops in Laos and Cambodia, complicated the Chinese wish for a friendly atmosphere that would encourage continued discussions at the conference. The leader of the Chinese delegation, Zhou Enlai, therefore met with Pham Van Dong on 8 May and urged him to issue a statement that the Vietminh would arrange to release all seriously wounded enemy captives at Dien Bien Phu. Zhou also contacted Wei Guoqing, the chief Chinese military advisor at the Vietminh headquarters and told him that Geneva should at all times be updated on the Vietminh handling of this matter.[51]

However, at the same time the Vietminh victory also strengthened the Chinese belief that they could achieve a result in Geneva. A member of the Chinese delegation, Wang Bingnan, said that when he heard the news of Dien Bien Phu 'we spread it to each other. We were very much encouraged and felt more confident in solving the Indochina issue.'[52] As a result, the Chinese delegation came to Geneva with ambitious instructions from the leadership in Beijing. Their main aim during the conference was to exercise active diplomacy to break the American policy of isolation and embargo against China, as well as strive to reduce world tensions. Further, they should try to conclude agreements so as to set a precedent for solving international problems through Great Power consultations. Under all this lay the most basic objective of the Chinese government, namely to prevent an internationalization of the Indochina conflict. The Chinese would at all costs try to avoid a situation similar to the one they had experienced in Korea.[53]

The Chinese side has also argued that Moscow had only a limited interest in Indochina, and that to the Soviet leaders it was more important to undermine German rearmament than to continue revolutionary war in Southeast Asia.[54] An examination of available Soviet documents supports the view that China played the most active role in Geneva. Both Soviet and Chinese sources point to an active Chinese Foreign Minister, Zhou Enlai, as the man who secured a settlement at Geneva. However, a settlement of the Indochinese problem was of great importance to the Soviet Union as a means to prevent a possible outbreak of war in Indochina, and not only in terms of its impact on policies elsewhere.[55]

Moderating the Vietnamese stand became even more important after the new French Prime Minister, Pierre Mendès-France, took office on 16 June. Mendès-France had promised to resolve the situation in Indochina within 20 July, or resign. With the new climate and a renewed French eagerness to reach an agreement on Indochina, the Soviet Union and the PRC used all their influence on Ho Chi Minh and Pham Van Dong to convince them that now was the time to negotiate with France, and that they should not insist on keeping the demarcation line on the 14th or 15th parallel.[56] The idea of partition was initially presented by the Chinese. They hoped for a partition at the 16th parallel but realized that such a solution would cut off one of the essential French colonial highways, and decided to be willing to accept a partition at the 17th parallel.[57]

With Pierre Mendès-France in charge, Zhou saw an opportunity to reach agreement in the midst of French distress over the situation in Indochina. Moscow fully agreed with Zhou's stand in this question. It was time to settle while Mendès-France was in power, also probably because it now seemed possible to get a negative vote in the French National Assembly on the European Defence Community. The United States exerted much pressure on the French, and both Moscow and Beijing feared that if the Vietminh continued to present the French Prime Minister with unacceptable demands, the French government would collapse.[58]

A collapse of the Mendés-France government could possibly lead to a worsened situation in Indochina and ruin the chances of a settlement at that point. Soviet analysts further argued that the one of the main aims of Mendès-France' threat to resign unless agreement was reached in Geneva was to put pressure on the Soviet Union, the PRC and the DRV in order to improve the French position in the negotiations. Through conversations with close associates of the prime minister, diplomats at the Soviet embassy in Paris were given the understanding that the Mendès-France government needs

> a certain amount of 'help' to achieve a cease-fire in Indochina on conditions 'honourable' to France and announced that in case they did not succeed, Mendès-France would resign and a new government would take power, which would probably contribute to an internationalization of the war in Indochina.[59]

Such an outcome would, according to the informer, not be in the interest of either the French or the Soviets.

Thus, with the threat of yet another change of government in France, combined with the failure of the conference participants to reach agreement on the Korea question, the pressure to reach an agreement on the Indochina issue would become even greater. As earlier, the problem was the DRV attitude, and their refusal to admit the existence of their forces in Laos and Cambodia. At a meeting between the Soviet, Chinese and Vietnamese delegations on 15 June, Molotov, Zhou Enlai and Pham Van Dong agreed that the Communist camp should adopt a new policy with emphasis on the complete withdrawal of all foreign forces, including the Vietnamese volunteers from Laos and Cambodia. These concessions would in turn be used to opt for a more beneficial situation with regard to the division of Vietnam into two separate zones. According to Chinese sources, Molotov and Zhou had discussed this in several private conversations, whereas Pham Van Dong needed to be persuaded and pressured to concede to this new strategy.[60] To Hanoi, the question of forces in the two neighbouring countries was difficult because the Vietnamese Communists did not regard Cambodia and Laos as clearly foreign states and because for military logistical reasons, Indochina had to be considered one battlefield.[61]

In every sense of the word, Moscow considered China to be in charge of dealing with the Vietnamese Communists, as well as to add the necessary pressure to secure their consent for the negotiating strategy. Therefore, during the conference the Chinese delegation and Zhou Enlai in particular, invested much effort into reaching consensus with the Vietnamese comrades. In later accounts of the conference, the Soviets put particular emphasis on the Chinese role underlining that 'the Chinese delegation presented a number of specific suggestions, and played a vital role in reaching a settlement on the peaceful regulation in Indochina'.[62] Moscow further emphasized that this was particularly important in July, during the last stage of discussing the Indochina question. At that point there was a sharp increase in closed sessions and unofficial meetings between the parties, and the general opinion was that these meetings played an important role in the work of the Geneva conference. It was during these sessions and meetings that the Soviet and Chinese delegations did a tremendous amount of work in order to bring together the views of the opposing sides. According to the Soviet evaluation of the conference, it was in particular the strong effort of the Chinese delegation that led to a favourable decision in the question of reaching a ceasefire in Indochina.[63]

One very important meeting between the Chinese and the Vietnamese took place during the conference break at Geneva, when Zhou Enlai travelled to the Chinese city of Liuzhou to meet the leaders of the VWP.[64] Realizing the difficulties of discussing only through telegraphic exchanges, Zhou took this opportunity to personally discuss the problems of the conference with the Vietnamese leaders. However, before meeting with the Vietnamese leaders, Zhou Enlai met with the new French premier, Mendès-France, and promised him to help persuade the DRV to speed up negotiations. Thus, it was with the hope of concluding a peace settlement the Chinese leaders began the meeting with the Vietnamese on 3 July. Zhou's key argument during the meetings was the danger of a possible direct American intervention in Indochina. It was of vital importance to prevent an internationalization of the war, which could eventually lead to American involvement and create a situation similar to the one the Chinese had met in Korea.[65]

The result of the Liuzhou meeting was a general consensus between the Chinese and the Vietnamese on the strategies for the next phase of the negotiations in Geneva. During the meeting, the two parties agreed that they would propose the 16th parallel for the regroupment of troops, and that the 17th parallel should be proposed as the provisional military demarcation line. In addition, the Vietnamese side wanted general elections to be held within six months at the latest, whereas the Chinese proposed two years. The Chinese proposal was unpopular with the Vietnamese, who felt that the 'situation would be very difficult, once our troops had withdrawn to the North and we had to wait two years for the election'.[66] However, upon Ho's return to Vietnam the VWP Central Committee issued an instruction on 5 July (to be known as the 'July 5th Document') which apparently reflected the agreements reached in Liuzhou. It also included the new strategy in which the Indochina problem would be solved through a ceasefire based on a temporary division of Vietnam into two zones, as well as the suggestion of a nationwide election that would take place after the withdrawal of the French forces and, eventually, lead to a reunification of the whole country.[67] Ho's acceptance of these conditions, and his emphasis on the danger of American intervention, shows the strong Chinese influence.

Certain that they had reached consensus with the Vietnamese, the Soviet and Chinese leaders focused their attention on presenting a deal in Geneva that Mendès-France could accept. When briefing Molotov on the discussion during the Liuzhou meeting, Zhou admitted that Ho Chi Minh had agreed to the possibility of accepting the 17th parallel as the provisional demarcation line, if it should prove impossible to reach consensus over the 16th parallel. However, at the same time Pham Van Dong was still reluctant to carry out the agreements reached in Liuzhou, and Zhou once again met with Dong to reach a compromise that could be presented in the negotiations. During the meeting, Zhou emphasized both the danger of an American intervention and the need to act while Mendès-France was still in power in France to make Dong agree to the present plan for establishing the demarcation line. Finally Dong yielded, and at the end of the conversation Zhou had apparently promised to Dong that once the French had withdrawn their troops, 'all of Vietnam will be yours'.[68]

The Chinese performance during the Geneva conference was decisive, not only in the eyes of the Western powers but also to the Soviets. In his report to the Central Committee Plenum in late June, Soviet Foreign Minister Molotov once again praised China's role and emphasized that the most important aspect of the Geneva conference was the participation of the PRC,

> for the first time, on equal terms with the other Great Powers – the USSR, the United States, Great Britain and France. China's participation in the discussion of both questions – the Korean and the Indochinese – is important not only because the new, democratic China has now entered the international arena and assumed its rightful place among the Great Powers, but also because the Geneva Conference clearly shows that without the participation of the People's Republic of China, it is no longer possible to solve a number of international problems, and in particular those that concern the situation in Asia.[69]

This statement was made even before the conference had reached a final settlement and showed the extent to which Moscow appreciated China's effort in Geneva. The Soviets also went as far as to characterize the Chinese participation in Geneva as the 'actual international recognition of the People's Republic of China'.[70] At the Geneva conference the Chinese also had the opportunity to establish new contacts, in particular with countries that had yet to recognize the new Chinese regime. The first meeting between Chinese and American officials took place in Geneva, and the conference also improved Chinese relations with the countries of both South and Southeast Asia, in particular with the Indians.[71]

How close were relations between the Soviets and the Vietnamese on the eve of the conference? The Soviet Union and the DRV had no bilateral meetings either before or during the conference. All meetings were at least tripartite and took place with Soviet, Chinese and Vietnamese representatives present – and the occasional North Korean. In contrast, we have seen that there were several Sino-Vietnamese strategy meetings without the Soviets attending. An obvious question then is how close Sino-Vietnamese relations were on the eve of the conference? The very fact that everything went through the Chinese might indicate two things: first, that Moscow had other priorities in Geneva, in addition to reaching an acceptable solution to the problems in Indochina. Second, it could also mean that Moscow considered this still to be mainly China's responsibility. To this day it remains difficult to evaluate the status of Soviet–Vietnamese relations during the Geneva conference because of the continuous presence of China whenever the Soviets and the Vietnamese met. The setting further confirms the picture of China playing the vital role of intermediary all through the conference. It also shows how Moscow used the Chinese to achieve their own goals during the conference and that such a strategy was acceptable to the Chinese because to them the most important underlying aspect was to be accepted as an equal partner among the other Great Powers. In addition, the Chinese had in contrast to the Soviets, a clear geostrategic interest in securing the situation in Indochina.

Geneva and the future of Soviet–Vietnamese relations

In the early morning of 21 July 1954, the Geneva conference reached a settlement on the Indochina problem, just in time for Mendès-France's deadline.[72] The result of the Geneva conference was a settlement of the war in Indochina based on two separate but connected agreements: the Cease-Fire Agreement and the so-called Final Declaration. The first agreement was a ceasefire signed by the representatives of the belligerents: Ta Quang Buu, Vice Minister of National Defence for the DRV, and Brigadier General Henri Deltiel for the French Union Forces in Indochina. This agreement contained provisions for the regroupment of troops, and under its terms the troops of the PAVN (the Vietminh) would regroup north of the 17th parallel, while French union forces would regroup south of it.[73] In anticipation of the reunification elections, the provisions of the Agreement stated that the 'civil administration in each regrouping zone shall be in the hands of the party whose forces are to be regrouped there in virtue of the present Agreement'.[74] In addition, the provisions agreed upon in the ceasefire part of the Agreement stated that there were to be no troop reinforcements, no augmentation of weapons, no military bases and no foreign military alliances on the part of the administration of either zone. The conference also clearly recognized Laos and Cambodia as independent, sovereign states.

The second agreement, the Final Declaration, was dedicated to Vietnam's political future. It took note of several particulars of the ceasefire prohibiting any increase in troop levels, armaments, foreign military aid or the signing of alliances. The declaration also stated that the 17th parallel should not be interpreted in any way as a political or territorial boundary, and that free general elections by secret ballot were to be held two years later in July 1956 under the supervision of an ICC.[75]

The ICC consisted of representatives from India, Poland and Canada, with India holding the chairmanship. It was established at the time of the ceasefire to provide for control and supervision, while the actual responsibility for the execution of the Agreement rested with the parties. Consultations between representatives of the two zones to prepare for the elections were to start on 20 July 1955. However, this declaration was not signed by any of the heads of delegations, only verbally endorsed by some of them.[76] The agreement also provided for a joint commission composed of an equal number of representatives from the two zones, whose task was to facilitate the execution of those provisions of the Cease-Fire Agreement concerning the joint action of the two parties.[77]

Moscow considered the Geneva conference a success. Within the international context, Moscow had three equal issues on the agenda in Geneva: first, to promote Soviet objectives in Europe, more specifically to put pressure on the French government and thereby remove the threat of the proposed German rearmament through the EDC. Second, to remove the threat of escalation in Indochina through a US military intervention, and third, to introduce the PRC to the international diplomatic scene and possibly also reduce the tensions in China's relationship with the West, especially the United States.

The Soviet policy with regard to all three issues was a success. The most notable was probably the effect it had on the future of European military cooperation. In France, the slow progress at Geneva led to a government crisis and subsequently to the establishment of a government headed by Pierre Mendès-France, who was not enthusiastic about the idea of the EDC. On 30 August 1954, the French National Assembly refused to ratify the EDC proposal and thereby undermined the plans for German rearmament at that point.[78] Sino-Soviet cooperation during the conference was also a huge success. With their common desire to end war in the region, Moscow and Beijing shared the responsibility of advising the Vietnamese Communists both before and during the conference. Together the two powers exerted a restraining influence on the DRV, thereby illustrating how international strategic considerations took precedence over the ideological obligation to support the struggle of a fellow Communist party.

From the Soviet policy makers' point of view, the Vietnamese situation was a problem that needed to be solved in order to pursue larger and more important goals. And while the situation in Indochina was the problem, China was the means to solve it. The increased attention to China, and Beijing's eagerness and possibility to put pressure on the Vietnamese, was seen as a great benefit in Moscow. The change of government in France made the situation easier and gave the Communists a better opportunity to put positive pressure on the French while they at the same time tried to alienate the Americans. However, while Moscow wanted a conference to solve the problems of both Korea and Indochina, it did not want to sacrifice anything else to achieve results in Asia. They used the Chinese fear of American invasion and a Korea-like situation to make the Chinese pressure the Vietnamese. Moscow and Beijing had the same goals in Geneva, but for very different reasons. Both sacrificed a swift Vietnamese reunification in order to safeguard their own priorities. Moscow's priorities were a better relationship with the West and the French rejection of the EDC. Beijing needed to prevent an American intervention, a second 'Korean War', and, not least, to secure their southern border by the establishment of a Communist state between themselves and the imperialists.

In later accounts of the conference and its results, however, the Chinese and the Vietnamese were bitter to both China's and the Soviet Union's performance at Geneva. In a conversation between Mao and Pham Van Dong in mid-November 1968, Mao claimed that the Chinese had made a mistake when going to the Geneva conference in 1954. He emphasized that President Ho Chi Minh had not been satisfied that he had to give up the South, and, Mao continued, '[. . .] when I think twice, I see that he was right. The mood of the people in the South at that time was rising high. Why did we have the Geneva Conference? Perhaps, France wanted it'. Pursuing Mao's argument Zhou Enlai added that the suggestion to hold a conference had come from Khrushchev, who had wanted to solve the problem in Indochina. Without directly criticizing the Soviet involvement, Mao argued that the general public opinion had been in favour of such a conference but that it had been unfavourable to the Vietnamese Communists, who could have seized the whole country, had they not been forced to withdraw to the North. According to Mao, the Chinese and Vietnamese lost an opportunity by agreeing to participate at the Geneva conference.[79]

In spite of how the Chinese evaluated their own participation during the Geneva conference in later accounts, the preparations for and the actual conduct of the Geneva conference have shown that Moscow regarded China as an integral part of Soviet policies towards Vietnam. Once preparations for the conference began, Moscow's first priority was to secure the participation of both Beijing and Hanoi at the negotiating table. Soviet policy makers soon realized that without the active participation of China it would not be possible to conclude an agreement in Geneva.

But is it true that only strategic considerations played a part when Moscow elaborated its policies towards the conference and its main objective – Indochina – or is it possible that Soviet thinking with regard to Vietnam also reflected the ideological views of the Kremlin leadership? There is no doubt that Soviet conduct at Geneva has shown how self-interest played an important role in Soviet foreign policy-making both before and during the conference. However, if ideological considerations did play a role, it would, in this case, be in consensus with, and not in opposition to, the self-interest of the Soviet leaders. While on the one hand, the conference gave Moscow the perfect opportunity to introduce a new and by all means large player from the Communist camp, it also permitted the Soviets to play their policies of 'splitting the unity among the imperialist powers' together with their Chinese ally. Such a policy was reflected in how they tried to ally with the French and alienate the Americans.

One possible reason why Moscow found it rather easy to accept an agreement that seemed disadvantageous to the Vietnamese Communist leaders could have been based on what Moscow (from a Communist ideological point of view) thought was both possible to achieve and, not least, appropriate for the DRV at the time. To Moscow, the idea of consolidating the North while waiting for elections to reunite both zones was fully compatible with how a Communist society should develop. In other words, Moscow was satisfied with the results of the conference, both in terms of their larger strategic goals both in Europe and Asia and with regard to the prospects for future development of Communism in Vietnam.

As such, Geneva served the Soviet leaders well but would have serious implications for future relations between Moscow and the Vietnamese Communists. One can only assume that the conference most probably added to Hanoi's suspicions that the Soviet leaders were ready to sacrifice the DRV whenever that could benefit Soviet foreign policy interests.

4 Together for Communism?

Sino-Soviet cooperation and the rebuilding of North Vietnam, 1954–1957

The main concern of Moscow's Vietnam policy in the first few years after the Geneva conference was how to succeed with their 'peace offensive' towards the West, while at the same time strengthening their relations with China. However, during 1955 and 1956 these two policy goals were not always easy to reconcile, especially not without at times sacrificing the best interests of the Vietnamese. While focusing on China's role, the Soviet leaders failed to understand the seriousness of the developments that took place within the Lao Dong from early 1956 onwards. Publicly the Lao Dong leadership still promoted political struggle within the Geneva framework, but privately more and more individuals within the party leadership viewed a strategy of limited military actions as a possible supplement to the political struggle. From that point onwards Moscow gradually encountered an increasing distrust among the leaders in Hanoi, who feared that their Soviet allies were content with a more permanently divided Vietnam. Thus, in the latter half of the 1950s Moscow wanted a well-functioning relationship with the DRV, and to achieve that there was no way around China.

China played an important role in Vietnam during these years, not least because of its contributions to the reconstruction of Vietnamese society, in terms of both money and manpower. Cooperation with China soon became a condition for Soviet engagement in Vietnam, and Beijing's announcement in late 1955 of partial Chinese withdrawal from Vietnam was viewed with much concern in Moscow. Nonetheless, Moscow continued to emphasize both the importance of a well-functioning Sino-Soviet partnership in Vietnam and China's vital role as the main provider and organizer of 'aid and advice to the Vietnamese friends in deciding important questions in their foreign and domestic policies'.[1]

Four topics were particularly central in these first years after the Geneva conference: the reconstruction and consolidation of Vietnam; the struggle to implement the provisions of the agreement reached in Geneva, especially the consultations for and holding of all-Vietnamese free elections; the Twentieth Congress of the Soviet Communist Party and its effect on Moscow's relations with the Lao Dong and the CCP, with particular emphasis on its impact on the North Vietnamese land reform campaign; and finally Hanoi's discussions about a new, and more militant, strategy for reunification.

Reconstruction and consolidation in Vietnam

After the conclusion of the Geneva agreement, the North Vietnamese had their hands full with the reconstruction process, and emphasis was on consolidating the state north of the 17th parallel, rather than political developments in the South. In the North, the Lao Dong had a solid grip on power, and its leader, Ho Chi Minh, was a popular and charismatic leader. It was the Communist forces originating from the Vietminh who took power in the North after the Geneva partition. By 1954 the Lao Dong's control over the police, the military, the administration and the people at large was almost total, and accordingly there was no real opposition in that part of the country. Ho Chi Minh was in a favourable situation as the unquestioned leader of most of the people north of the 17th parallel and, in addition, some groups south of it.[2] Even so, some groups resisted, such as many of the Catholics in the North. In the early months after Geneva almost 1 million Catholics, encouraged by the Catholic hierarchy and organized by Ngo Dinh Diem's American advisors, fled from the North to the South.[3]

In the first months after the Geneva conference contact between Hanoi and Moscow consisted mostly of official communiqués referring to the Soviet assistance to the DRV during the negotiations at Geneva. The few appeals for assistance were made discreetly, and Moscow's assistance was kept on a low level. As long as the situation in Vietnam was calm, Moscow saw no need to interfere. Until the end of the Franco-Vietminh war the unstable situation in Vietnam had been considered a hindrance to a further elaboration of Soviet–Vietnamese contacts. However, with the new situation after the partition of Vietnam, the Soviet Union was able to establish an embassy in Hanoi, to maintain close contact with the DRV leaders. The first Soviet ambassador to the Democratic Republic of Vietnam, Aleksandr Andreevich Lavrishchev, arrived in Hanoi in late September 1954.[4] The establishment of a Soviet embassy in the DRV enabled Moscow to opt for a more active policy in Vietnam and relieved the Soviet leaders of their dependence on Chinese intelligence from Vietnam.

Ambassador Lavrishchev's main priorities should, according to Moscow, be to oversee the implementation of the ceasefire agreement, provide analyses of the degree of foreign presence in Vietnam and assess the chances of a reunification within the Geneva framework. More specific instructions were given on the need to carefully study both capitalist and Communist presence in Vietnam. The growing American influence in Southeast Asia was a serious concern, especially as a result of US efforts to include most of the countries in the region in a defence pact – the Southeast Asia Treaty Organization (SEATO).[5]

In addition, Moscow wanted the embassy to give priority to the study of the Soviet Union's closest ally in Vietnam – the People's Republic of China. The embassy should take particular interest in China's role in Southeast Asia as such, with emphasis on the continuation of friendly relations between China and the DRV.[6] Soviet policy makers were, of course, well aware of the close relationship that existed between the Vietnamese and Chinese Communists. But at the same time, the instructions do indicate that from a Soviet point of view the absence of such relations was seen as a possibility, and could be exploited to Moscow's advantage.

With regard to the internal developments in Vietnam, the Soviet foreign ministry focused on the political, economic and military situation. In politics, the main study object would be the Lao Dong, with emphasis on the condition of its ideological policy and organizational work, conditions within the leadership, and its contact with the mass organizations, primarily the Lien Viet (Unified National Front).[7] Moscow also signalled its willingness to provide the DRV government with the 'necessary assistance [...] to strengthen the democratic system in the country'. Financially the Soviet Union should assist in the restoration and development of the economy and the carrying out of land reform. Militarily Moscow should give 'necessary assistance [...] to strengthen the forces of the People's Army'. In addition, Moscow revealed its intention to establish formal relations between the two countries in both the economic and military fields.[8]

Although the Soviet leaders showed their intent to support and advice the North Vietnamese both economically and to some extent militarily, they maintained that the Lao Dong would remain the authority on internal Vietnamese affairs. However, contrary to this attitude the instructions to the Soviet ambassador contained a number of suggestions aimed at future North Vietnamese policies towards the South. According to Soviet policy makers, the DRV's most important task was the reunification of Vietnam within the Geneva framework, to be achieved through free general elections as stated in the Final Declaration of the Geneva agreement. The North Vietnamese should adopt a policy of establishing, as well as strengthening, already established relations with all patriotic, religious and political organizations in the South. From a Soviet point of view the aim of this policy would be to unmask, and then subsequently isolate, the government of Ngo Dinh Diem as well as the parties, organizations and officials supporting it. It was also important to eliminate possible provocation by the United States and France in Indochina. The main aim of the two states, as the Soviets saw it, was to prevent general elections in Vietnam, Laos and Cambodia.[9]

In South Vietnam the consolidation of the new state proceeded somewhat differently from what we have seen in the North. In June 1954 the United States pressured Vietnamese Emperor Bao Dai to appoint Ngo Dinh Diem Prime Minister, and in July Diem returned to Saigon to formally take control of the government. From an American point of view, Diem was a logical choice for the premiership of an independent Vietnam. He was anti-French and had impeccable credentials as a nationalist and, even more importantly, as a staunch anti-Communist. He was also a devout Catholic and had long administrative experience.[10] Once in position, it was soon obvious that Diem lacked many of the qualities required for the imposing challenges he faced in a divided Vietnam. He loved his country but was an elitist who had little understanding of the needs and problems of the Vietnamese people. His ideals were taken from an imperial Vietnam that no longer existed. In contrast to the leader in the North, he had no plan for modernizing the nation or mobilizing his people. He lacked the charisma of Ho Chi Minh, as well as broad support among people in the South.[11]

Diem's position in Saigon was insecure. Without support from the United States Diem would not have been able to cope with the enormous problems he confronted in his first year. The first crisis came with the massive exodus from the North to the South, consisting mostly of Catholics who, encouraged by Diem with promises of land and livelihood, fled from the northern Communist regime. Thereafter followed the sect crisis lasting until the spring of 1955. During his first year in office Ngo Dinh Diem consolidated his power in all possible areas. He eliminated his main opponents – the three sects – and as American advisors gradually replaced French officials in South Vietnam, Diem's position was solidified.[12]

In the aftermath of Geneva, the DRV economy was far from strong enough to finance the costly reconstruction of the country, and the Lao Dong leaders found it natural to turn to the Soviet Union and China for assistance. The requests for assistance in the fall of 1954 were modest. They ranged from military assistance to fulfil the ceasefire agreement to appeals for immediate aid to prevent famine. Most of the appeals for assistance were, after some internal discussion, eventually sanctioned by Moscow. When DRV Prime Minister Pham Van Dong asked permission to use Soviet ships to transfer North Vietnamese forces back from the South, the Head of the Southeast Asia Department in MID, Kirill Vasilevich Novikov, declared that he would not recommend providing such assistance to the DRV.[13] But Novikov's recommendations were not followed. Higher officials within the MID bureaucracy sanctioned the request from Hanoi. Thus, in the end Soviet ships were used to carry both North Vietnamese forces and civilians, and at a later stage to transport rice from China to the DRV.[14]

It was Foreign Minister Vyacheslav Molotov who disagreed with Novikov and approved the assistance to Hanoi. During the 1950s Molotov was the Soviet foreign minister who showed the most interest in Vietnam. He had personally met several of the Vietnamese leaders, and we have already seen that he played an active role both during preparations for the Geneva conference in the spring of 1954 and during the conference itself. As one of the engineers behind the agreement, Molotov was well acquainted with the current situation and also aware of possible future complications in Vietnam. We have not gained access to his personal papers, but his active involvement in the decision-making processes concerning Vietnam, compared with his successors in the foreign ministry, Dimitrii Shepilov and Andrey Gromyko, indicates that he had a special interest in a successful development in the area.

In addition to transport assistance, the North Vietnamese also requested more direct military assistance. Pham Van Dong stated that he would be pleased if a group of Soviet military colleagues would arrive in Vietnam to assist in the implementation of the ceasefire agreement.[15] Moscow was aware of the DRV's need for advice and suggested that a group of advisors should be dispatched to Vietnam. The decision was not made without concern for possible Chinese reactions. Chinese military advisors had been active in Vietnam since 1950, and the Soviet leaders did not want to risk any complications with the Chinese. As a result Moscow decided to engage the military advisors as assistants to the Soviet military attaché in Hanoi.[16] The Head of the Southeast Asia Department in the Soviet Foreign Ministry, Kirill Novikov, did not specify what kind of complications with the Chinese that could be feared. However, based on what is know about the Chinese role in Vietnamese military affairs on all levels, it would be safe to assume that he was afraid the Chinese could be offended if the Soviet Union offered military assistance without coordinating it with Beijing in advance.

In the autumn of 1954 the Soviet Union and the DRV had not yet signed any formal agreements on either economic or military assistance. Assistance was given on request and in most cases without further discussion, but no long-term plans for assistance was made until Ho Chi Minh's first official visit to the Soviet Union as DRV head of state in July 1955. With regard to support to reconstructing the country, Moscow constantly reassured the leaders in Hanoi of the priority given to the rebuilding of North Vietnam. However, the Soviet leaders emphasized that this was considered very important not only by the Soviet Union itself but also by the other members of the Socialist camp.[17]

The leaders in both Moscow and Beijing realized that in order to substantially support the Vietnamese, Sino-Soviet cooperation was vital. The Soviet leaders argued that they saw economic as well as technical assistance to the DRV as an important factor in the struggle for the reunification of Vietnam. But Moscow had no intention to assist the DRV without any backing from the rest of the Socialist camp. The absence of a Chinese statement on aid to the DRV was viewed with special concern.[18] From the very start of the official relationship between Moscow and Hanoi the Soviet government underlined that cooperation with China was a significant factor in Soviet economic and military assistance to Hanoi. At the same time this was one of the first occasions when these two countries actively cooperated to rebuild society in a small Communist state, and in that regard, from a Soviet point of view, the DRV would become a test case for Sino-Soviet foreign policy cooperation. Such a picture was further strengthened by the fact that this cooperation continued even when relations between Moscow and Beijing began to deteriorate, and also when the Chinese announced their decision to withdraw from North Vietnam.

Economic assistance was the most important part of Soviet policies towards Vietnam in the early years after Geneva. The first formal economic assistance agreement between the two countries was signed in July 1955. The signing took place during DRV President Ho Chi Minh's visit to Moscow from 12 to 18 July 1955. It was mainly an aid programme under which the Soviet Union promised to assist North Vietnam in a large number of projects. But economic assistance was only one of several subjects during Ho's visit, and before the meetings with the DRV delegation began, Soviet negotiators were coached on what to discuss with the Vietnamese. The instructions outlined before these meetings would also become the basis for Soviet engagement in Vietnam in the years to come. They touched upon political, economic, military and cultural relations between Moscow and Hanoi. They outlined the Soviet position in most areas of the relationship through suggestions on how to respond to requests forwarded by Ho Chi Minh and his colleagues.[19]

In general terms the Soviet negotiators had clear instructions: support would be given within the framework of the Geneva agreement, and the Soviet Union would raise the question of political regulation in Vietnam at the next Big Four meeting in July 1955. The instructions also contained assurances to Ho Chi Minh and the other North Vietnamese delegates that the Soviet government was ready to provide, in cooperation with the Chinese friends, 'the necessary support to the Democratic Republic of Vietnam in the struggle for independence and reunification of the country, as well as in the case of the economic and cultural reconstruction of the Democratic Republic of Vietnam'.[20] However, Moscow said nothing on the issue that was of most interest to Vietnam, namely the reunification of the two Vietnams. In 1955 unification was not on the agenda as far as the Soviets were concerned.

In the first years after Geneva, Soviet economic support for the DRV was very low key. The kind of assistance provided was identical to that given to other members of the Socialist bloc, and by no means more important. It might even be that Soviet financial assistance to some non-Socialist developing countries exceeded that given to the DRV, even though the Hanoi leaders had eagerly committed themselves to the ideals of the Socialist world.[21] Moreover, during the first two years after Geneva, the general policy of the Lao Dong seems to have made little difference in the economic relations between the Soviet Union and the DRV. Agreements like the one signed in July 1955 were renewed on a regular basis, and there was no significant increase in the amount of aid given during the first years after Geneva.[22]

Military cooperation and Chinese withdrawal

While the economic relationship was fairly well-established by the summer of 1955, the question of military relations between the two countries was much more delicate. A clear-cut example can be found during the negotiations in the summer of 1955. The instructions to the Soviet negotiators were clear: if Ho Chi Minh should raise the question of establishing a joint Sino-Soviet economic and military mission, he would be told that 'such a step would not be expedient, as there had already been established a practice of cooperation in these fields between the Vietnamese and the Chinese'.[23]

Is it possible that Moscow had already gotten the impression that the Vietnamese were suspicious of Chinese intentions and therefore opted for a stronger Soviet engagement, also militarily? If that was the case, in 1955 Moscow did not seem to be sensitive to the Vietnamese wishes with regard to practical military support. Nevertheless, this did not exclude the possibility that the DRV could receive technical aid from the Soviet Union. The question had also been raised earlier. In a telegram from General Antonov, at the General Staff in the Soviet Ministry of Defence, to Deputy Minister of Foreign Affairs V.A. Zorin in early June 1955, General Antonov underlined the inexpediency of establishing a joint Sino-Soviet military mission to coordinate questions related to the construction of the armed forces of the People's Army of Vietnam (PAVN) in Hanoi.[24] His argument was rooted in the Chinese military presence. Antonov emphasized that 'at present PAVN has Chinese military advisors. These advisors know the peculiarities of the country and its army. They have many years of experience in advising the Vietnamese friends on questions of constructing the armed forces, including the instruction and education of troops.'[25] Antonov's answer indicates that the military command in Moscow was unwilling to engage in Vietnamese military affairs. It preferred the military mission in Hanoi to remain strictly Chinese and did not want to give promises of military aid to the Vietnamese.

In spite of General Antonov's views, the Vietnamese military leaders continued to meet with both Chinese and Soviet officials to discuss military affairs. On 27 June 1955 a Vietnamese military delegation led by Defence Minister Vo Nguyen Giap made a secret trip to Beijing. While there, they discussed the reconstruction of the DRV armed forces, as well as future war plans with Chinese Defence Minister Peng Dehuai and Lieutenant General Petroshevskii, a senior Soviet military advisor in China. We first met Petroshevskii when he delivered reports from Vietnam during the preparations for the Dien Bien Phu offensive in the spring of 1954.[26] A similar trip to Beijing, also led by Giap, took place in mid-October 1955, and this time the Vietnamese general discussed the same questions also with the Soviet general Gushev, of the General Planning Division of the Soviet General Staff.[27]

Thus, in the late summer of 1955, when Beijing announced its decision to withdraw the military advisors who had been sent to North Vietnam in July–August 1950, the Soviets were forced to rethink their own position in Vietnam and their efforts to provide support for the Vietnamese Communists. The withdrawal was supposed to be carried out in three phases – first in September/October 1955, at the end of 1955 and finally in the spring of 1956. At the request of the North Vietnamese leaders the military advisors would be replaced by military specialists assigned to help with the modernization process in the PAVN. Thus, this decision did not mean an end to the close ties between the People's Liberation Army and the PAVN.[28]

Although Beijing was prepared to continue its military assistance to the DRV, the decision to withdraw the advisors caused concern both among the Vietnamese and the Soviets. Soviet ambassador Zimyanin informed his superiors in Moscow of the Chinese plans to withdraw all political and economic advisors working in the DRV before the end of 1955.[29] To prevent a total Chinese withdrawal from the DRV, Moscow turned to Beijing with a plea to retain Chinese assistance to the DRV. However, the situation must have been seen as somewhat delicate, since the decision was to present the Soviet discontent to Beijing in 'a tactful way' and make them understand that the Soviets were in favour of more long-term assistance from China to the DRV.[30] In early December 1955 the Chinese Ambassador to the DRV, Luo Guibo, informed the Soviets that the Chinese advisors would be allowed to stay only until the end of 1955.[31]

According to Chinese scholar Chen Jian, on 24 December 1955 the Chinese Defence Minister, Peng Dehuai, informed his Vietnamese counterpart, Vo Nguyen Giap, about the decision to call back the CMAG. The group had been in Vietnam since July 1950, but by mid-March 1956 all members of the group had returned to China.[32] It is difficult to say whether the Soviet leaders knew about the Chinese decision in advance. If so, it could explain why they emphasized the Vietnamese need for Chinese assistance, even before Beijing made the final decision to withdraw all military advisors. What does seem clear, however, is that the Soviets relied on the Chinese presence in Vietnam, politically and economically, as well as militarily. A Chinese withdrawal in any of these fields would complicate the situation for the Soviets and deprive the DRV of much-needed resources. With no Chinese presence the Soviets might be forced to engage themselves more deeply in Vietnam.

The above account shows that in the mid-1950s the Soviet Union still preferred to leave the major part of the responsibility for military affairs to China. Why were the Soviet leaders willing to give away influence to the Chinese in such an important field? Apart from the costs of taking on such a responsibility one reason could be that at the time, in spite of the growing Soviet interest in the country's political affairs, Vietnam was not of primary interest to the Soviet Union when it came to active military engagement. The Soviets were of course much more concerned about the military situation in Eastern Europe.[33] By leaving the military responsibility to the Chinese, the Soviets would retain their control within the Communist sphere without being directly responsible, and at the same time they would avoid the risk of getting too greatly involved.

Another reason can be traced to the state of Sino-Soviet relations in Vietnam in 1955. Although it has been claimed that tension between the two had started to surface, the further record of Sino-Soviet cooperation in Vietnam indicates that with regard to Vietnam, the relationship between Moscow and Beijing was still functioning. The two powers agreed on the necessity of assisting the DRV. Beijing had long military experience in Vietnam, and it was therefore natural to both the Soviet Union and China that the present arrangement continue. In addition, the Soviets wanted a peaceful, not military, reunification of Vietnam.

Sino-Soviet relations and the Geneva agreement

The Soviet leaders considered the implementation of the agreement, as well as the existence and work of the ICCs in all three Indochinese countries, as an important part of its strategy in this area in the latter part of the 1950s. As co-chairman of the Geneva conference, the Soviet Union was perceived by many, and among them the Vietnamese, as having a special responsibility for the implementation of the agreements. According to the provisions in the Final Declaration of the Geneva conference, general elections should be held in all of Vietnam in July 1956. The purpose of the elections was a reunification of the two zones under a government freely chosen by the Vietnamese people. Consultations for elections should start on 20 July 1955, between competent representatives from both the zones.[34]

The Soviet Union strongly emphasized the diplomatic struggle for the fulfilment of the Geneva agreement, both through public statements and through the promotion of the work of the three ICCs. At the same time the Hanoi government worked hard to initiate consultations, but in spite of all efforts the elections were not held. The reason was the attitude of the South Vietnamese government of Ngo Dinh Diem and his American allies. The prevailing assumption in both the North and the South was that the Communists would most probably receive enough votes in both zones to gain the upper hand in a future national government.[35] Without Diem's consent it would be impossible to hold the consultations. In the North the Lao Dong continued, in spite of the unfavourable situation, to fight for implementation of the Geneva agreement. To succeed, however, Hanoi depended on the full support of its Communist allies.

While Hanoi strove to initiate consultation talks, Ngo Dinh Diem continued to consolidate his regime in the southern zone. The prospects for consultations and an achievement of a solution through diplomatic means were not good. The French were getting ready to pull out completely, leaving no one in charge of implementing the provisions agreed upon. The Diem government, which was supposed to succeed the French and undertake their obligations with regard to the agreement, refused to participate, claiming that since South Vietnam was not a signatory of the Geneva accords, it had no obligations whatsoever. During the autumn of 1955 Diem further consolidated his power.[36] On 23 October 1955 he arranged a referendum in South Vietnam, by which he dethroned the former emperor Bao Dai and had himself elected president. Shortly afterwards he broke off economic relations with France, left the French Union, and finally proclaimed the Republic of Vietnam (RVN) on 26 October 1955.[37] The referendum provoked no major protests from either the Soviet Union or China, indicating that the two Communist powers accepted the idea of a divided Vietnam. In other words, during the autumn of 1955 Hanoi was alone in protesting both Diem's refusal to hold consultations and the referendum. To both the North Vietnamese and the Soviets, it was now clear that the government of Ngo Dinh Diem would stay in power for a while.

During the spring of 1956 the Lao Dong leaders were worried not only because of the reluctant attitude of the South Vietnamese government but also by the French position in this matter. On 3 April 1956 the French gave formal notice of their withdrawal from Vietnam and announced that they would dissolve their High Command by 15 April. On 9 April DRV's Prime Minister Pham Van Dong sent a letter to the Geneva co-chairmen, insisting that the Diem regime take over France's legal obligations in regard to the agreement. In reality the French were forced out of Vietnam. Disagreements between the French and Diem over the French presence in Vietnam and the American readiness to take on support of the South Vietnamese was the background for French withdrawal.[38] From a South Vietnamese point of view it would be more convenient to have Americans than French in the country. Both the North Vietnamese and the Soviets were negative to the French withdrawal.[39] As long as the French had formally been responsible, there had been a certain chance of a fulfilment of the Geneva agreement. With the French gone and the Americans gradually taking over their role, the hope for a peaceful solution was diminished.[40]

When the Chinese proposed to convene a second Geneva conference in early 1956, the North Vietnamese soon supported the proposal, hoping that it could help to improve the political situation in Vietnam. The Soviets, although positive to such a meeting, were not convinced that it would be possible to convene as long as the Western powers were reluctant about the idea. Since it was clear at the time that no elections would be scheduled by July, North Vietnamese were searching for new solutions. Truong Chinh in this regard expressed the Vietnamese point of view in a meeting with Soviet Deputy Foreign Minister V.V. Kuznetsov during the Twentieth Congress in Moscow in February 1956. Encouraged to report on the current situation in Vietnam, Truong Chinh emphasized that 'in the present situation the necessary conditions for conducting these elections do not exist. At the same time the CC has pointed to the necessity of using all forces in order to keep the initiative in the political struggle for the regulation of Vietnam's political problems.'[41]

Hanoi's suggestion in order to keep the initiative was to postpone the elections. The Lao Dong leaders feared that disbanding entirely the idea of holding elections could provoke a strong reaction from the people of Vietnam. 'To inform people of this now, would' – according to Truong Chinh – 'result in a serious worsening of their spirits'.[42] Based on this the Vietnamese acknowledged, during the spring of 1956, that 'to insist on a full implementation of the Geneva agreement will be difficult'.[43] Accordingly, they claimed that from a tactical point of view it would be necessary to 'on the one hand, continue the fight for a fulfilment of the agreement, but on the other hand, to take new steps'.[44]

The new steps were basically a plan with two alternatives that was presented to the Soviet and the Chinese ambassadors in Vietnam. Both alternatives would provide a solution within the Geneva framework, and both were based on a postponement of the date for the elections to May 1957. In the first alternative, labelled the 'maximum plan', the North Vietnamese expected that the Diem government and the French fulfil the provisions of the Geneva agreement and that Diem take over the French obligations. The goal of this plan was to achieve full implementation through the postponement of elections. The second option, labelled the 'minimum plan' or 'modus vivendi', implied that the opposite side would fulfil only the basic provisions of the agreement such as securing democratic freedoms and normalizing relations between the two zones.

In response to the two plans, the Soviets and Chinese agreed that Hanoi would eventually have to make concessions, but not when it came to questions of principle. Since a postponement of the elections would count as a very large concession, neither the Soviets nor the Chinese were unreservedly positive to the North Vietnamese suggestion.[45] In the spring of 1956 the Soviets and Chinese agreed that the best solution in Vietnam at the time, taking into account that there would not be any general elections in the foreseeable future, would be to hope for a new Geneva conference.[46] At the same time, neither the Vietnamese nor the Chinese attempted to put any pressure on the other powers that had participated in Geneva to call for a new conference. The outcome of the North Vietnamese initiative was just some further meetings between the two co-chairmen of the conference.

Parallel to these developments, the Soviet embassy in Hanoi advocated what seems to have been a more active policy to secure fulfilment of the Geneva agreement. Expressing concern over the situation that was developing in the region, and especially the attempt of the United States, Great Britain and France to undermine the agreement, the Soviet ambassador suggested that the Soviet Union, China and the other Socialist states should strive to exploit the existing disagreements between these powers, and especially India, in order to strengthen the influence of the Socialist camp in the region.[47] One of the suggestions Zimyanin advanced was that the two co-chairmen, during their scheduled meeting, could support the Indian suggestion that Ngo Dinh Diem take on the French obligations with regard to the agreement, thus guaranteeing that South Vietnam would not join SEATO and also creating conditions that the ICC would be able to work under. Under such conditions it would be possible to agree to the British suggestion of a postponement of the elections, especially because political consultations between South and North Vietnam had yet to begin.[48]

Zimyanin's thoughts were not reflected in the message that eventually resulted from the meeting in London between the two co-chairmen on 8 May 1956. In the public message issued, the two foreign ministers, Andrey Gromyko and Lord Reading, emphasized the need to preserve peace in Indochina and proclaimed that the co-chairmen and the ICC would continue their responsibilities. The 8 May message left the world in no doubt that the Communist powers would allow Vietnam to stay divided. After the meeting, DRV Prime Minister Pham Van Dong sent a letter to Ngo Dinh Diem on 11 May demanding the normalization of relations between the two zones.[49]

On several occasions the Chinese appeared to be more determined to hold on to the Geneva agreement than the Soviets. The London Talks in May had made quite clear that there would be no general elections in July 1956, or even in the very near future. This had, of course, been clear to all concerned parties for a long time, but the message from London put an end to the last drop of hope. Still, the Chinese continued to voice their commitment to fulfil the pledge and under-lined that they would strive, together with the North Vietnamese, 'for the full implementation of the Geneva Agreements'.[50] The Chinese lack of actual commitments with regard to the agreement, stood in contrast to that of the Soviet Union, who still held the position of co-chairman of the conference together with Great Britain and therefore could not just make promises without any plans of keeping them. In the end, however, both Moscow and Beijing let the election deadline in July pass in silence. Neither the Soviets nor the Chinese wanted to provoke another crisis in Vietnam over the question of national reunification and may even tacitly have considered a continued partition of Vietnam to suit their interests. Policy makers in both Moscow and Beijing had more pressing issues coming up – the Soviet Union in Eastern Europe, and China first and foremost on the domestic arena.

Hanoi and the Twentieth Congress

Nikita Khrushchev's secret speech at the Twentieth Congress of CPSU in February 1956 had an immense effect on the Communist world and not least on the Sino-Soviet relationship. Khrushchev's overall arguments in favour of a peaceful transition to socialism and his insistence that war between the two world camps could be avoided led to drawn-out discussions in both Hanoi and Beijing. The new Soviet foreign policy line endorsing peaceful coexistence would be difficult to adapt to China's more offensive attitudes.[51] But to the Chinese the hardest pill to swallow was the lack of consultation in advance. Mao and his fellow CCP leaders felt deeply offended by the manner in which their Soviet comrades handled this matter.[52]

Within many Communist parties the revelations would have significant implications for how they viewed the role of their own leadership. Just like the Chinese participants, the two Lao Dong representatives at the congress, General Secretary Truong Chinh and Politburo member Le Duc Tho, were both totally unprepared for the revelations in Khrushchev's speech. In the period immediately after the congress, the Lao Dong leaders in both private conversations and public speeches acknowledged the new Soviet foreign policy line. However, they never revealed in detail how the resolutions of the congress would affect their own policies. In later political analyses the Soviets accused the Vietnamese of sharing the Chinese point of view with regard to the Twentieth Congress, accusing the Central Committee of the Lao Dong of sharing 'the points of view of the leaders in the Chinese Communist Party and the Albanian Workers Party on the personality cult question. They did not agree with the decisions of the Twentieth Congress of the CPSU condemning the personality cult of I.V. Stalin, but preferred to pass this over in silence.'[53] The discussions between Soviet and Vietnamese officials in the period after the congress further confirm the Vietnamese unease, and not least their reluctance to take a definitive stand with regard to what happened during the Twentieth Congress.

Hanoi's first official reaction to the speech came in an editorial published in the Lao Dong daily *Nhan Dan* on 28 February 1956. It stated that the DRV fully supported the results of the CPSU congress but added that the Lao Dong 'would further endeavour to study Marxist-Leninist theory and to apply it creatively to the concrete situation in Vietnam, to combine this theory with the practice of Vietnam's revolution'.[54] Comments in the editorial indicate that the Lao Dong had not yet decided whether they wanted to accept the whole concept of this new Marxist-Leninist doctrine. Before giving their full endorsement, the Lao Dong leaders wanted to properly discuss how this new foreign policy line could be applied to the specific situation in Vietnam.

During the spring of 1956 the Lao Dong leadership had several discussions about the Twentieth Congress, and on 31 March the Politburo in Hanoi issued a communiqué that fully supported the resolutions of the congress. In the end of April, after the extended 9th Plenum of the Lao Dong Central Committee, Nguyen Duy Trinh, a member of the LD CC, presented the results of the discussions and the evaluations of its implications for the Vietnamese situation to Moscow. In his conversation with Soviet ambassador Zimyanin, Trinh reported that the Plenum 'unanimously and warmly approves the decisions of the Twentieth Congress of the CPSU'.[55] This was the official version, but the truth was that Hanoi's approval was a result of long discussions within the party. Its background can be found in the months preceding the 9th Plenum.

Starting in mid-March 1956 the Central Committee was evaluating a proposal from Le Duan, Secretary of the Regional Party Committee in the South, which contained suggestions for a new strategy in South Vietnam.[56] This new strategy included preparations for a resumption of the armed struggle, and a 14-point plan for military consolidation of the Nam Bo region, the southern part of South Vietnam, including the surroundings of Saigon.[57] The Lao Dong CC had extended its 9th Plenum to thoroughly discuss the resolutions of the Twentieth Congress and their impact on Vietnam's domestic and international situation. During the Plenum the discussions were separated into two interlinked parts. The first part was dedicated to the examination of the principal questions of the DRV's foreign and domestic policies and the international situation in the light of the decisions of the Twentieth Congress. The second part of the Plenum focused on a discussion of questions related to the party work of the Lao Dong based on the resolutions of the Soviet congress, the report from the CPSU CC and Khrushchev's secret speech on the cult of personalities and its consequences.[58] Le Duan's suggestions for a new strategy towards South Vietnam could have been discussed in either of the two sessions.

The discussions during the Plenum shed some light on developments within the Lao Dong during this period. They indicate that the North Vietnamese considered seriously Khrushchev's revelations of misconduct within the Soviet party, and immediately focused on their own internal party life to ascertain whether similar errors had been committed. The Lao Dong leaders acknowledged that mistakes had been made also within their organization and pointed to the role of Ho Chi Minh. A certain degree of personality cult had been developed around Ho, but according to discussions at the Plenum, not to the same degree as around Stalin.[59]

Moscow was not able to extract much information on Hanoi's future policies towards South Vietnam from their knowledge about the Plenum. The discussions centred mostly on the domestic policies of the DRV and the situation within the Lao Dong. The only remark targeting directly the Southern situation concluded that 'the general line of the Vietnamese people's fight to strengthen the DRV and reunify the country by peaceful means, which had been outlined in the programme of the Fatherland Front, was the correct line to follow'.[60] The decision to continue the political struggle indicates that those in favour of Le Duan's proposed strategy did not officially prevail in the spring of 1956 and that the further strategy of the Lao Dong would be at least close to the new Soviet line.[61] As a result, the discussion on Southern strategy would continue through 1956, and while Soviet leaders steadily continued on a course of action in which accommodating the US was more important than the peaceful reunification of

Vietnam, Hanoi's hardliners promoting a more militant strategy gradually gained more influence within the Lao Dong Politburo.

Moscow made no outright attempts to influence the DRV views at this juncture. However, in the beginning of April 1956, shortly before the 9th Plenum of the Lao Dong, Anastas Mikoyan, the Soviet deputy premier, made a visit to North Vietnam. Mikoyan's visit was the first by a senior Soviet official. At the time of his arrival the Lao Dong had issued its statement of support for the resolutions of the Twentieth Congress but had not explicitly stated its full commitment to the policies outlined there. Neither the Soviets nor the Vietnamese have outlined the purpose of Mikoyan's visit, and no official communiqué was issued during his stay.[62] Still, it is safe to assume that the purpose was to discuss the results of the Twentieth Congress. The lack of an official communiqué at the end of the stay has led to speculations about the results of the discussions, but it may just indicate that his visit was a working trip, rather than an official visit.[63]

Comments in the following period further support the idea that the two main subjects during Mikoyan's visit were the Twentieth Congress and the DRV's political and economic development.[64] According to Nguyen Duy Trinh, Mikoyan gave some advice to the Vietnamese regarding the issue of exclusion from the party, and the Plenum agreed with the advice of comrade Mikoyan and decided to show more caution when excluding members from the party.[65] In August the same year the Vietnamese once again raised the question of problems with Stalin's theories, and argued that during his visit in April Mikoyan had remarked that some of the theoretical theses developed by Stalin were wrong. The Vietnamese now wanted to know more specific details regarding the areas in which the Stalin theories had been wrong, as this was important both to their propaganda work and to their theoretical work.[66]

Parallel to Mikoyan's visit the Lao Dong experienced internal turbulence. In late April 1956 the Vietnamese acknowledged that a certain personality cult had developed around Ho Chi Minh himself, but these accusations did not lead to any practical consequences for Ho's position in the party and were soon abolished.[67] However, the discussion around Ho's role was, as we shall see, only the start of a larger rearrangement within the party leadership, which led to a greater number of Politburo members with close ties to the South. After the Twentieth Congress there had been serious disagreements within the Lao Dong leadership. Lack of unity and the differences of opinion that existed among the leaders was a source of worry for Soviet officials, as well as for other DRV government officials. The reason for this lack of unity was, according to an official at the prime minister's office, Buy Kong Chung, that the members of the Politburo were too preoccupied with theory. He argued that when serious problems were raised, the Politburo members often differed in opinion, although they would rarely end in open disagreement. This was, according to the DRV official, due to the lack of 'ideological' unity among the members of the Politburo, a situation that occurred because the party had yet to work out a general line or programme.[68]

Soviet perceptions of China's role in Vietnam were clearly expressed by the Soviet ambassador in Hanoi, Zimyanin, in July 1956. Chinese withdrawal and the revelations during the Twentieth Congress set aside, he reemphasized China's role as Hanoi's closest advisor and ally '[...] with regard to aid and advice to the Vietnamese friends in deciding important questions in their foreign and domestic policies [...] the People's Republic of China plays a leading role in organizing such assistance to the Vietnamese friends'.[69] Zimyanin's statement was characteristic of the way Moscow viewed developments in Vietnam in the first years after the Geneva conference, and how they, in spite of China's decision to withdraw many of their specialists and advisors from the DRV, still regarded China's role as vital.

Land reform and its critics

The most important stage of Lao Dong's social revolution in North Vietnam was the land reform. This not only involved the transfer of land from the landlords to the poor peasants but was more generally aimed at all sources from which the old rural elite drew its power.[70] Based on modified Chinese models, the Communist authorities in Hanoi introduced land reform in 1953, and during the last phase of the Franco-Vietminh War the poorer peasants were mobilized into a victorious military force. The land reform gave the Communists an opportunity to win the gratitude of the poor and to develop a political structure in the villages while simultaneously recruiting cadres from among the peasants. To many Vietnamese peasants the land reform campaign represented their first encounter with communism and may help to explain why the relationship between the peasants and the ruling Communist party was better in North Vietnam than it was in the Soviet Union after collectivization.[71] After the Geneva conference, during the latter part of 1954, the same land reform was said to increase agricultural output and efficiency. Through land reform the party leadership expected to achieve rapid change in the whole structure of North Vietnamese society, and thereby create conditions on which their power monopoly could safely rest.[72]

In the early phase, land reform was carried out on a small scale, but from 1955 the campaign intensified. Control was exercised by cadres reporting to a central land reform committee working outside of the ordinary party channels and in close cooperation with local village committees. As a part of the campaign, peasants were categorized into five classes ranging from 'landlord' to 'farm worker'. The leaders concluded that landlords and other feudal elements represented 5 per cent of the rural population, and cadres were sent out to liquidate these. But few farmers in the North possessed more than three or four acres of land, which meant that few peasants actually would fall into the 'landlord' category. Nevertheless, from 1955 the so-called agricultural reform tribunals were set up, and the cadres started to execute the 5 per cent who according to their statistics had to belong to the landlord category.[73] The DRV government has never published an official count of those killed in the land reform, but historians working with the subject have given estimates of executions ranging from 3,000 to 50,000.[74]

In North Vietnam land reform grew more radical as it went on, and by the spring of 1956 the Lao Dong leaders had started to realize the seriousness of its excesses. Still, it was not until the autumn that the party leaders fully understood the consequences of the campaign. Since charges were being made against old cadres and against men with whom party leaders were personally acquainted, the Lao Dong leadership began to question the accusations.[75] The land reform and the errors committed during its implementation constituted one of the most important issues in the DRV in the autumn of 1956. Time had come to disperse responsibility for the excesses of land reform, a process that also led to changes within the higher echelons of the party.

As soon as it had been admitted that serious errors had been committed, North Vietnamese leaders started to encourage criticism from below.[76] At the 10th Plenum the party collectively assumed responsibility for the excesses during the campaign, but pointed out that certain comrades were personally responsible for what had happened. The Plenum concluded that the instructions of the Lao Dong Central Committee on the elimination of enemies within the party organization had been misunderstood and, as a result, had led to massive repression and physical punishment. Their newfound understanding was, according to Nguyen Duy Trinh, based on their careful studies of the materials of the Twentieth Congress. It was now much clearer which mistakes had been committed. However, most of all they blamed themselves for the uncritical acceptance of Chinese advice.[77]

Although the Central Committee and the Politburo of the CC assumed collective responsibility for the errors, some party officials also had to be sacrificed to demonstrate the Lao Dong leaders' sincerity in rectifying the errors committed. Several top officials within the Lao Dong were held personally responsible, the most prominent of these was Truong Chinh, the General Secretary of the Lao Dong. He was removed from his post but remained a member of the Politburo.[78] Truong Chinh was at the time considered to be close to the CCP. The pseudonym he had chosen in his youth, Truong Chinh, means 'long march' in Vietnamese.[79] The North Vietnamese blamed themselves for having unconditionally followed the Chinese example on land reform, something that may have led them to choose Truong Chinh as the official scapegoat. He was the leader most Vietnamese associated with land reform and was a ruthless ideologue who had often emphasized the necessity of eliminating class enemies.[80]

The dismissal of Truong Chinh led to changes within the Lao Dong top leadership. Ho Chi Minh himself took over the post as general secretary and would therefore, until the next scheduled congress of the Lao Dong, hold the positions of both president of the DRV and general secretary of the party. At the same time, Vo Nguyen Giap, commanding general of the PAVN, was appointed deputy (second) general secretary of the Lao Dong CC. These changes left the Politburo of the Lao Dong CC with the following members: Ho Chi Minh, Pham Van Dong, Truong Chinh, Vo Nguyen Giap, Hoang Quoc Viet, Le Duc Tho, Nguyen Chi Thanh and 'the comrades working in South Vietnam'.[81]

According to Nguyen Duy Trinh, the rearrangement of the party leadership was part of a broader campaign aimed at mending some of the damage caused by land reform. The Vietnamese variant of de-Stalinization was named the 'rectification of errors campaign', and one of the most important tasks of this campaign was 'to achieve unity within the ranks of the party'.[82] But an even more important aspect of this was the impact such changes would have on Hanoi's strategy towards the southern zone. It reflected a new and more militant attitude within the top echelons of the party. While the list of Lao Dong Politburo members from September 1956 refers to 'the comrades working in the South' and makes no direct references to important figures such as the future general secretary Le Duan and his southern associate Pham Hung, in December that same year both of them were listed as Politburo members, and Le Duan singled out as working in the South.[83] Together with Le Duc Tho, Le Duan and Pham Hung were to become the leading advocates of stepping up the struggle in the South.[84]

During the autumn of 1956 there was only one incident of revolt against the DRV government. It took place in the North Vietnamese province of Nghe An in early November.[85] When presenting the Nghe An incident to the Soviet chargé d'affaires, A.M. Popov, Nguyen Duy Trinh emphasized that the revolt was staged to undermine the rectification of errors campaign. He also accused the participants in the demonstration of being used by the reactionaries to spread false information for the purpose of undermining the people's government. The disorder this activity created enabled the reactionaries to make even more trouble. After the situation in Nghe An had calmed down, Hanoi could reassure Moscow that in spite of the temporarily difficult situation in that province, the present conditions in Vietnam would not lead to events like the ones in Poland or Hungary.[86]

The rectification of errors campaign and the subsequent changes within the Lao Dong leadership do not seem to have had any direct influence on the bilateral relationship between the Soviet Union and the DRV. Moscow approved of Hanoi's efforts to mend the damage made during land reform but did nothing to interfere in the campaign itself. Nor do the foreign ministry materials indicate any reaction to the changes within the party leadership. The Soviet reaction to Hanoi's rectification of errors campaign and its rearrangements in the top leadership was expressed as follows in a note from Deputy Foreign Minister Andrey Gromyko to the CC CPSU:

> Taking into consideration that the questions related to the situation in the country was recently discussed at the 10th Plenum of the Lao Dong CC, and taking into consideration that it was the Plenum that took the decision to rectify the errors committed in the past by the Party, it seems to be inexpedient at the present time to give any advice to the Vietnamese friends on inner-political [domestic] questions from our side.[87]

On the Sino-Vietnamese relationship, however, the rectification campaign and the changes within the Lao Dong leadership had a much greater effect. There can be no doubt that the negative Vietnamese attitude towards the Chinese advisors played a considerable role in the Chinese decision to withdraw from Vietnam.

In its yearly report from 1956 the Soviet embassy in Hanoi argued that the sharp criticisms of the Chinese advisors for mistakes made during the conduction of land reform in the DRV played an important role when the Chinese government decided to withdraw most of their advisory teams in North Vietnam.

The PRC government has made a significant contribution to the development and strengthening of the DRV, and therefore the Chinese friends were indeed not pleased to hear the opinions of individual Vietnamese friends that contained accusations towards the Chinese advisors for mistakes made during the conduction of land reform in the DRV. One could suppose that such opinions with address to the Chinese advisors also served as a reason for the decision of the PRC government to withdraw these from Vietnam.[88]

The embassy also discussed the problem of nationalist tendencies within certain parts of the Vietnamese intelligentsia, emphasizing that 'these have an anti-Chinese focus and turn, at times, into direct and open attacks against Chinese representatives in the DRV'.[89] The possible problems that this 'anti-Chinese' focus could create, especially in terms of future Chinese involvement in Vietnam, worried the Soviet leadership.

In the mid-1950s there were several examples of how Sino-Vietnamese cooperation did not always work to the satisfaction of both parties. One such incident was reported to the Soviet ambassador to Beijing, Pavel Iudin, in January 1956, around the time when many Chinese advisors were about to leave the DRV. The Chinese economic advisors were closely involved in the reconstruction of North Vietnam, but the Vietnamese initiatives with regard to economic planning and reconstruction were not always to the liking of the Chinese. One example was the Vietnamese plans for large industrial and mining facilities and their plans to use most of the assistance received for these purposes. The Chinese emphasized their disapproval of the plans and encouraged the Vietnamese to concentrate on plans for increasing the living standards in the North.

According to the Chinese point of view, the Vietnamese should now use all means to develop their agriculture, produce consumer goods and strive to compete with South Vietnam in terms of living standards for the population. They should not try to develop industrial production, which demands large sums of capital investment, because Vietnam was not yet ready for such development. With regard to the mining industry they should extract only those minerals demanded by the Soviet Union and China. In spite of such clear advice, the Chinese had to admit that they had not been able to fully convince the Vietnamese, who were prone to speed up the industrialization of their country.[90] In spite of the ongoing process of withdrawal, the Chinese took an active interest in the organization of Vietnamese production and economy. The Soviets had no comments on the Chinese complaints, perhaps because the Vietnamese plans were more in line with Soviet ideas than with Chinese.

The Vietnamese dissatisfaction with its Chinese allies, and the subsequent Chinese decision to withdraw their advisors from Vietnam, should be understood within the wider context of the new ideological foreign policy line of the Soviet Communists beginning under Nikita Khrushchev. During 1956 these changes allowed the Vietnamese to display their dissatisfaction and in public condemn those responsible for the errors committed during the land reform. Most of these leaders were, as we have seen, very close to Beijing. However, as the rectification campaign began long after the Chinese decision to withdraw their advisors, this must be seen only as a result of a long period of criticism against the Chinese example, in which the outright criticism in the autumn of 1956 was the final drop.

Moscow, Beijing and Hanoi's new Southern strategy

Ever since the preparations for consultations collapsed in the summer of 1955 the Vietnamese had signalled their readiness to pursue a new kind of policy, a policy that would imply an increased level of violence compared with the first year after Geneva. From a Soviet point of view, a change in Lao Dong policies towards the South should probably have been a source of worry, since it was unlikely to correspond with the new Soviet foreign policy line with its emphasis on a peaceful transition to socialism. A new Hanoi strategy would no doubt imply a more militant approach leading to severe reactions from both the South Vietnamese authorities and the Americans. Even though the North Vietnamese, in the spring of 1956, gave several indications of the need to revise their Southern strategy, they never outlined explicitly to the Soviets what their plans were if a political solution was impossible.

In April 1956 the 9th Plenum of the Lao Dong CC decided to continue the political struggle as the correct way to achieve reunification; this decision caused much protest in the South. Pursuing the political struggle was the pragmatic course for the Lao Dong in the mid-1950s. There were many reasons for this; one was the losses of the last war and the reluctance to enter into another bloody encounter with the West. The main goal for the majority of the leadership was to create a solid Socialist base in the North before expanding for the purpose of overthrowing the American-supported government in the South.[91]

However, many southerners were still bitter about the outcome of Geneva and therefore called for a reversal of the peaceful strategies and all-out attacks against the Saigon regime. The main proponent of armed violence in the South was, as we have already seen, Le Duan. During the 9th Plenum in April his 14-point March proposal was not officially approved, but in the months following the Plenum the climate within the Lao Dong leadership apparently began to change, and coming up to the date scheduled for all-Vietnamese elections there were several hints from Hanoi to the Soviets on intentions to revise the Southern strategy. In late June 1956 Ho Chi Minh stated during a meeting with Soviet Ambassador Zimyanin that one could no longer count on the holding of general elections.[92] Referring to the present situation in Vietnam, Ho said,

at this point one can no longer count on the holding of consultations with South Vietnam and general elections for Vietnam. Diem refuses to follow the Geneva Agreement. In South Vietnam a referendum was held, and also separate elections. The armed resistance of the sects has been smashed. Diem has to some extent strengthened his armed forces. The French have left South Vietnam. As a result a new situation has arisen that one must take into account in the fight for the unification of the country.[93]

Ho Chi Minh also pointed to the new measures that needed to be taken as a result of the new situation and said that the Lao Dong CC was preparing instructions for the comrades working in the South on the tasks and methods for the further struggle. Ho also underlined to the Soviets that the Communist networks in the South had not been completely destroyed in spite of Diem's repression. The Vietnamese people themselves constituted another important factor that, according to Ho, had to be taken into consideration when planning the future of Vietnam. He claimed that some of the people had started to ask what needed to be done to obtain reunification of the country under the present circumstances. Those who were most worried were the ones who had fled from the South to the North after partition.

To emphasize to the Soviets the importance of fulfilment of the Geneva agreement, Ho Chi Minh used the respect for the people of Vietnam as an argument. It would be necessary to give the people an explanation as to why the provisions of the agreement had not been fulfilled as planned. Thus, several meetings must be held to help the people of both the North and the South understand the DRV's fight to reunite the country. The Lao Dong also acknowledged that they had not done enough in their fight for the fulfilment of the Geneva Agreement. One of the problems was that they had underestimated the force of their opponents. Political struggle was the correct option, but too many insufficiencies had surfaced when they had tried to follow this direction. One example was the programme of the Fatherland Front – the VNFF. It was a good programme, but it had been drawn up too late, at the time when the armed forces of the DRV had already left the South. To overcome these difficulties, Ho Chi Minh recommended that one should study Diem's tactics more carefully and react more seriously to them. He also underlined that it was now clear to Hanoi that the government in Saigon did not want to enter into any consultations.[94]

Some have claimed that the Lao Dong leaders already in the autumn of 1954 knew that there would not be any general elections on schedule in 1956, or even at a later date for that matter.[95] In June that year Ho Chi Minh told Soviet ambassador Zimyanin that they knew for certain there would be no elections and declared that the failure to hold elections could lead to serious trouble.[96] Ho's argument was further elaborated by DRV Deputy Foreign Minister Ung Van Khiem and member of the Politburo Pham Hung, in a conversation with the Soviet ambassador. Pham Hung said that 'at present it is necessary [...] to strengthen the fight in North and South Vietnam for the fulfilment of the Geneva Agreement', and to achieve that it is necessary to send another letter to the two co-chairmen. Zimyanin said that both he and his Chinese colleague, Ambassador Li Zhimin, agreed with Pham Hung's idea of sending another letter to the co-chairmen, but that all emphasis should not be on calling a new Geneva conference. There would be no elections in July, and no new Geneva conference in the near future. To remind people of the conference was good tactics, but not the purpose of the fight.[97]

In 1956 Moscow and Beijing agreed that the struggle for preserving peace and reuniting the country was the just fight of the Vietnamese. The main task was to mobilize the whole people to struggle for a full implementation of the agreement. The fact that the elections had not been held should not be left unnoticed by the people of the world and should be emphasized in diplomatic documents. The Soviet and Chinese ambassadors then gave advice on the order in which to send the letters: one now, and the other after the date scheduled for elections. They also underlined that none of them should express any form of defeatism or pessimism, as that would undermine the basic task as it was seen from the Vietnamese side: that is, emphasis on mobilizing the broader masses of the people.[98]

Ho Chi Minh's and other Lao Dong leaders' opinion must be seen in connection with the 8 May messages from the Geneva co-chairmen emphasizing the need to preserve peace in Indochina.[99] Nothing was said about the general elections scheduled to take place about two months later. At this stage the North Vietnamese leadership could not have been pleased with the behaviour of its Communist allies. Moscow's lack of interest in the election implied their tacit satisfaction with the situation in Vietnam. By late June 1956 the decision from April to support the new Soviet line, and to keep to the political struggle, had already been modified. The Lao Dong Politburo now passed a resolution in which they decided that even though the struggle was mainly political, it did not exclude the use of force in limited situations to secure the task of self-defence. The resolution also stated the need to strengthen the military and half-military units and create strong bases for these, while at the same time increasing the Lao Dong influence among the people, as the support of the people was the basic condition for preservation and development of the armed forces.[100]

The ascendancy of Le Duan and Pham Hung in the leadership coincides with a shift in policies towards the South. Sometime between the Lao Dong's 10th and 11th Plenums, held in September and December 1956, respectively, Le Duan presented another suggestion for policy revision in the document entitled *The Path of Revolution in the South* (*Duong Loi Cach Mang Mien Nam*). The policy guidance incorporated in the document was aimed both at solving the Lao Dong leaders' problems with the failure of their policy of reunification, and at the problems arising from the conduct of land reform in the North.[101]

In December 1956 the Nam Bo Regional Committee met to discuss, among other issues, Le Duan's *The Path*. Considering the needs of the revolutionary movement in South Vietnam the meeting concluded that it was to a certain extent, necessary to allow 'military activities' to supplement the political struggle. However, removing the restriction on the use of force did not imply that encouragement was given to its immediate employment. It rather suggested that force would be used at a future time, when circumstances were ripe. One small exception was made, and a secret document allowing a policy of limited violence known as 'killing tyrants' was authorized for high-level party members only. This was to prevent confusion among lower-level cadres, who were instructed to continue to build a mass organization in the South.[102] Hence, with this approval of tactical violence the Vietnamese Communists were embarking on a new strategy. The failure of the policy of reunification, the lack of support from their Communist allies, and finally, the increase in the number of Politburo members in favour of a new policy were important reasons behind this change.

At the time when the Lao Dong began to re-evaluate its reunification strategy Moscow's attitude can at best be characterized as expectant. Available sources indicate that Moscow did possess enough information to realize that a change was taking place. Soviet leaders also realized that these changes would, in one way or another, influence the Soviet–Vietnamese relationship. The Lao Dong leaders knew that a resurgence of armed struggle in the South was unlikely to be accepted by the Soviet party, thus they preferred to make their own decisions rather than consulting Moscow.[103] In 1956, however, this was not necessarily done with the purpose to conceal ongoing discussions within the Lao Dong leadership, but as much due to the fact that many of the major decisions concerning the Southern struggle were not yet taken and were, furthermore, internally controversial in the Vietnamese leadership.

Both Moscow and Beijing did probably have a rather clear idea about what was going on behind closed doors in Hanoi. Obviously, to Moscow the early changes in Hanoi came at a time when there was much turmoil in both Eastern Europe and the Middle East, which meant that less attention was focused on the situation in Southeast Asia. Moreover, the Soviets did seem quite content with the continued partition of Vietnam. The Chinese, on the other hand, were, according to some, only keeping their revolutionary ambitions at bay, waiting for better times.[104] If such was the case, one might suggest that both Moscow and Beijing, rather than being kept in the dark without any say in the matter, did signal, through their non-involvement, that the Vietnamese should continue to develop their strategies for reunification. At the same time, this is not to say that Moscow approved the insurgence, but rather to suggest that as long as Hanoi's plans did not directly threaten Soviet foreign policy objectives in the world at large, Moscow did not see the need to interfere in Vietnamese politics. That, however, was not the case in the early 1960s, when Moscow strongly advised the Vietnamese to refocus on the political struggle for reunification.

Two particular issues made the difference in these two cases: first, in 1956 both the Soviets and the Chinese doubted that the Vietnamese would actually be able to reunify the country by force, and second, by the beginning of the 1960s the Vietnamese had had time to considerably strengthen their military and economic forces and thus were much better able to carry out a prolonged struggle. But even more important were the changes in the Sino-Soviet relationship, meaning that in the early 1960s Moscow could no longer be certain that Beijing would continue to play on their team with regard to constraining the Vietnamese.

A balancing act

Soviet policies towards Vietnam in the first years after Geneva reflect how Moscow's attempts to balance the wishes of the Vietnamese and Chinese against their own need to come to better terms with the West, and in particular the United States, with few exceptions went in the Vietnamese Communists' disfavour. The introduction of peaceful coexistence as the new line in Soviet foreign policy, which was further strengthened at the Twentieth Congress in February 1956, influenced domestic Vietnamese policies, and did, to some degree, inspire the Vietnamese Communists to re-examine some of their practices during land reform in their own de-Stalinization: the 'rectification of errors campaign'.

As a result, from 1956 the interests of Soviet leaders and Vietnamese Communists with regard to the future development in Vietnam diverged for a while. In line with its policy of peaceful coexistence the Soviet Union was relatively satisfied with a divided Vietnam and would not assist the Lao Dong if such assistance could hamper the improvement of Soviet–American relations. Hanoi, on the other hand, still considered reunification its main goal, and was slowly realizing that to achieve a unified Vietnam it would have to seek support from elsewhere than Moscow.

In 1956 the Vietnamese Communists were still officially promoting a purely political struggle as the best way to achieve reunification. However, there were individuals within the party leadership, and certainly in South Vietnam, who had lost faith in the political struggle and turned increasingly to a strategy in which military action would complement the political struggle. To those within the party in favour of a new strategy, the Soviet bid for peaceful co-existence was a problem. In spite of the new line in politics outlined at the Twentieth Congress, and the Lao Dong statement fully endorsing it, Hanoi continued to discuss alternative routes towards reunification. The changes in the Lao Dong leadership had two effects: first, it downgraded or removed those who had been in charge of land reform and especially those with the closest bonds to China, with Truong Chinh as the most prominent example. Second, after the changes the Politburo would from late 1956 consist of more high-ranking members likely to support a strategy of insurgence in the South.

The failure to hold elections did not reduce Sino-Soviet cooperation in Vietnam. Moscow and Beijing were still inclined to continue to cooperate in Vietnam, and in a comment on Sino-Soviet cooperation in Vietnam the Chinese ambassador to Hanoi, Luo Guibo, underlined that 'the Soviet Union and the People's Republic of China should continue to assist their Vietnamese friends in deciding important questions'.[105] But Luo's friendly remarks disguised problems just below the surface of the triangular relationship. Even though the Sino-Soviet cooperation in Vietnam continued in the same pattern, developments in the two years after Geneva had on several occasions dealt serious blows to both the Sino-Soviet and the Soviet–Vietnamese relationship.

Chinese withdrawal posed a serious challenge to Moscow's Vietnam policy. The reasons for the withdrawal were many and may be found both on the PRC domestic arena based on Beijing's wish to focus more on its own domestic needs and in Vietnam itself. But among the most important reasons were the Vietnamese criticism and their sometimes outright refusals to follow instructions by the Chinese advisors. Through 1955 and 1956 Beijing had to deal with repeated Vietnamese criticism of the overall aspects of China's role in Vietnam. In addition, it is fair to assume that the changes in Moscow's foreign policy line after the Twentieth Congress further accelerated the Chinese wish to withdraw from its commitments, primarily because the new political environment within the international Communist movement enabled the Vietnamese to initiate even stronger criticism of the Chinese. These criticisms must have worried the Soviet leadership, who depended on the Chinese presence in Vietnam, especially in the question of sharing the burden of assistance. Absence of Chinese personnel could possibly force Moscow to take a more active interest in the practical aspects of the Soviet–DRV relationship, a situation Moscow most likely would try to avoid.

The underlying principle of Soviet policy towards Vietnam was the 'use' of China as a 'foreign policy sub-contractor' in Vietnam. During the good days of the Sino-Soviet relationship this strategy was successful, but as cracks began to appear in the relations the whole concept became increasingly difficult for Moscow. However, in spite of the growing foreign policy differences leaders in both the Soviet Union and the PRC realized the necessity of a continuing good working relationship with regard to Vietnam.

5 Reunification by revolution?

The Soviet and Chinese role in Vietnamese reunification plans, 1957–1961

The Vietnamese decision of January 1959 to resume armed struggle as a means of reunification was made exclusively by the Central Committee of the Lao Dong. It was not a move initiated by either the Soviet Union or China, although the actions of the two were important parts of the Lao Dong's decision to embark on a new and more militant strategy. In the years after the Geneva conference, both the Soviet Union and China failed to give Hanoi the necessary support to enable them to hold elections, and thereby reunification within the framework of the Geneva agreement. By the end of the 1950s there was, from a Vietnamese Communist perspective, only one other option left – reunification through armed struggle. Based on Soviet attitudes and behaviour in the preceding years – Moscow's urge to promote détente and the peaceful transition to socialism – there was no reason at all for the Vietnamese to believe the Soviet Union would support them in, or even encourage, the launch of armed struggle to achieve reunification. Thus, from the early 1960s the Vietnamese Communists pursued the new strategy against the advice of Moscow, and initially also against the advice of Beijing.

Parallel to the radicalization of the Vietnamese strategy, Sino-Soviet relations deteriorated. The disagreements within the Communist camp were of great concern to the Vietnamese, who depended on the combined assistance from Moscow and Beijing to reconstruct their economy, and not least to prepare for a reunification struggle in the South. Until early 1961 Moscow and Beijing agreed that the Vietnamese should continue to emphasize political struggle, but from the summer of 1961 the Chinese leaders became increasingly positive to the additional use of military struggle to achieve reunification of Vietnam. The development of Soviet and Chinese positions with regard to the Vietnamese reunification strategy shows how cooperation in Vietnam survived the initial Sino-Soviet disagreements, and how the Vietnamese were eager to mend the conflict to prevent it from ruining cooperation between their major allies.

This chapter centres on three main topics: first, Soviet and Chinese cooperation and their views on the future of the Geneva agreement; second, Moscow and Beijing's approach to changes in the Vietnamese reunification strategy; and finally, the role of the emerging Sino-Soviet conflict and Hanoi's attempt to reconcile its allies.

Accepting two Vietnams

The first real test of the sincerity in the Soviet–Vietnamese relationship after the failure to carry out elections in July 1956 came in January of the following year. On 23 January 1957 the United States proposed the acceptance of both South Vietnam and South Korea as independent members of the United Nations. The American suggestion immediately provoked a Soviet counterproposal on 24 January: to admit North Vietnam and North Korea as well.

The Soviet proposal led to a quick North Vietnamese protest sent to all the members of the United Nations Security Council. This protest was signed by DRV Foreign Minister Pham Van Dong and contained references to the Final Declaration of the Geneva Accords and its § 6: 'the military demarcation line is provisional and should not in any way be interpreted as constituting a political or territorial boundary'.[1] Thus, according to Pham Van Dong, South Vietnam could not be seen as a separate state and could also not become an independent member of the United Nations. He also sought support in the declaration of the Bandung Conference of April 1955, which states, 'Vietnam could only become a member of the United Nations as a reunited Vietnam', meaning that none of the two parts of Vietnam could become a member of the United Nations as long as the country remained divided into two zones. Pham Van Dong's protest was dated 25 January, the day after the Soviets sent their counterproposal.[2] The protest was directed not only against the US proposal but also completely contradicted the Soviet counterproposal. With their counterproposal the Soviet Union was by many, among them Ngo Dinh Diem, seen as accepting a two-state solution for Vietnam.

Except for a few critical comments on behalf of the Vietnamese, Beijing was not ready to criticize the Soviet counterproposal. Accusations in the French and South Vietnamese press implying that there were inconsistencies between Hanoi and Moscow's declarations regarding this question were strongly denied by the Soviet ambassador to Hanoi in a conversation with his Chinese colleague. He underlined that 'there were no inconsistencies', and that 'the Soviet Union stead-fastly defended the fundamental interests of the DRV'.[3] But of course there was an 'inconsistency', which was taken seriously indeed by the Vietnamese themselves, although to a lesser extent by the Chinese. In September 1957 the Chinese chargé d'affairs in Hanoi told the Soviet ambassador that some of the 'Vietnamese friends' had expressed their disagreement with the Soviet proposal to admit the two states in Vietnam as independent members of the UN. However, according to Li Zhimin, the Chinese considered the Vietnamese friends to be too concerned with details regarding any steps from the Socialist camp that could be interpreted as an indirect recognition of South Vietnam.[4] It is not unlikely that Beijing would consider it an advantage for the two parts of Vietnam to be further consolidated as it would secure the state in North Vietnam and also the southern Chinese border.

The prevailing understanding in the literature is that the Soviet counterproposal was a surprise for the Hanoi leadership.[5] My reading of the Soviet documents confirms this. In an extract of a directive from the CC CPSU to the Soviet delegation at the Second Session of the UN General Assembly in late January 1957, the Soviet policy was outlined as follows: 'The Soviet Union shall not take the initiative in posing the question of adopting as members of the United Nations the DRV and DPRK.'[6] However, in its second subsection the extract contains orders on how to proceed if a formal proposal of accepting only South Korea and South Vietnam was put forward. In that case 'the delegation should come forward with a proposal of simultaneous admittance as United Nation members North Korea, North Vietnam, South Korea and South Vietnam'.[7] The Soviets asserted that an acceptance of the two Korean and the two Vietnamese states as members of the United Nations would contribute to their reunification, while the acceptance of only one of the parties as a UN member would be an obstacle on their road to reunification. The directive from the Central Committee of the CPSU also emphasized that if the question of admitting South Korea and South Vietnam was raised without any connection to the simultaneous admittance of North Korea and North Vietnam, the delegation should object, and vote against it in the Security Council, i.e. use their veto.[8]

What was the background for the Soviet proposal? Historian Marilyn Young claims that Khrushchev made the proposal because he was anxious to strengthen détente but also because of the difference in political and economic structure between the two states in Vietnam and the fact that they existed separately.[9] In the United Nations the Soviet representative argued that to admit only South Korea and South Vietnam would create the false impression that the whole of Vietnam and Korea were fully represented in the United Nations. To admit one state and not the other would discriminate the state left out and tend to aggravate and perpetuate the division of the two peoples concerned.[10] Soviet attitudes in 1957 indicate that Moscow saw Vietnam as consisting of two independent states, although that was not an argument they used when explaining their action to their Vietnamese friends. However, time would show that the Soviet leaders thought increasingly of Vietnam as a permanently divided country.

In Hanoi the leaders were worried about the propaganda effect of the Soviet proposal. The Lao Dong officially still aimed at achieving reunification of the country on a democratic foundation and within the Geneva agreement. In his attempt to explain the Soviet position to Ung Van Khiem, the Soviet ambassador emphasized that the Soviet position in the UN defended the fundamental interests of the DRV, and as such, there were no contradictions in the positions of the Soviet Union and the DRV. Moscow supported the Vietnamese friends in their campaign to reunify the country, and the UN proposal did not contradict that objective. Nevertheless, it had to be taken into consideration that 'the fight for a reunified Vietnam unquestionably would be long, and that there was no need to hold an illusion that the reunification may occur from one day to the next'.[11] In other words, the Soviets underlined to the Vietnamese that the reunification would take time, and that what they had done in the UN question would have no negative influence on the question of an eventual reunification. Thus, according to Moscow there were no contradictions between the Soviet and Vietnamese positions.

Evidently, Zimyanin's explanations to Ung Van Khiem were not satisfactory in Vietnamese eyes; Zimyanin also had to explain Soviet behaviour to Ho Chi Minh. Once again he argued that the Soviet Union was defending the fundamental interests of the DRV, and that the Soviet position in the UN in no way contradicted the Geneva agreement and the Vietnamese people's fight for a peaceful reunification of the country. When explaining the Soviet position to Ho Chi Minh, ambassador Zimyanin described it as being 'guided by principle while at the same time flexible'.[12] The flexibility was explained by emphasizing that if the Soviet Union had been forced to veto the proposal to admit South Vietnam into the United Nations, the United States would have been forced to do the same with regard to North Vietnam. These facts should, according to ambassador Zimyanin, be thoroughly presented in DRV propaganda to show that there were no contradictions in the positions of the Soviet Union and the DRV.[13]

In the end, nothing came of the Soviet proposal. And on 30 January 1957 the General Assembly's Special Political Committee approved a US-backed resolution recommending that the Security Council reconsider the membership applications of the Republic of Korea and of Vietnam. The Committee also rejected the Soviet resolution to consider both Vietnams and Koreas as members. On 28 February the General Assembly carried the matter further, when it voted 40 to 8 to recommend to the Security Council that the Republic of Vietnam and of Korea be admitted into membership.[14]

It has been argued that the Soviet Union withdrew the proposal after pressure from Hanoi.[15] Due to the lack of documents reflecting internal Soviet discussions, it is difficult to determine how the Soviets themselves evaluated the pressure form the Vietnamese side. The obvious North Vietnamese displeasure with the proposal can be part of the reason why it was withdrawn. Nor were the Chinese unreservedly positive to Moscow's position on this question. However, as long as the Soviet Union remained a permanent member of the Security Council, it had the power to block the admission of South Vietnam to the UN. Moscow continued to oppose South Vietnam's application for membership, and the Council was unable to recommend its admission.[16]

To the Vietnamese Communists the Soviet behaviour in 1957 was only another of those incidents that made them aware that Moscow could not be trusted to preserve the interests of the Vietnamese. With the counterproposal, Moscow indirectly recognized the Republic of South Vietnam and signalled its acceptance of two independent states in Vietnam. The episode also illustrates the general Soviet attitude towards Vietnam in the period – by forwarding the proposal without prior consultations with the Vietnamese, Soviet leaders showed their readiness to make decisions with serious implications for the future of Vietnam, without letting Hanoi participate in the process. In January 1957 the Soviet Union, apparently, did not see any reason why they should have consulted their allies in North Vietnam, or the Chinese for that matter.

Renewed interest in the Geneva agreement

The UN proposal led to a renewed interest in the Geneva agreement. From Hanoi's point of view the UN proposal and the fulfilment of the Geneva agreement were closely linked. Did Soviet behaviour in the United Nations imply that Moscow no longer had any interest in implementing the Geneva agreement? With their proposal that both Vietnams should be admitted into the UN as independent members, the Soviet leaders indirectly said what the North Vietnamese feared the most, namely that they had accepted the idea of two separate states in Vietnam. The events of January underlined to the Vietnamese that for the moment they were further away than ever from their goal of a united Vietnam under Communist leadership.

In early 1957 neither Hanoi nor Moscow had completely abandoned the idea of a full implementation of the Geneva agreement – the holding of all-Vietnamese elections. From the Soviet point of view the implementation should be done in coordination with China. In response to Hanoi's insistence that one had to think of further steps to obtain fulfilment of the agreement, ambassador Zimyanin told the North Vietnamese that Moscow would have to discuss this question with the Chinese.[17] The Soviet attitude shows that in regard to Sino-Soviet cooperation the pattern from 1954 to 1956 continued. Despite signs of growing differences between Moscow and Beijing they agreed on the necessity to cooperate in Vietnam.

Moscow was positive to the DRV's chances for a fulfilment of the agreement. In March 1957 the Soviet ambassador stressed to Pham Van Dong that the political position of the DRV was significantly stronger than that of South Vietnam, and it was also likely that a weakening of the struggle for reunification within the Geneva framework would be beneficial to the United States (and its position in South Vietnam). According to the Soviets, the strong position of the DRV and the danger that abandoning the Geneva agreement would benefit the United States were two good reasons for continuing the fight for implementation of the agreement. An important part of this strategy was to preserve and support the work of the ICC. Although the principal task of the ICC was not to fight the United States and their interference in the affairs of South Vietnam, the Soviets emphasized that to the extent it was possible the ICC should be used to unmask American intrigues in South Vietnam, because 'to fight for peace in Indochina at present, and for the reunification of Vietnam, it is necessary to concentrate all forces on driving back American interference. The principal policy is political struggle against the aggressive policies of American imperialism.'[18]

During 1957 Moscow continued to encourage the DRV leaders to call for a second Geneva meeting. However, the Soviet policy makers were also apprehensive of a second meeting, because it could possibly reach conclusions less beneficial than the ones from the 1954 Geneva agreement and have unfavourable consequences. But on the positive side, they concluded, Hanoi could use such a meeting to expose the aggressive policies of the United States and its agents in Indochina. Thus, in 1957 both Moscow and Beijing encouraged Hanoi to target their propaganda and their political anger against the United States, while at the same time they should use all efforts to establish relations between North and South Vietnam.[19]

Hanoi were positive to the idea of establishing relations between the two zones. The North Vietnamese leadership was eager to keep the door between the two states open. Moscow's indirect acceptance of two separate states in Vietnam, indicated in the UN proposal, and the general reluctance in both Moscow and Beijing to pursue a solution in Vietnam based on Geneva must have made the Vietnamese leaders realize that they were now the only remaining party still hoping for a fulfilment of the Geneva agreement.

Sino-Soviet cooperation

Through the increase in diplomatic exchanges between the DRV and other countries during 1957 and 1958, the North Vietnamese leaders made long visits to their largest allies, the Soviet Union and China, but they also turned their attention to the East European countries, as well as friendly countries in Asia.[20] The main aim of these trips was to secure economic support for the DRV and also support for the reunification of the country.[21] These visits show how during 1957 and 1958 the North Vietnamese were working hard to gain more friends and allies both within the Socialist camp and in Asia at large, something that would make them more independent of the two major economic and military contributors, the Soviet Union and China.

As in previous years, Soviet and Chinese aid remained essential to the Vietnamese. Even after the withdrawal of many advisors in 1955 and 1956 Beijing was still in charge of the major part of practical assistance to the DRV. It has been argued that one reason for leaving the practical responsibility to the Chinese was that Chinese specialists were more easily integrated into North Vietnamese society than Soviet specialists. Vietnamese complaints over problems with the interaction between Soviet specialists and Vietnamese citizens support such suppositions. Moscow even wanted to reduce the number of Soviet specialists in Vietnam for such reasons.[22] Accounts from earlier years, however, have shown how also the Chinese specialists encountered many problems in their interactions with the Vietnamese, even though they, at least according to the Soviets, should have been more easily integrated into Vietnamese society.

Both Moscow and Beijing were sceptical of Hanoi's extensive use of foreign specialists and the DRV's total dependence on aid from fraternal countries. In January 1957 the Soviet Union and China jointly criticized the DRV for relying on fraternal countries to help them raise over 50 per cent of the budget.[23] According to the Vietnamese, Chinese Premier Zhou Enlai was sceptical about using foreign specialists in Vietnam, as he feared that the more specialists were involved, the more mistakes would be made. In 1956, as a part of the rectification of errors campaign, Lao Dong leaders claimed that part of the mistake was that the Vietnamese had so uncritically followed the Chinese example when conducting land reform. Grudges after these accusations were instrumental in

1957, when the Chinese were reluctant to send new specialists to the DRV. To explain this move to the Soviets, the Chinese argued that they feared a high number of foreign specialists would reduce the initiative among the Vietnamese. Vietnam should first of all rely on its own resources.[24]

Dissatisfied with the Chinese attitude, Pham Van Dong revealed to the Soviet ambassador that Chinese Premier Zhou Enlai had little faith in Soviet assistance to the DRV. In the spring of 1957 Zhou had told the Vietnamese that they had to decide for themselves whether they should ask Moscow for assistance or not, but that they had to bear in mind 'the USSR had many obligations'.[25] Hanoi was dependent on assistance from both the Soviet Union and China. Thus, Pham Van Dong's ulterior motive in revealing the Chinese attitude to the Soviets could have been to push Moscow into proving the Chinese wrong, by showing that the Soviet Union did care about the situation in Vietnam and would give aid to the Vietnamese. But most important in this context were probably the memories of the rectification of errors campaign. It is possible that Beijing wanted to hear the Lao Dong leaders apologize for the campaign, which had seriously hurt leaders inspired by the Chinese example, such as Truong Chinh, before they would provide further assistance to the DRV.

An essential part of Soviet advice to Hanoi was the need to elaborate detailed plans for the economic development of the country. In his conversations with the DRV leadership ambassador Zimyanin emphasized the need for careful planning in Vietnamese requests for economic assistance. Before Ho Chi Minh's 1957 visit to the Soviet Union the ambassador urged the North Vietnamese to have fully elaborated plans for material aid from the Socialist countries to the DRV.[26] The fact that the Vietnamese had intended to use much more of the Soviet aid than announced for military purposes in 1956 meant that this time the fraternal countries wanted to see explicit plans for the use of the aid to avoid similar diversification.

By 1958 the trend within the Vietnamese armed forces was to reduce rather than enlarge the army. In February 1958 Defence Minister Vo Nguyen Giap could inform the new Soviet ambassador, Leonid Ivanovich Sokolov,[27] that the Vietnamese military leaders had decided to reduce the PAVN to 1,60,000 troops before 1960. The ambassador responded by suggesting that the demobilized forces should be used in the national economy.[28] During the years 1957–59, PAVN underwent a process of technological modernization, and at the same time party political controls over the military were instituted at all levels. As a result of decisions taken by the party's 12th Plenum in March 1957, military units were assigned tasks in the civilian economy, and in 1958 the Army's involvement in this sector was increased as units assumed responsibility for running state farms.[29]

From 1960 onwards Hanoi again expressed a strong will to accelerate the tempo of their economic development, and to acquire the necessary assistance the leaders turned to the Soviet Union. The immediate background, according to Pham Van Dong, was that they were afraid of falling behind South Vietnam in economic development. If they could win the economic competition with the

South, it would not only heighten their prestige in Southeast Asia but also have an important impact on the outcome of the fight to reunify the country. In other words, without saying it outright to the Soviets, this acceleration was also part of the preparation for a future war. But a more intensive development did, according to Pham Van Dong, also require more intensive assistance. However, this time Moscow was more reserved when responding to the request. Pham Van Dong emphasized that he understood the Soviet Union could not constantly increase the amount of aid; nor did the DRV have any right to expect that. To accommodate Moscow, Pham Van Dong suggested that they redirect the aid and use all forces to more intensively exploit it in order to increase the tempo of development.[30] In response to the Vietnamese requests the Soviet Union provided two assistance payments (long-terms credits) during 1960; the first amount of approximately 79 million roubles came in June, and a second amount of approximately 97 million roubles came in late December. Thus the total amount of Soviet assistance provided in 1960 was 176 million roubles. According to Soviet sources the Vietnamese only used a total of 83 million roubles, not even half of what they were offered.[31]

In the sphere of economic and military assistance the changes in the Vietnamese reunification strategy during 1959 and 1960 seem to have had no drastic impact on the amount of assistance from the Socialist camp to the DRV. Soviet estimates show that the development of the national economy of the DRV was fulfilled according to the Three-Year Plan for 1958–60. The financial part of the plan had been fully balanced due to the help of Soviet and Chinese experts and included Soviet credits of 100 million roubles and Chinese credits in the amount of 600 million yuan. Although the situation so far was favourable, it was not precluded from the Soviet side that Hanoi would ask for an additional credit from the Soviet Union. The Soviet attitude to that was positive, and it was underlined that if such a request came, Moscow would consider assisting the North Vietnamese in developing their economy also beyond 1960.[32] All in all, assistance from the Soviet Union to the DRV was kept on the same level as in previous years, implying a gradual increase, but no substantial change in 1959–60.[33]

The Lao Dong debates its policy on reunification

Towards the end of 1958 the Vietnamese Communist Party leadership was unified in its decision to change the course of the struggle in South Vietnam. Between the 14th Plenum held in November 1958 and the 15th Plenum of the Lao Dong Central Committee held from December 1958 to February 1959, Politburo member Le Duan made a trip to South Vietnam to evaluate the situation.[34] The contents of his report are not known, but it must have concluded that the situation in South Vietnam demanded a new strategy allowing military actions to complement the political struggle. In sum, it was the growing desire for reunification in the North combined with Le Duan's report, which underlined similar strong sentiments for a swift change in the South, that prompted the Vietnamese Communists to change the strategy of reunification.

Although Moscow had settled for a permanent partition of Vietnam, the debate in Hanoi over what kind of policy to pursue to obtain reunification continued. As we have already seen, the Lao Dong leaders had started to discuss alternatives to political struggle as early as 1956, but consensus was not reached until the end of 1958, when they decided to supplement the political struggle with military action. There are few signs indicating that Hanoi discussed the change of strategy with Moscow, since the Lao Dong leaders already knew the Soviet preference for a peaceful solution to the Vietnam problem. The party leadership repeatedly stressed to Soviet officials the need to revise the Southern strategy and reported on measures the party had taken in this regard. Soviet diplomats must have been aware of the ongoing debate within the Lao Dong, but whether they realized its seriousness is difficult to assess. The records of conversations between Soviet officials, the party leadership and Chinese representatives in the DRV show that the Vietnamese expressed, though not always directly, the need to make changes in the policy towards the South.

Soviet and Chinese positions towards the Vietnamese reunification struggle up to 1959 were not dissimilar. Although Beijing in general seemed more prone to accept a more militant strategy on reunification than Moscow, in the late 1950s the Chinese supported the Soviet position calling for a peaceful reunification within the Geneva framework. At the same time the Chinese were conscious of possible disagreements between Moscow and Hanoi. In September 1957, PRC chargé d'affaires in Hanoi, Li Zhimin, spoke to the Soviet ambassador about what he considered to be differences of opinion between the representatives of the Soviet Communist Party's Central Committee and the Vietnamese Communists with regard to Vietnamese reunification.[35]

The Soviet ambassador rejected the allegations. The Soviet Union supported the reunification of Vietnam within the Geneva framework. However, for the future the tactics of the struggle had to be carefully thought out and, if necessary, changed according to the situation. It had to be taken into consideration that at present two different states existed in Vietnam, and Vietnam could possibly remain divided for a rather long period of time. What complicated the situation was, according to Zimyanin, that some Vietnamese friends did not quite understand this. The problem was those 'independent Vietnamese friends, working in South Vietnam, who believed it was necessary to organize separate attacks against the Diem regime as a means of inspiring the masses to fight. This manifested an oversimplified, un-Marxist approach to the situation and to the question of armed insurrection.'[36] These independent Vietnamese comrades were, according to Zimyanin, still not willing to bear in mind that the principal target in this political fight was the United States and that the best solution would be to stop criticizing Diem and to start considering how to establish contact between North and South.[37]

In late 1956 members of the Lao Dong complained about the absence of a general line of policy and a lack of ideological unity. The party had obviously faced the problem when, in June 1957, Politburo member Truong Chinh informed Zimyanin that the party saw it as one of its most urgent tasks to work out a general line in politics. It was especially important in the period of transition towards a Socialist state and in finding a direction for unification of the country. The basis for this general line would be to secure common views and to strengthen unity within the party with special emphasis on ideology and politics. Truong Chinh referred to Khrushchev's speech at the Twentieth Congress, a speech that he said had been carefully studied within the Lao Dong and had made them understand the importance of criticism, particularly from below. The speech also had grave consequences for the structure of the party leadership in the Lao Dong and the principle of collective leadership.[38]

In conversations with Soviet officials the North Vietnamese leaders repeatedly underlined that the changes in the Vietnamese situation required a new strategy to achieve reunification. The Soviet reaction to the Vietnamese attitude is not all that evident, although the archival documents indicate that Soviet embassy officials received enough information to see a change of attitude within the Lao Dong leadership. One example is how Hanoi informed them of changes within the Politburo, which clearly indicated the ascendancy of individuals from the South or working in the South. On several occasions during 1957 and 1958 North Vietnamese officials discussed the changing historical conditions in Vietnam with the Soviet embassy and underlined that because of the new situation, it was possible that the forthcoming Third Congress of the Lao Dong would make changes in both the programme and statutes of the party. At present the party was elaborating separate strategies for the Northern and Southern parts of the country. Such an approach had been chosen because the party leaders felt that the difference between the situations in the two parts was so important that separate tactics had to be worked out. The most important task was to develop the revolutionary line of the party in all of Vietnam under the new conditions.[39] The fact that Southerners gained increasingly more power within the higher echelons of the party should have told Moscow that changes were being prepared.[40] The question, however, is whether the Soviet embassy in Hanoi and the leadership in Moscow grasped the serious signals inherent in these changes.

Although hinting on several occasions that changes in the Southern strategy was underway, there is little evidence in available documents of the Vietnamese speaking to the Soviets in a direct sense of armed struggle or overthrowing the Southern regime. The only such direct information can be found in a conversation between second secretary at the Soviet embassy in Hanoi, G. Kadumov, and an official at the DRV Ministry of State Security, 'Thum', held on 4 April 1958.[41] Thum reported that the DRV Ministry of State Security had concluded the discussion of two documents approved at the Moscow Conference of Communist and Workers Parties in November 1957. In the course of the discussion a particularly animated debate had unfolded over the question of Vietnamese reunification.

The background for the heated debate was the large number of regrouped Southerners in the ministry; these so-called 'regroupees' were regrouped Vietminh cadres who had moved to the North after partition in 1954. Like Southerners in other ministries they had started to lose faith in the peaceful reunification of Vietnam in the near future. Some comrades declared that they no longer believed in peaceful reunification, since the South Vietnamese government would never agree to such a solution. The regrouped Southerners did, however, realize that the only acceptable policy for the countries of the Socialist camp, including the DRV, was a policy of deciding all vexed questions by peaceful means. The problem, according to Thum, was that this apparently insoluble contradiction worried some Southern comrades who now believed the country would never be reunited. As a result, some comrades had come to the conclusion that it was necessary to decide whether to reunify the country through armed struggle, even if that meant sacrificing their lives.[42] Thum also reported that when some of the Southern regroupees had volunteered to return to South Vietnam in order to activate underground work to overthrow Ngo Dinh Diem's regime, the response from the party leaders, particularly Le Duan, was negative. According to Le Duan the comrades in the South had their methods, and the Southern regroupees in DRV were not updated on these. This refusal of their services apparently led to even more dissatisfaction among the Southern regroupees.[43]

This conversation shows that the Soviet embassy personnel did obtain the necessary information to capture the general mood among the Vietnamese. However, Moscow's continued emphasis on the need to follow a peaceful line in politics, and the outright lack of comments with regard to Vietnamese unification, imply that the Soviet leaders either had not yet grasped the seriousness of the ongoing debate on DRV policy towards the South, or were convinced that the Vietnamese would not attempt to embark on a new, more militant strategy of reunification without the consent of their major allies.

While the debate of 1957–58 over future strategy towards the South unfolded in Hanoi, the Soviet leaders were still inclined to see a peaceful solution to the Vietnam problem. The preferred solution would be within the framework of the Geneva agreement. If that proved impossible, Moscow seemed willing to settle for a two-state solution in Vietnam. In the instructions from the Soviet Ministry of Foreign Affairs to the Soviet ambassador in Hanoi, Leonid Ivanovich Sokolov, three areas of priority were accentuated. First, Moscow emphasized the need to realize the peaceful initiative of the Soviet Union; in other words, no policy contradicting it should be allowed. Second, it stressed that the difficult situation due to the temporary partition of Vietnam was likely to continue for some time. Third, it expected the embassy officials to conduct a more thorough analysis of US influence in the area. Embassy personnel were instructed to send home reports on the situation in Vietnam, as well as suggestions on how to handle the situation.[44]

Thus, the Soviet instructions from 1958 indicate Moscow's changing view on the situation. In 1954 the emphasis had been on the reconstruction of the DRV in various fields, and only to a lesser extent on the international context of Vietnam's situation and, as a part of that, Soviet aims in the region. After four years of experience in Vietnam, and as a result of the changing international situation, the instructions of 1958 reflected to a larger degree Soviet aspirations in the region. The importance of peaceful co-existence, the growing American influence and, not least, the long-lasting temporary partition of Vietnam were now integral factors in Soviet policy planning towards Vietnam. As reflected in Moscow's priorities in Vietnam for 1958, Soviet policy makers were apparently not yet worried about the changing mood among the Vietnamese leadership. There are two possible reasons for this. Either the Soviet leaders, just as in the fall of 1956, did not consider the changes in the Lao Dong a threat to stability in the region, and thus saw no immediate need to interfere. Or it could be that Moscow still reckoned that the Chinese had a certain amount of control over the Vietnamese and thus would see to it that Hanoi neither seriously challenged the RVN nor provoked their American allies enough to unleash an attack. These reasons, however, would no longer be valid once the Sino-Soviet split intensified.

During 1957 and 1958 the situation in South Vietnam deteriorated. Diem's move to further consolidate his regime led to a new wave of repression in both the urban and rural areas. To the people of South Vietnam that meant another sequence of denunciation, encirclement of villages, searches and raids, arrests of suspects, plundering, interrogations, torture (even of innocent people), deportation and 'regrouping' of populations suspected of contacts with the rebels.[45] Ngo Dinh Diem's Anti Communist Denunciation Campaign initiated in 1956 continued and was supplemented by other campaigns aimed at opponents of the Diem regime, including both Communists and non-Communists. The background for these campaigns was the continuing competition for rural legitimacy between Diem and the various opponents of his regime. The RVN had to devote a large amount of its resources to establishing and maintaining its authority in rural areas. From 1957 to 1959 Diem failed to cope successfully with problems in the rural areas, a situation the Lao Dong attempted to exploit.

American economic assistance to the Republic of Vietnam amounted to US$1.7 billion in the period from 1955 to 1961. In May 1958 Saigon housed the largest US aid mission in the world, and by 1961 the RVN was the third-ranking non-NATO recipient of American aid after Korea and Taiwan. The growing American influence in South Vietnamese affairs and the increased acceptance of the RVN on the world stage only served to convince party leaders that they had to redouble their efforts to reunify Vietnam before the Southern republic became too strong.[46]

Chinese attitudes during this period were another factor that reassured Moscow that there was no imminent need to worry about Vietnamese strategies. Although recent studies of the Sino-Vietnamese relationship indicate that the North Vietnamese leaders might have been more direct when asking for advice from Beijing than from Moscow, the Chinese were no more willing to go down that path than Moscow. Chinese sources reveal that in the summer of 1958 the Vietnamese Politburo formally asked Beijing's advice about the strategy for the 'Southern revolution'; in response, Beijing emphasized that Hanoi's most important task was 'to promote socialist revolution and reconstruction in the North'.[47] At the current stage it would not be possible to realize a revolutionary transformation in the South, and therefore Hanoi should adopt in the South a strategy of 'not exposing our own forces for a long period, build up our own strength, establishing connections with the masses, and waiting for the coming of proper opportunities'.[48] The Chinese position indicates that, just like Moscow, Beijing's leaders were not particularly enthusiastic about the Vietnamese plans to initiate military struggles in South Vietnam at that point.[49]

Thus, the Chinese neither hindered nor encouraged Hanoi at that stage. The attitude may well have been rooted in the country's current situation, as China was entering a difficult period in both the domestic and international sphere. Despite the Soviet emphasis on peaceful coexistence the international situation grew tenser through 1958, and the first direct Sino-Soviet disagreements surfaced. Moreover, China was in the process of accelerating the Great Leap Forward, a radical domestic programme aimed at rapid industrialization of the country. The programme was officially approved at the CCP's 8th Congress in May 1958. China's domestic radicalism soon spilled over into the foreign policy sphere. In mid-1958 it announced plans to liberate Taiwan, and on 23 August the Formosan Straits crisis was precipitated when mainland gunners opened fire on the nationalist-held offshore islands of Jinmen and Mazu. The attack on the US-supported nationalists brought to the fore Sino-Soviet differences, as China now adopted a more militant attitude than the Soviet Union towards Washington.[50]

The Lao Dong Politburo never formally asked Moscow for advice on the Southern strategy before they made their decision to start the insurgency. In their approach to the Chinese, Hanoi counted on the more radical Chinese attitude, which developed during 1957 and 1958, but even the Chinese wanted to contain the Vietnamese situation for the time being. Since Moscow was still promoting its line of peaceful coexistence, it was clear to the Vietnamese Communists that it would prove difficult to obtain support for a more radical line towards reunification. Also, the Soviet lack of reference to the changes in the Vietnamese Communists' attitude to means of reunification indicate that Soviet leaders refused to believe that Hanoi would embark on a new and more militant road to reunification, especially if it stood in contrast to the general Soviet policy in the area.

Moscow was further reassured in its position by the attitude of Beijing. The majority of the Chinese leaders were not willing to support the new Vietnamese strategy, as that could provoke a stronger American interest in Vietnam. Did the Soviet Union and the PRC more or less turn their backs on the DRV to avoid involvement, while at the same time tacitly condoning their change in strategy? If so, Moscow's policies must have been rather confusing to the Vietnamese Communists. This would also imply that Moscow did, to some extent, support Hanoi's plans but was reluctant to do so openly. Especially with China gaining more and more ground in North Vietnam, and the Sino-Soviet relationship showing increasing signs of fatigue, it remains possible that the Soviets were afraid to provide too much active support.

Embarking on a new Southern strategy

The major strategy change in Hanoi's policy towards the South came in 1959 and 1960. Three significant political events took place during these years. The first was the decision made during the 15th Plenum of the Lao Dong Central Committee held from December 1958 to February 1959 to resume armed struggle in the South; the second decision was made at the Third Party Congress of the Lao Dong in September 1960 and reemphasized this new attitude and the third was the establishment in December 1960 of an organization that would carry through these plans, the National Liberation Front of South Vietnam (NLF(SV)). Together these three events forced Moscow to pay more attention to the developments in Vietnam and the new Lao Dong strategy. Initially the Soviets and Chinese tried to restrain the Vietnamese plans, which they perceived as a threat to stability in the region, but this task became increasingly difficult as Soviet and Chinese views on foreign policy visibly began to diverge from the early 1960s onwards.

At the 15th Plenum the Lao Dong approved in principle the resumption of armed revolt in the South. The official communiqué with the resolutions of the 15th Plenum was not presented until 13 May 1959, nearly five months after the meeting itself. The communiqué did not specifically refer to armed struggle but did outline a change in the course of the Southern strategy. Prior to the announcement in May, Soviet diplomats had repeatedly asked the Lao Dong leaders for information on the Plenum resolutions. In January, during the Plenum sessions Ho Chi Minh told Soviet ambassador Sokolov, 'the present situation in South Vietnam can be characterized as ripe for revolution'.[51] In March, when the embassy once again requested materials from the Plenum, the response was still negative. According to Nguyen Duy Trinh, it was because the final resolution had not yet been edited, and the main speaker at the Plenum, Pham Hung, had left for Indonesia together with Ho Chi Minh.[52] Barely a month before the official announcement, on 15 April, records show that Le Duan informed Sokolov of the subjects of discussion at the 15th Plenum. However, Sokolov wanted more than just vague information. What he was most interested in were those decisions of the Plenum directly concerned with the basic problems of the evolution of the revolutionary movement in South Vietnam, and the fight for reunification of the country.[53] Moscow never got a clear answer to that question in April. It was not until after the official communiqué was released on 13 May that the Soviet embassy was informed in some detail as to what the new strategy consisted of.[54]

The second decision, made at the Third Party Congress in September 1960, acknowledged the expansion of armed struggle in South Vietnam with the purpose of overthrowing the regime of Ngo Dinh Diem.[55] The resolutions of the Third Congress further expanded the resolutions of the 15th Plenum. The aim was now to 'set the general policy of the "liberation" of the South – i.e., the overthrow of the Diem regime and the establishment of a coalition government favourably disposed toward reunification with Communist North Vietnam'.[56] In contrast to the resolution from 1959, the decision made at the Third Congress had been discussed with both the Soviets and the Chinese in advance. During a visit to Beijing in early October 1959 Nikita Khrushchev evidently discussed the future strategy in South Vietnam with Ho Chi Minh.[57] Evidently, from the autumn of 1959 Soviet leaders developed a new interest in the situation in Vietnam. North Vietnam now showed itself as much stronger and more independent than the Soviets expected. Such a situation thus called for a stronger Soviet interest in the area.

In the spring of 1960 Soviet and Chinese policies on Vietnamese reunification were still coherent, and they jointly advised the Lao Dong on how to proceed with the political preparations for the Third Congress. In May that year the Lao Dong Central Committee had consultations in Moscow with the Central Committees of the Soviet and Chinese Communist parties, to discuss the thesis in the Lao Dong political account for the Third Congress. The section of the thesis dedicated to the struggle for the reunification of Vietnam indicated an intention to expand armed struggle in South Vietnam with the purpose of overthrowing the regime of Ngo Dinh Diem and create liberated areas governed by the people in the South. To convince the Soviets and the Chinese that there were really no drastic changes in the new strategy, the Vietnamese underlined that it was simply a continuation of the war of resistance (1946–54), and as such the creation of liberated areas was 'the form of gradually accomplishing the reunification of the mother country'.[58] However, at this point Soviet policy makers had started to realize that the Vietnamese could become harder to restrain than previously thought, and together with the Chinese they attempted to influence the Vietnamese views.

Although neither Moscow nor Beijing did, according to Soviet documents, agree with the offensive strategy proposed by the Vietnamese Communists, they did nothing to actively oppose it either. In 1960 most protests were still rather modest from both of Hanoi's allies. While in Moscow for consultations with the Soviets and Chinese, the Vietnamese comrades were told that due to the developing situation in Vietnam, it would be inexpedient to deny the slogan of peaceful reunification of Vietnam on the basis of the Geneva agreement. The Vietnamese apparently agreed with the Soviet and Chinese position and in the opening address of the Lao Dong CC at the Third Congress 'set forth a position envisaging a peaceful reunification of the country.'[59] To the Soviets it now seemed as if the Lao Dong had accepted the Soviet and Chinese advice, as the party leaders set forth a policy promoting a peaceful reunification of the country. In 1960 that was the only form of Vietnamese reunification the Soviet Union would accept.

Nevertheless, through 1959 and 1960, parallel to this development, the Lao Dong gradually managed to rebuild its strength in South Vietnam, and there was a sharp increase in the number of guerrilla attacks in that part of the country. From May 1959 the Vietnamese Communists started to infiltrate Southern regroupees back to the South. Two different groups first made these preparations. One was in charge of the inland area, the 559th transportation group, directly under the command of the party centre, and in charge of what has later been known as the Ho Chi Minh Trail. The other, group 759, a maritime unit, was based at the naval headquarters of Quang-Khe and given the responsibility for infiltration by sea. Before the end of 1960 these groups had succeeded in introducing some 4,500 cadres into the South, a most valuable resource for the decimated underground party. The sharpest increase in assaults against RVN officials came in the last quarter of 1959, continuing into 1960. Gradually the party rebuilt its strength in the South, while the Army of the Republic of Vietnam was cut off from rural areas, where the party developed large military units.[60]

Hanoi's goal during these years was to establish strong points in the South and become self-sufficient. To achieve that goal party bases were established and cadres from the party were present in all parts of the administration. According to the Lao Dong, such a strategy would enable them to gradually take power in South Vietnam with a minimum of bloodshed. According to Hanoi officials, the Southerners did not even need weapons from the North. It was also emphasized that in the present international situation a resumption of the partisan war in the South would be considered unfavourable to the cause of peace and was therefore undesirable. The most important task in the South was therefore to preserve peace at any price while simultaneously preserving and strengthening the revolutionary forces in the South in order to complete the national people's democratic revolution for the whole country.[61] The establishment of a mass movement in South Vietnam was, as we have seen earlier, an important part of the Lao Dong strategy for the South. In 1960 the Lao Dong sent more than 10,000 Communists to work in the South, and by early 1961 they had managed to establish active and well-organized party organizations in more than 850 of 1,000 villages.[62]

Meanwhile in Saigon the government and its American allies were worried about the decisions of the Communist side in the spring of 1959. While the leaders in Hanoi had elaborated their new Southern strategy, the Americans had started to rethink their own military assistance to foreign governments such as the South Vietnamese. The eventual outcome of this thinking with regard to Southeast Asia was that the Communist military forces were unlikely to embark on a conventional war so long as the American commitment to its allies remained firm. The problem at the time, particularly in South Vietnam and Laos, 'was how to deal with a revolutionary movement operating from political bases inside a "threatened" country and gradually acquiring a capability for anti-government violence.'[63] The solution to the problem was a new strategy – the doctrine of counterinsurgency, a solution based on the following concept: First, a guarantee of the political and economic stability of the threatened government by means of increased aid, enabling improvement of administrative efficiency at grassroots levels. Second, it was also important to provide counter-guerrilla assistance, to enable the armed forces of the threatened country to defeat rebel terrorist and guerrilla units in the field.[64]

The third major event in Hanoi's strategy change during 1959 and 1960 was the establishment, in South Vietnam, of the NLF(SV) on 20 December 1960.[65] According to reports from the Soviet embassy in Hanoi, the front was designed to counter the growing American influence in South Vietnam and exploit all patriotic forces opposed to the regime of Ngo Dinh Diem. The creation of the front had, according to the embassy, a positive effect in developing widespread political work among all layers of the Southern population, and the main task was to eventually overthrow Diem's regime and establish an independent, peaceful and neutral state in South Vietnam under the governance of a national democratic coalition government. Quoting Vietnamese propaganda, the embassy underlined how 'the activities of these patriotic forces created an immediate threat to the regime of Ngo Dinh Diem, which troubled the United States in its effort to preserve South Vietnam as an American outpost in Southeast Asia'.[66] Thus, the front was a formalization of the work we have seen in South Vietnam in the years after 1955 but now took on the role of a more active opponent to the Southern regime.

The Soviet embassy further described the establishment of the NLF as 'another important step in the development of the national-liberation movement in the south of the country'. The initiator was, according to the embassy report, the Lao Dong, and until a permanent Central Committee of the NLF was in place all orders came from the leadership in Hanoi. However, directives from the Lao Dong would also in the future to some extent determine the activities of the organization. In the south, the NLF cooperated with a number of organizations sympathetic to the cause of the DRV.[67] Although not positive to a stepped-up armed struggle in Vietnam, Moscow took note of what had happened but did not take any immediate action to discourage the formation of the NLF.

In Hanoi the Lao Dong leadership continued to work with a radicalized strategy for reunification. As seen, this strategy was first suggested in the spring of 1956 as an alternative to the so far fruitless political fight for reunification within the framework of the Geneva agreement. The fruitless efforts to secure a diplomatic solution in the years after Geneva had convinced the Vietnamese Communists that armed struggle represented the only successful way to reunification. This decision was upheld in spite of the initial advice to the contrary from both Moscow and Beijing. However, in late 1961 Soviet policy makers had become increasingly convinced that the Chinese were about to develop a more positive attitude towards the new Lao Dong strategy and concluded that the Vietnamese friends had 'not without influence from the Chinese friends in 1961 taken a course toward initiating armed struggle'.[68]

Mediating the emerging Sino-Soviet conflict

Although relations between Moscow and Beijing rapidly deteriorated during the late 1950s, Sino-Soviet cooperation continued in Vietnam. The first obvious signs of difference in the Sino-Soviet relationship came during the Jinmen and Mazu crisis in mid-1958, when China adopted a more militant attitude towards the United States than the Soviet Union. The first major crisis in the relationship came in 1959, when Khrushchev took a neutral stand during the Sino-Indian border dispute. When arriving for a diplomatic visit to Beijing after the crisis, Khrushchev unsuccessfully attempted to act as an intermediary, a move Mao and the Chinese took as a sign of Soviet perfidy. Through the spring of 1960, especially after the U-2 incident in May, relations seemed somewhat better. In June, the Rumanian Communist Party's Congress, and the Bucharest Conference of Communist parties that followed it, was the scene of a bitter exchange between

Khrushchev and the Chinese representative, and in July Khrushchev decided to withdraw all Soviet specialists from China.[69]

The withdrawal of Soviet specialists from China was viewed with special concern by the Vietnamese. In response to the Vietnamese ambassador in Beijing, Chan Ti Binh, who was eager to understand why the Soviet specialists had been withdrawn, Soviet ambassador Chervonenko explained that there were mainly two reasons. The CCP had made several efforts to influence the views of the specialists on important problems related to the current international situation. As a part of this, they had even showed the specialists confidential notes sent between the Soviet Union and China and asked the specialists to give their personal opinion on these documents. Secondly, during 1958 and 1959 there had been an increasing number of cases in which the Chinese ignored the advice given by the Soviet specialists and thus put them in situations where they seemed to be giving false instructions.[70]

Chan Ti Binh then explained to Chervonenko how the Chinese had hinted to the Vietnamese that the departure of the Soviet specialists not only had an impact on the fulfilment of plans in China itself but would also have a serious impact on the Chinese ability to provide assistance to the DRV.[71] Realizing that there were those who accused the Vietnamese of 'following the Chinese comrades', Chan Ti Binh underlined that the disagreements between the Soviet and Chinese Communist parties had caused much grief and distress among the Vietnamese and that they would do all they could to improve relations between the two parties.[72]

The growing differences between Moscow and Beijing worried the Lao Dong leaders, and efforts were made to bring the two together to settle the differences in private. At the time of the Bucharest Conference in late June 1960 Ho Chi Minh wrote a letter to Nikita Khrushchev expressing his worries over the developing situation within the Communist camp. The contents of the letter were presented in a conversation between Ho and Soviet chargé d'affaires Nikolai I. Godunov on 22 June. Ho Chi Minh emphasized the possible serious consequences of these differences being exposed in the press and underlined that the present development was not in the interest of the Communist world. With regard to the effects of the conflict on the Vietnamese Communists Ho Chi Minh said, 'within our party [. . .] we have already faced, in connection with these differences, perplexing questions, but we are trying to avoid raising them and call upon the members of the Lao Dong to wait and not to make any hasty conclusions'.[73]

Watching the controversy, which took place during the Bucharest Conference, Ho obviously feared a similar scenario could occur at his party's Third Congress scheduled for September that year. At a meeting with representatives of the Socialist countries held in late August 1960, shortly before the congress, the Lao Dong leaders presented the results of a Lao Dong Central Committee visit to the Soviet Union and China. The issue was once again Sino-Soviet differences, and the discussion was based on a four-point text containing the Lao Dong view on the conflict.[74] However, to what extent Ho's pleas to mend the conflict saved the congress from becoming a victim of the differences is difficult to estimate based on available materials.

As the differences with Beijing intensified, Moscow devoted more attention to Hanoi's stand in the conflict. In October 1961 the Soviet embassy in Hanoi presented a report entitled 'Some questions related to the activities of the CC Lao Dong after the Moscow meeting of Communist and Worker's Parties in 1960'. The report underlined Chinese influence on the Vietnamese Communists and the Lao Dong leaders' preference for the CCP's points of view in questions related to both building socialism in the DRV and the Twentieth Congress of the CPSU. Another insufficiency in the Soviet–Vietnamese relationship was, according to the report, the lack of information from the Vietnamese to Soviet diplomats with regard to party plenums and policies towards the South. Lao Dong leaders had promised to report on steps to be taken in South Vietnam, but according to the report no information was provided because 'our friends evidently think that by openly presenting their views on how to solve the problem of South Vietnam they will not receive the necessary support from the Soviet Union'.[75] In 1961 Moscow must have been rather frustrated with its grip on the situation in Vietnam. The Chinese were clearly increasing their influence at the expense of Moscow, and in the light of the deteriorating Sino-Soviet relationship the Soviets could no longer fully count on China as a support in Vietnam, especially not if Soviet policies contradicted those of China. Years of neglect and focus elsewhere were catching up with Soviet policies towards Vietnam.

Moscow and the new Southern strategy

When President John F. Kennedy took office in early 1961 there were 800 American military personnel in South Vietnam. When he died in November 1963 the number was 16,700.[76] Parallel to the escalation of the American commitment, the Lao Dong sought China's assistance to counter the increased American military involvement in South Vietnam. In June 1961 Pham Van Dong went to Beijing, where Mao expressed a general support for the armed struggle of the South Vietnamese people, while Zhou Enlai was more moderate and advised the Vietnamese to stress flexibility in tactics and stay on a course of combining political and military approaches.[77] Beijing's position was now about to change and became increasingly positive to the use of armed struggle to achieve reunification, in contrast to Moscow's continued emphasis on the political struggle.

In the fall of 1961 the Lao Dong reorganized and strengthened its Central Office for South Vietnam (COSVN) and passed a resolution advocating an intensification of the anti-American struggle. These actions were soon reflected in a sharp increase in the number of NLF operations in the autumn of 1961. During the early autumn US intelligence officers reported a total of 200 guerrilla incidents: 50 incidents in September and 150 in October. The successful advance of the Communist insurgents was definitive when they captured a provincial capital only 55 miles from Saigon.[78]

With the increased military activity in South Vietnam, Moscow now had to decide on their own stand in relation to the new strategy developing in Vietnam.

The Chinese role in Vietnam played an important part in this, and in Moscow the numerous signs of pro-Chinese tendencies among Lao Dong leaders were indeed taken seriously. The special relationship between the Lao Dong and the CCP was carefully studied by Soviet officials in both Hanoi and Beijing, as well as in the Soviet foreign ministry's Southeast Asia Department. As Soviet Ambassador Suren Akopovich Tovmasyan phrased it in a political report to the Foreign Ministry: 'the CC CCP has a definite influence over the political line and activities of the CC Lao Dong'.[79] To illustrate the extent of the Chinese influence, Tovmasyan explained that the Vietnamese leaders shared the points of views of the leaders in the CCP and Albanian Worker's Party on the personality cult. They did not agree with the decision of the Twentieth Congress of the Communist party of the Soviet Union condemning the personality cult of Stalin, but preferred to pass this over in silence. And with regard to the case of Albania, the ambassador argued that Ho apparently felt sorry for Enver Hoxha and therefore did not share the Soviet opinion of him.[80]

In May 1961 Le Duan discussed the situation in South Vietnam with Nikolai I. Godunov, then councillor at the Soviet embassy in the DRV. After a detailed account of the development of the patriotic forces in the South from February to April, Le Duan told Godunov that the Politburo of the CC Lao Dong had decided to 'now take a course to prepare for a general uprising in the South of Vietnam'.[81] This decision was, according to Le Duan, made on the basis of the present situation in the area. Gradually armed struggle would play the most important role, especially in the mountain areas. With regard to the plains, Le Duan said that there would be a combination of political and armed struggle, while in the cities main emphasis would be on the political forms of struggle. He also maintained that a full general uprising in the South would come in two or three years at the earliest. On a direct question from Godunov, Le Duan underlined that the political course of the CC Lao Dong with regard to South Vietnam remained unchanged; what had changed, however, 'was only the form of the struggle'.[82] In July, DRV Acting Foreign Minister Hoang Van Tien further explained to Godunov that 'the purpose of this phase of the struggle is to expand the liberated areas of South Vietnam'.[83]

The Vietnamese use of Soviet planes to transport troops to the South may serve as an example of how Hanoi from 1961 kept Moscow in the dark about their strategy in South Vietnam. Due to the work of the NLF the situation in the South was developing in favour of the patriotic forces. The unstable situation in Laos provided an open road connection from the DRV into South Vietnam via the southern part of Laos – what was later known as the Ho Chi Minh Trail. To fully exploit the situation the Vietnamese decided, according to Soviet sources, to use Soviet aircraft, originally provided to the DRV in order to assist Laos, to fly in equipment for their own bases in South Vietnam. These measures taken by the Vietnamese to organize large-scale aid to the patriotic movement in South Vietnam, primarily show that North Vietnam was determined to effect change in the South, with no concern for the eventual consequences and negative reactions from their allies. As a part of that, Hanoi attempted to influence the regulation of the Laotian problem, according to Soviet sources, by trying to preserve the unstable situation in Laos in order to keep the supply route to South Vietnam open.[84]

The Soviets did, of course, disapprove of Vietnam's use of these aircraft but did nothing to actively prevent the use of them either.[85] It is very unlikely that Moscow would officially have sanctioned the Vietnamese plans for these aircraft. In 1961 Moscow was reluctant to encourage such behaviour in South Vietnam because it feared that it could trigger even greater American involvement in the region. But the idea of being kept completely in the dark, without any decisive powers with regard to further developments in Vietnam, was also not tempting. Tacit approval, or rather the absence of refusal, is a much more likely scenario. If that is correct, it emphasizes the hypothesis that Moscow could have overlooked certain North Vietnamese actions and thereby given some measure of support without giving their full support to an insurgency in the South.[86] In the end of 1961 Soviet policy makers seemed to be without any other good alternatives in their dealings with Vietnam.

The end of diplomacy?

The first few years after the Geneva conference were characterized by a wish for coordination and cooperation from both Moscow and Beijing to secure what they viewed as a positive development of the situation in the DRV. In the mid-1950s neither of the two large Communist powers wanted to initiate a policy in Vietnam that could endanger the relative peace in Southeast Asia. Not even the failure to hold all-Vietnamese elections in July changed Soviet and Chinese views on future policies towards Vietnam. Despite the growing differences between Moscow and Beijing after the Twentieth Congress of the CPSU, the two powers both wanted to continue the cooperation in Vietnam with the implementation of the Geneva agreement as the ultimate goal.

When the Vietnamese Communists made the decision to start, and subsequently expand, the armed struggle in South Vietnam, Moscow found itself in a difficult situation. Soviet leaders had not been consulted prior to the decision. It was made without any active involvement of the Soviet Union, or even China. During the early part of 1959, Moscow did little to either encourage or, for that matter, stop the change in the Vietnamese course of reunification. However, from the autumn of 1959 Soviet interest in the Vietnamese situation was strengthened. One reason was that Hanoi's policies now clearly contradicted Moscow's line of peaceful coexistence; another was the growing Soviet fear that the increased guerrilla activities in South Vietnam could instigate a greater American involvement in Vietnam. Together with Beijing, the Soviets intervened and told the Vietnamese to tone down the military strategy and focus on the diplomatic road to reunification. The immediate result of that intervention was that the Lao Dong leaders now set forth a policy envisaging a peaceful reunification of the country.

However, when the Third Congress of the Lao Dong reaffirmed the new strategy in September 1960, and the NLF was established in December that year, the situation was once again changed. The establishment of the NLF provided the

Lao Dong with a front organization in the South. Thus, by the end of 1960 the Vietnamese policies clearly contradicted the wishes of the Soviet leaders, who had now clearly expressed that they would not condone an armed struggle for reunification of Vietnam.

Moscow's policies towards Vietnam were further complicated by a deteriorating relationship with Beijing. The Soviet leaders depended on Chinese cooperation in order to contain the Vietnamese wish for a military reunification struggle. Likewise, the Vietnamese regarded a continued good relationship between Moscow and Beijing as instrumental for their survival, and continuously appealed to both powers to end their disagreements. In spite of the many appeals for unity Hanoi was not able to reconcile the two opponents, and the Vietnamese leadership now worried that neither of the two powers would support their fight for reunification. However, from May 1961 Beijing showed signs of approval with regard to the new Southern strategy, and there were forces in Beijing that were willing to support the Vietnamese struggle. The change in Chinese foreign policy strategies was one reason for the deterioration in Sino-Soviet relations.

Notwithstanding these diverging views on how to handle the situation in Vietnam, the Soviets and Chinese were still able to cooperate in the area. The most prominent example was Sino-Soviet cooperation during the Geneva conference on Laos. Starting in the autumn of 1960, parallel to the changes in Vietnamese Southern strategies at the Lao Dong Third Congress and the establishment of the NLF, the focal point of Sino-Soviet interest in Indochina switched from the situation in Vietnam to that in its neighbouring country Laos.

6 The fight over Laos, 1961–1962

We work well together at the international arena, like for example in Geneva, although we do not agree on everything else.[1]

From the autumn of 1960 Laos became equal to Vietnam in importance in the eyes of both Soviet and Chinese policy makers. The reason for this renewed interest in Laos was Prince Souvanna Phouma's return to office after a coup d'etat in August 1960. Phouma, who was in favour of a neutralized Laos and wanted to reduce American interest in the country, started to negotiate with the Communist led Pathet Lao. Due to his positive view on the Pathet Lao, Souvanna Phouma was attacked by troops led by the government he had ousted in August. To counter these attacks he requested, and received, military support from the Soviet Union and the DRV.[2]

The interest in Laotian affairs on the part of the DRV, as well as Moscow and Beijing, began long before the autumn of 1960. During the 1954 Geneva negotiations one of the major problems was Hanoi's refusal both to admit to having forces in Laos and to withdrawing them. Ever since the signing of these agreements in July 1954, Moscow had carefully followed the internal development in Laos, focusing primarily on the position of the Communist-led organization Pathet Lao.[3] Like in Vietnam, Moscow did not wish to see an escalation of the struggle in Laos and, until the spring of 1960, Soviet policies in Laos coincided largely with the policy towards Vietnam, namely an emphasis on the fulfilment of the Geneva agreements.

However, the outbreak of civil war in August of 1960 forced Moscow to reconsider its policies towards Laos. In cooperation with the North Vietnamese the Soviet Union established an air bridge, through which they carried supplies for the Communist-led organization Pathet Lao. The situation in Laos soon became a test of cooperation between Moscow, Hanoi and Beijing in times of trouble and was the last example of extended Sino-Soviet cooperation before the total breakdown of relations. To solve the problems in Laos, a second Geneva conference was scheduled to begin in May 1961. The situation was, however, so complicated that consensus was not reached before 23 July 1962, when the 'Declaration on the Neutrality of Laos' was signed by the foreign ministers of the fourteen nations assembled at the Geneva conference.

In the period leading up to the conference, Soviet and Chinese leaders seemed to share a common view on how to best solve the conflict. This unity, however, soon began to crack once the conference started in early May 1961. The possible change of attitudes on the Chinese side, and the Soviet reaction to this, forms the background for one of the major questions in this chapter, namely how the Sino-Soviet relationship developed during the conference and how the conference influenced the future of these relations. A second, but equally important, question concerns the role of Hanoi. The vital Ho Chi Minh Trail went mainly through Laos, and its existence might be threatened if Laos were to be neutralized or governed by forces more hostile to the North Vietnamese. As such the question is why the Vietnamese failed in their attempt to manipulate the Soviet Union in order to fulfil their own policies. This chapter aims to answer these two questions and give a new and more detailed account of the inner life of the second Geneva conference. The first part of the chapter will serve as an introduction to the situation in Laos during the latter part of the 1950s and early 1960s and show how Soviet, Vietnamese and Chinese interests came into conflict with one another already at an early stage.

The civil war in Laos

While the leaders in Hanoi were discussing the new strategy for Southern Vietnam, the Soviet Union became increasingly involved in the affairs of its neighbour, Laos. The situation in Laos deteriorated rapidly in the late 1950s. The United States had been deeply involved in Laotian politics since 1954. Washington's main aim was to strengthen the Royal Laotian Government and Army and defeat the Pathet Lao, a guerrilla force led by Communists, which had been established with the help of the Vietminh during the First Indochina War and remained closely linked to the DRV. After the Geneva conference in 1954 Laos was governed by a coalition led by Prime Minister Prince Souvanna Phouma.

The strongest group within the coalition was the Communists, and fearing that they were exercising excessive influence, the Eisenhower administration encouraged anti-Communist elements to vote Souvanna Phouma out of office. During the turbulent period starting with the government crisis in January to May 1957, the situation in Laos rapidly deteriorated. Prince Souvanna Phouma resigned his post as premier on 31 May but was reinstalled on 8 August. At that point he finally received support from the National Assembly to improve relations with the Pathet Lao. The developments in Laos during summer and early autumn of 1957 were not popular in Washington. From July 1958 the government had become progressively neutralist with a pro-Western tilt. This government was then challenged by the Communist Pathet Lao, who were backed by North Vietnam. The Americans worked hard to keep a US-backed government led by Phoui Sananikone, which opposed cooperation with the Pathet Lao, but their efforts proved insufficient. After the military seized power from the US-backed government in a coup d'état in August 1960, the leader of the Neutralist faction,

Prince Souvanna Phouma, could return to office. This marked the start of the civil war in Laos.[4]

During this period, Moscow and Beijing both carefully followed developments in Laos. In February 1959 DRV Foreign Minister Ung Van Khiem informed the Soviet ambassador that Beijing had urged Hanoi to take measures to assist the Laotians in the current situation. The Chinese were ready to provide the Pathet Lao with the necessary support, and the Central Committee of the CCP underlined once again that 'the Laotian friends ought to continue their legal struggle in combination with illegal activities . . . ' and that it was necessary to be prepared in order 'not to be taken unawares in case of a reaction, and be able to give a resolute response, if necessary, with arms'.[5] As a neighbouring country bordering on both North and South Vietnam, Laos was of tremendous strategic importance to the Vietnamese Communists. By 1959 there had already been lengthy discussions within the Lao Dong on whether to assist the Pathet Lao and, if they were to assist, what form the assistance should take. After a discussion of the Chinese points of view the majority of the Lao Dong Politburo did in principle agree with the Chinese.[6]

But despite the consensus between the Vietnamese and the Chinese on how to handle the situation in Laos, the situation seems to have changed during 1959. In conversations with Soviet Deputy Foreign Minister G.M. Pushkin in January 1960 Ung Van Khiem reported that 'the Vietnamese, after consulting the Soviet and Chinese comrades, had concluded that assistance to the Laotian friends should have the character of political support in an international scheme, since providing any other kind of assistance would not be in the interest of the common good and could lead to dangerous international consequences'.[7] The Soviet Union agreed with that position.[8]

The course of events described above suggests that sometime between February/March 1959 and January 1960 the leaders in Hanoi changed their official view on how to handle the situation in Laos. The decision was apparently taken after advice from both the Soviet Union and China. In the spring of 1959, when presented with first the Chinese and later the Vietnamese position, the Soviet Union did not disapprove. Almost one year later, in January 1960, Beijing had changed its point of view and agreed with Moscow that solving the situation legally would prove to be the best way to achieve a peaceful situation in Laos. China's domestic situation must also have been part of the reason why Chinese leaders gave in on their initial plans to support a more militant struggle in Laos. During 1959 and 1960 the Chinese were fully occupied with the continuation of the Great Leap Forward Campaign, which could possibly have drawn attention from their involvement elsewhere.

Although the Lao Dong leaders' official stance was to support the Soviet and Chinese point of view in the matter of Laos, there are indications that they in fact would gain more if the situation in Laos continued to deteriorate. In the late 1950s the Vietnamese Communists used a route through their neighbouring country to ship supplies and manpower from the North to the South, which has later been named the Ho Chi Minh Trail. With a stabilized situation in Laos it would be more difficult for the Vietnamese to defend the use of the trail, and accordingly, Soviet policy makers concluded that from a North Vietnamese point of view, disturbances in Laos were to the benefit of their reunification struggle.[9]

How did Moscow's policies fit into the Laotian picture? From 1959 until the spring of 1960 Soviet policies in Laos coincided with the policy towards Vietnam. Moscow did not wish to see an escalation of the struggle. In the autumn of 1960 the situation changed when Souvanna Phouma regained his position and started to negotiate with the Pathet Lao, despite the American effort to dissuade him. He was soon attacked by troops led by the government ousted in August, and subsequently he started receiving military material from the Soviet Union and DRV.[10] In December 1960 the Soviet Union launched a massive aid programme to help the Neutralists led by Prince Souvanna Phouma and the Pathet Lao. The government of Souvanna Phouma and the Soviet Union established diplomatic relations on 5 October 1960, and on 13 October the first Soviet ambassador, Alexandr Nikitich Abramov, arrived in Vientiane.[11] The programme was based on an airlift of goods into Laos from Moscow via Hanoi. Soviet planes and crews were sent to Hanoi to carry out the assistance, and the North Vietnamese played a vital role in its distribution.

Calls for a Geneva conference on Laos

The initiative to convene this new Geneva conference came from Cambodia's Prince Sihanouk at the United Nations in September 1960. He suggested that Laos and Cambodia should form a guaranteed neutral zone to safeguard themselves from foreign interference. The Neutralists in Laos, represented by Souvanna Phouma, concurred with this proposal. On 15 December India's Jawaharlal Nehru suggested to Great Britain and the Soviet Union that the ICC[12] should be reactivated in view of the renewed fighting after the coup by Royal Armed Forces Captain Kong Le and the great amount of foreign intervention.[13] On 23 December his initiative was followed up by the Soviet Union and China, whose leaders wanted to discuss the ongoing war in Laos. This Soviet proposal, which was essentially a reconvening of the 1954 Geneva conference, gained no support from the Western powers. On 1 January 1961 Prince Sihanouk suggested a larger, fourteen-nation conference, which would include those nations that had been at Geneva in 1954, the members of the ICC, and the Asian nations bordering Laos.[14]

Throughout the spring the Americans, in particular, were doubtful about the proposal and were not ready to support a new Geneva conference. But once an agreement was reached that the ICC would secure a ceasefire before negotiations began, the Americans agreed to participate at Geneva. On 24 April 1961 the two Geneva co-chairmen, Great Britain and the Soviet Union, issued a joint appeal for a ceasefire. They also proposed that the Indian government convene the ICC and announced that an international conference for settling the Laotian problem would be convened in Geneva on 12 May 1961.

With the prospects of a conference on Laos, the Pathet Lao and its Communist supporters hastened to seize as much ground in Laos as possible.[15] However, with the American demand for a ceasefire before talks could take place in late April, Great Britain twice had to approach Gromyko to warn that further military moves by the Pathet Lao would endanger the chances of a conference, and that an effective ceasefire should be arranged at once. In the period leading up to the Geneva conference the parties on the Socialist side spent much time preparing for the upcoming discussions. As a part of that, Laotian delegations from both the Pathet Lao and the Neutralists spent time in both Moscow and Beijing. While preparing for the conference Beijing improved its relations with Souvanna Phouma's government, and Souvanna visited China from 22 to 25 April 1961. At the same time Moscow tried to influence the Pathet Lao and convince them to agree to a ceasefire, and the Pathet Lao leader, Prince Souphannavong, was summoned to Moscow on Souvanna Phouma's insistence. On 25 April both princes agreed to go along with a ceasefire.[16] The ceasefire deadline was set for 3 May, and the ICC arrived in Laos on 8 May. On 11 May the ICC reported to the co-chairmen that there had been a general and demonstrable cessation of hostilities in Laos since the ceasefire order of 3 May. The conference could begin.

Despite the fact that the alliance might have looked like a tight ship from the outside, the Communist bloc did have difficulties reaching common ground on several questions during the conference. Grounds for disagreement may first of all be found in the different interests of the involved countries. The Socialist group at the conference consisted of four different countries: (1) the Soviet Union, (2) PRC, (3) Poland and (4) the DRV. Of these four Poland was the only country that had no direct territorial or national security interest in the final outcome of the conference – other than that a peaceful settlement would serve all countries in general. Poland was a member of this group owing to its role in the ICC, and as such it represented the Communist camp within the commission.

We have already seen that the Lao-Vietnamese relationship went a long way back and how the fate of the two countries had become particularly intertwined with the ongoing war of reunification in Vietnam after the Geneva conference on Indochina in 1954. We have also seen that North Vietnam was the major beneficiary of an unstable Laos due to its use of Lao territory to transport troops and equipment to its allies in South Vietnam. Hanoi therefore had a major stake in the outcome in Laos. In 1961 North Vietnam had approximately twenty thousand workers in Laos repairing roads and another thousand working as drivers. And during the spring of 1961 seven hundred North Vietnamese soldiers and auxiliary personnel were either killed or injured in Laos. According to Chinese historian Qiang Zhai the 'policy makers in Hanoi viewed their effort in Laos as a part of the protracted struggle for the liberation of the unified strategic area of Indochina'. Hanoi's advice to the Pathet Lao was to 'preserve its base area, maintain its alliance with the Neutralists, and work for the conditions that would strengthen its influence and appeal'. The main objective of the negotiations was, according to Hanoi, to achieve an independent and neutral Laos that would be recognized by other states, but without the need for any international guarantees. This North Vietnamese view clearly coincides with the Chinese approach to the Geneva conference, which also aimed at using neutralization in order to gain a position of strength for the Pathet Lao.[17]

The position of the PRC before and during the conference is somewhat ambiguous. Initially, the Chinese seemed to favour a continued unstable situation in Laos but did to some extent back down when the Soviet Union insisted. However, China was still inclined to think that the Communist force in Laos, the Pathet Lao, should continue its fighting until it had gained a position of strength that would help its cause during negotiations. The Soviet Union seems to have had an altogether different agenda in mind; its main purpose awaiting the conference was to strengthen its relationship with the Western powers. If they could show cooperation in the Laotian case Moscow hoped to become a more reliable ally to the West. Despite the differences in agendas the Soviet Union and China had managed to reach agreement before the conference began. As we shall see later, Soviet Foreign Minister Andrei Gromyko was rather surprised when the Chinese began suggesting further changes to the Communist strategy on the eve of the conference.

The PRC had not participated in any large international conference since their debut at the 1954 Geneva conference. In order to signal how important they regarded this second Geneva conference to be, the Chinese came to the conference with the largest delegation of all and with an intent to stay in Geneva for as long as it would take to secure a lasting settlement for Laos.[18] Five experienced diplomats and party officials led the large delegation. The head of the delegation was Foreign Minister Chen Yi, and he was accompanied by his deputy foreign minister, Zhang Hanfu; a participant at the 1954 conference, Qiao Guanhua; Wang Bingnan, the Chinese ambassador to Poland; and Huan Xiang, who was chargé d'affaires at the Chinese embassy in London.[19] When compared with the 1954 conference the Chinese had now gathered much more experience in foreign policy and were determined to show this in both numbers and diplomatic action. Although they welcomed close cooperation with the Soviet Union, they demanded a larger portion of influence at the conference than what had been the case roughly seven years earlier.[20]

Compared with the Chinese the Soviet delegation was less impressive. Soviet Foreign Minister Andrei Gromyko was present during the most central meetings, but most of the day-to-day business was led by Deputy Foreign Minister Georgi Pushkin, and in number also the Soviet delegation was less impressive than the Chinese. In terms of its international relations the Soviet Union expected much from the Geneva conference. Moscow's main goal for the conference was to reach a political settlement within a limited amount of time. Before the conference began the Soviet leaders expressed the opinion that they expected the conference to last for six weeks at the most. However, just like the Americans, the Soviets seem to have had a rather distorted view of the situation in Laos. The two superpowers both remained fixed on power relations and disregarded the power of the local forces. According to one author, Moscow was first of all concerned with its relationship with the United States and China, and was not up to date on the actual conditions inside of Laos.[21]

Examining the role of Laos, and especially the discussions that took place during the conference organized to regulate the situation in the country, is important because it shows how the relationship of strength between Moscow and Beijing in Asia had changed in the years since the 1954 Geneva conference. In 1954 Moscow was the natural leader of the two and took upon herself to introduce the PRC on the international diplomatic scene, but by 1961 Beijing had considerably increased her influence in international affairs and was no longer willing to automatically consent to the Soviet point of view. As for the North Vietnamese, they had almost no influence in 1954, but, like the Chinese, they had increased their influence especially through their close cooperation with the Communist-led Pathet Lao. Thus, when the 1961 conference began, relations between Moscow, Beijing and, to some extent, Hanoi were on a much more equal level than in 1954.

Negotiations begin in Geneva

On the eve of the conference the chances for successful Sino-Soviet cooperation did indeed look good. Although there were potential sources of conflict in the two countries, personal aims for the conference, there seems to have been a universal understanding between them that possible differences would not be allowed to surface. An example of this may be found as early as in the pre-conference talks that took place in Geneva during the last few days before the conference began. Internal discussions in the Communist camp show that the Soviet Union, in spite of the fact that China's handling of the Laos situation was a constant source of irritation, wished to continue Sino-Soviet cooperation. Soviet documents on the conference might contribute to a better understanding of how Soviet delegates perceived Vietnamese, as well as Chinese, attitudes and behaviour at the Geneva conference, taking into account the difference of interest among the three countries with regard to the situation in Laos.

On 14 May Chinese Foreign Minister Chen Yi expressed China's perception of its role in the Laos problem. In a meeting with Soviet Foreign Minister Gromyko, Chen told him that he often found it much easier to agree with the Soviets separately than when the other Socialist delegations were involved. So, he suggested that, in addition to the meetings involving all four Socialist delegations present in Geneva, the Soviet and Chinese representatives could sometimes meet alone. Chen Yi strongly argued that together the two countries possessed great strength and went on to illustrate this point by describing what he saw as the Western powers' attempts to discover differences in opinion between the Soviet Union and China. He also added that discovering contradictions and differences of opinion within the opposing camp could also successfully be used by the Socialist countries. During the conversation Chen Yi repeated his message on the necessity of close cooperation and contact between Beijing and Moscow all through the conference. He emphasized the need for them to stand together not only when facing the imperialists but also in front of the neutral countries. 'We think', said Chen Yi as if it was a less important remark, 'that the support of the People's Republic of China is important to the Soviet Union'.[22]

Chen Yi's comment is important because it illustrates the Chinese perception of their own position during the conference relative to that of the Soviet Union. Beijing's position had changed significantly during the seven years since the last Geneva conference, and the Chinese felt that they now, unlike during the 1954 conference, were in a position to set their own demands and have an equally strong say in the final outcome as the Soviets. Moreover, because of the increasing Chinese influence on the decisions of the Vietnamese Communists, Chen Yi knew that without Chinese cooperation and not least their leverage on the Vietnamese, the Soviets would not be able to secure a successful outcome at the conference.

In the written transcriptions of this meeting, Soviet Foreign Minister Gromyko endorsed his views and emphasized that 'during the conference they faced, unquestionably, a persistent struggle with the delegations from the Western powers, in which they would have to show much versatility and firmness to reach their goals'.[23] However, in spite of the immediate Soviet comment, the Chinese attitudes were not left in silence, and in later comments on the conversation, these are perceived as signs of suspicion and mistrust in relation to both the Soviet delegates and the delegates from the other Socialist countries. Chen Yi's attempts to suggest a possible 'division of labour between our delegations' when speaking to the conference and his views that the PRC and the Soviet Union should present a united front not only when facing the imperialist powers but also when dealing with the Neutralist powers, was viewed with suspicion by Moscow. The aim of this approach, a later report argued, was to ensure that in case there would arise differences in opinion between the Soviet and Chinese delegations, compromises would not be made in front of representatives from the other Socialist countries. Thus, it would be better to agree on matters first and then present the questions to the heads of the Socialist delegations.[24]

According to the Soviets, the Chinese also showed their suspicions and mistrust in meetings between the heads of the four Socialist delegations. In the afternoon of 15 May, the day before the conference was convened, the heads of the four Socialist delegations met to discuss and coordinate their strategies.[25] The meeting was chaired by Gromyko, who informed the other delegates about his meetings with the head of the British delegation – British Foreign Secretary Alec Douglas-Home. The two co-chairmen had agreed that the conference would be opened the next day by Prince Sihanouk; in case he would not be able to make it on time, the opening of the conference would be rescheduled to 17 May.[26]

The meetings between the four Socialist delegations would meet several needs during the conference, the first of which would be to inform the other Socialist countries of the discussions among the co-chairmen, and the second to allow the different delegations to voice their opinions on the strategy adopted by the Soviets in their meetings with the British. There is reason to argue that because of its position as co-chairman the Soviet Union had gotten a head start on the other

Socialist powers when it came to pushing through its own policies. Moscow seemed content with the pre-conference meetings and the efforts to reach a common strategy among the Socialist countries. Still, the Socialist delegations were not able to reach full consensus on all questions. Two particular issues were to some degree contested: one was the role of the co-chairmen and the other was the Chinese reluctance towards India's role within the ICC. Both of these were linked to the Chinese role at the conference.

Once the conference opened, the Soviet Union and Great Britain resumed their roles as co-chairmen. And although it was clear from the outset that the Soviets would function as co-chair together with the British, the Soviet foreign minister had, before the appointment was made official, several times emphasized to the Chinese that until the conference was convened the Soviet Union should not be considered co-chairman. Much of the reason behind the Chinese insistence on treating Moscow as co-chair was their own view of the 1961 conference as a widening of the original 1954 Geneva conference. Based on the continuous emphasis on this subject it is safe to assume that the Chinese considered it an advantage for the Socialist side if the Soviet Union be allowed to continue as co-chairman, not least because that would support the Chinese argument that the current conference was nothing but a continuation of the one held in 1954.

The Chinese view of the Geneva conference as a permanent institution led to a general discussion on the status of the Geneva conference within the Communist camp. Gromyko agreed with the head of the Polish delegation, who pointed out that the conference was not a permanent institution, and argued that the current conference had wider range of participants and was without doubt to be considered a new and independent conference. Gromyko further argued that regarding this as a new conference would be advantageous to the Socialist countries, especially if that would mean a confirmation of the co-chairmanship.[27]

Hanoi and Beijing both viewed the conference as a widening of the one held in 1954. They were also both negative to the role of India as Head of the International Control Commission.[28] During the 1954 conference India was named head of the ICC, mainly because of it status as a neutral state. However, the relationship between China and India had changed considerably during the seven years since the last conference, and China objected to India in the position as head of the ICC once again. In the autumn of 1959 the relationship between the People's Republic and India hit an all-time low when hostilities broke out on the Sino-Indian border. The hostilities were the result of a longstanding dispute about the line of the frontier between India and Chinese-occupied Tibet in the Himalayas. After a large-scale uprising against Chinese rule in Tibet the Dalai Lama fled to India, and a Sino-Indian border conflict lasting from July to October 1959 followed. In 1962 an actual border war broke out between the People's Republic and India. The situation was not improved by the fact that parallel to China's problems, the Soviet Union was trying to cultivate a relationship with India, as one of the leading countries in the non-aligned movement.[29] This was the background to Beijing's harsh words when Gromyko said that the two co-chairmen had decided to let the Indian representative, V.K. Krishna Menon, give a speech on the opening day in which he would suggest the order in which the co-chairs should speak at the conference.[30]

Differences between Socialist delegations other than the Soviet and Chinese also surfaced in these early meetings. One of the major issues was the unsolved differences between Beijing and Warsaw over the question of India's role. The Indian delegate Menon was scheduled as the first speaker during the conference, and the Chinese feared that he would suggest replacing the Soviet Union as one of the two co-chairmen of the conference. While the Poles agreed with Moscow that the Indian representative should be allowed to give his speech, the Chinese angrily argued that 'you, our Polish friends, have already criticized us during the meeting that was held not too long ago in Moscow. At that time the Chinese representatives were silent, but I have to tell you that we do not recognize a Polish right to evaluate any of our actions. How can you explain that you worry so much about India and why do you not worry just as much in relation to China?'[31]

According to the Soviet records, the Chinese outburst led to a strong polemic between the heads of the two delegations. But the Chinese attack on the Poles was also an attack on the Soviet stand in this question; however, it was more convenient for Beijing to attack the Poles than aiming directly at Moscow. After all, just like the Soviets depended on Chinese cooperation, Beijing was equally dependent on a good relationship with Moscow. What the Chinese feared most at this point was a total breakdown of negotiations, which could possibly lead to an American invasion of Laos. Thus, to Beijing the protests against India were yet another way of showing the Soviets that during this conference they were strong enough to have an independent position and follow a policy that primarily suited Chinese interests.

Soviet Foreign Minister Gromyko was confident that India would not suggest other co-chairmen than those who already had the positions. Moreover, he revealed that he was rather surprised by the sudden turn of the meeting due to the Chinese and Polish outbursts and that he hoped this would not spoil what had been achieved during the first five days of discussions and raise even more problems to consider.[32] He saw no reason to prevent the Indian head of delegation from speaking at the beginning of the conference and thought it would only create problems and misunderstandings if he, a Soviet representative, were to speak up against him. In a response to Gromyko's attitude Chen Yi admitted that since all the preliminary work for the conference was more or less completed, it would be difficult to make any changes in the British proposal, which held the suggestion that the Indian should give a speech on the opening day. As a result the Chinese would not object to an Indian speech on the question of co-chairmen and confirmed to the Soviets that they were in line with the tactical approach agreed upon by the Socialist countries with regard to Southern Vietnam and SEATO.[33] The Chinese back-down was a tactical move to maintain a good relationship with Moscow – more important issues would be at stake later, and at that point the Chinese would not be as ready to give in to Soviet pressure.

There were other ways of limiting the Indian role. On the last evening before the conference was convened, the Chinese suddenly came along with suggestions for changes in the two documents that the Soviet delegation had prepared for the first session the coming morning. They had two separate, but interrelated suggestions for changes. Their first suggestion was on how to stop military supplies to Laos, and the ICC's control of the import of weapons and ammunition. In addition, they wanted to add a special paragraph on the destruction and evacuation of left-behind Guomindang forces. Through these suggestions it was obvious that the Chinese argued in favour of a diminished, and as limited as possible, role for the ICC. They even suggested excluding the paragraph on the ICC's role in monitoring elections in Laos and wished to change the paragraph that allowed a majority in the ICC make decisions in questions of procedure.[34] Primarily, the changes suggested by the Chinese would undermine the position of the ICC and, of course, seriously weaken the role of India.

In what seems to have been an attempt to put more pressure on the Soviets to agree to these changes, Zhang Hanfu underlined the importance of unanimous decisions among the Socialist countries and how that would make their decisions and suggestions much stronger. He further argued along the lines that it was imperative to design the agreement so that the Western powers would be unable to change everything to their advantage and thereby discredit the Socialist camp.[35]

Once the conference was in session the Chinese returned to the Soviets with the question of left-behind Guomindang soldiers in Laos.[36] According to Zhang, these forces, which were remnants of the Chinese Nationalist Army that retreated into Laos after the Chinese civil war, were now used actively by the United States to increase the strength of the anti-Communist forces in Laos. However, Soviet Deputy Foreign Minister Georgii Pushkin was worried that if the Socialist powers should interfere in this matter, it could make the United States refrain from agreeing to a final settlement on the Laotian question.[37] The question of the former Guomindang forces is one example that shows the Chinese as much more aggressive and hostile to Western governments than the leaders in Moscow. There is no doubt that on several issues the Soviets shared the Chinese concern that the Western countries wanted to destroy the conference. There was, however, a significant difference in the Soviet and Chinese view on how to approach situations like this one. By emphasizing the need to play down the issue of the Chiang Kaishistovs throughout the summer, Moscow was able to convince the Chinese to let this question go and not push it any further.[38] A US withdrawal from the conference could prompt the invasion the Chinese were so eager to avoid.

The Soviet leaders did indeed take the issue of Guomindang forces in Laos seriously. Deputy Foreign Minister Georgii Pushkin returned to the question and reassured Zhang Hanfu that the Soviet Union agreed that these forces should be thrown out of Laos. On this question there was, according to Pushkin, full consensus between the Soviet and Chinese governments, and that both Chen Yi and Gromyko would mention this in their speeches to the conference.[39] As a response to Pushkin's comments, Zhang Hanfu repeated his arguments on the necessity of fighting against imperialism and pointed out that the Chinese delegation saw it as expedient to include the point on the Guomindang forces in the declaration. This suggestion, however, took Pushkin somewhat by surprise since there had been no talk about this during the meetings in Moscow prior to the conference.[40]

The discussion above exemplifies how representatives from the People's Republic viewed developments at the conference. These attitudes are also mirrored in Soviet records from the discussions showing that the Chinese were convinced that without a struggle they would not be able to reach any agreement with the Western powers. The Soviets, on their part, underlined that the battle at the conference would be strong and persistent and that there were of course no warranties that the Western powers would accept all positions and provisions of the projected agreement. However, it was emphasized from the Soviet side that much would depend on which questions were posed and in what form they were presented by the Socialist countries.[41] Zhang Hanfu, on his part, repeated that the Chinese delegation did not proceed on the basis of what would be acceptable to the Western powers. In the face of this, Pushkin answered that nevertheless the task of the Socialist countries was to achieve an agreement that would be satisfactory to themselves. The Chinese, however, had a more aggressive stand in this question. Zhang said that they too wanted an agreement but believed that it could be reached only through a persistent struggle against the Western powers. It could also be, he continued, that taking that into account, it might not be possible to reach an agreement on Laos.[42]

Soviet recollections of these first days of the conference and the many disagreements that surfaced illustrate the mood within the Socialist camp at the time. Every single word uttered by the Chinese was analysed by the Soviets and at times clearly overestimated. It is very likely that this was also the case on the Beijing side, in spite of the friendly words uttered by Deng Xiao Ping to Soviet ambassador Chervonenko at the end of September 1961 that Sino-Soviet cooperation in Geneva worked well, in spite of the many disagreements between the two powers.[43] In such a context the controversy over India was to some extent blown out of proportion due to the Chinese fear of a hidden Soviet agenda during the conference.

A temporary setback

While the Geneva conference was in session, Khrushchev and Kennedy met in Vienna from 3 to 4 June. The Soviet leader saw the meetings in Vienna as a perfect opportunity to improve relations with the West. During the meetings Khrushchev told Kennedy that he was not very interested in Laos, and that the Soviet Union had no interest in taking on responsibilities in such a remote geographical area. In addition the Soviet leader promised that he would do his utmost to influence the Laotian forces to establish a truly neutral government, and also cooperate with the ICC to secure a continued ceasefire.[44]

In spite of the kind words and promises of Vienna, it soon became evident how fragile the ceasefire in Laos really was, and how little leverage Khrushchev really had with regard to the actions of the Pathet Lao, as well as those of the North Vietnamese forces. When negotiations began in Geneva in May 1961 it was on the condition that a full ceasefire had been achieved on Laotian territory. However, the ceasefire in Laos was of the transient kind, and on 6 June negotiations were halted due to a break of the ceasefire when North Vietnamese and Pathet Lao forces captured Ban Padong, a base of the Royal Laotian Government. The battle almost led to a total breakdown of the Geneva conference.

According to Marek Thee, the Soviets were not informed of the plans to attack Ban Padong beforehand.[45] Thee's account coincides with available sources in the Russian archives, where there are no indications that the attack was either supervised or supported by Moscow. On the day of the attack the main topic of conversation was a totally different one, namely the forthcoming event of a possible meeting between the three Laotian princes Souvanna Phouma, Souphanouvong and Boun Oum in Zurich.

On 6 June, not long before the meeting was scheduled to take place in Zurich, Soviet Deputy Foreign Minister Georgii Pushkin was approached by DRV Foreign Minister Ung Van Khiem, who sought advice in relation to the Zurich meeting. It turned out that Pathet Lao representative Qinim Folsena intended to have a draft project ready for Souvanna Phouma once he arrived in Geneva. Ung Van Khiem thought it would be useful if the DRV delegation helped Folsena with the draft so that Souvanna Phouma would not turn to the French for assistance. However, there was not much time left, and Ung Van Khiem wondered whether the Soviets could purposely delay the Pathet Lao leader Souphanouvong in Moscow in order to buy the North Vietnamese some time with Souvanna Phouma.

The Soviet response to Ung Van Khiem's request was purely negative. Moscow would, under no circumstances, involve themselves in internal Laotian affairs at that point. In the delicate situation that Laos was in for the time being, it would be inexpedient to interfere in internal Laotian affairs. Pushkin then further added that there was no way the Soviets would hold back the prince in Moscow.[46] Based on the available facts there can be no doubt that the events at Ban Padong had taken the Soviet leaders by surprise and that due to the current circumstances there was no way the Soviets would compromise their role at the conference by holding back the leader of the Pathet Lao in Moscow.

On 7 June Ban Padong and the adjournment of the conference were the main subjects of conversation at the meeting between the four Socialist delegations. Delegates were confronted with a statement from Great Britain saying that they (the British) had agreed to a conference under the precondition of a ceasefire in Laos and that the current situation could lead to a total abandonment of the conference. In response to this the Chinese delegate said that if there were no session tomorrow (8 June), the Chinese would organize a press conference to tell who was responsible for ruining the conference, namely the Western governments. After taking note of the Chinese point of view, Pushkin attempted to calm down the situation and said that he would inform the others as soon as he had received more details from the leader of the American delegation, Averell

Harriman.[47] The attack at Ban Padong only led to a temporary halt in the Geneva negotiations. On 12 June negotiations were resumed with all parties present.

Once the conference was back in session the next item on the agenda was the possibility of a meeting between the three Laotian princes, Souvanna Phouma, Souphanouvong and Boun Oum in Zurich. By mid-June 1961 the general discussions had come to an end, and both the French and the Soviets had presented their proposals on how to solve the Laotian situation. The conference now awaited the outcome of the Zurich meeting, since that would, inevitably, have an influence on the conference's future work. In conversations with the Soviet delegates the Chinese emphasized that their hope for the meeting was that the three princes could agree to establish one united delegation that could represent Laos at the conference table. The Chinese viewed an agreement between the three princes as extremely useful to achieve a final agreement on Laos.[48]

The strong Chinese interest in a meeting between the three princes was, according to historian Qiang Zhai, strongly promoted by Foreign Minister Chen Yi in conversations outside the formal sessions, and he had urged Sihanouk as well as the French and Indian delegates to bring the three together for a meeting. The meeting took place in Zurich on 22 June 1961, and the three princes agreed to a set of principles that would allow them to create a government of national union representing the three parties. This government would follow a foreign policy of peace and neutrality in accordance with the 1954 Geneva accords and would reinstitute the electoral law and democratic liberties of 1957. However, in spite of his enthusiasm for the Zurich communiqué, Chen Yi was aware that it had not solved all internal problems in Laos and emphasized that it would still be difficult to unite the three forces in a coalition government.[49]

Although the major part of the discussion was over by the time the three princes met in Zurich, the parties still had another year to go before an agreement was signed. However, in spite of several unresolved issues, in particular the role of SEATO with regard to Laos, in December 1961 the conference was able to reach provisional agreements on the international aspect of Laos's neutrality. At the same time the negotiations between the three Laotian factions reached a deadlock, and it was not possible for the conference to move ahead and reach a final solution.[50]

During the spring of 1962 the Chinese urged the Pathet Lao to negotiate with the rightist group from a position of strength. To achieve such a position, in March the Pathet Lao attacked the town of Nam Tha, where Phoumi Nosavan had assembled 5,000 soldiers. In conversations with the Chinese in Beijing Souphanouvong was told that the final settlement in Laos would be decided by force and that the Pathet Lao should work to increase their own strength before joining a coalition government. The Chinese provided Souphanouvong with material assistance during that period, and on 6 May the Pathet Lao captured Nam Tha. The defeat at Nam Tha weakened Phoumi Nosavan's negotiation position with regard to his role in a future government. After this turbulent period the three princes signed an agreement on 12 June, distributing the portfolios in a government of national union.[51] The battle of Nam Tha further contributed to the disagreements between Moscow and Beijing on how to handle the situation in Laos. Apparently, the Soviets had made an attempt to stop Souphanouvong from attacking Nam Tha without any success. China showed dislike over the Soviet wish to solve local problems with superpower dialogues and disagreed with the Soviet emphasis on the importance of the Kennedy–Khrushchev summit in Vienna in June 1961 for the Geneva conference on Laos.[52]

In the light of the developments in the Sino-Soviet alliance during and after the Geneva conference on Laos, Deng Xiao Ping's references to the well-functioning cooperation in Geneva seems ironic. The conference was one of the very last examples of international cooperation between Moscow and Beijing and as such represents an interesting remnant of a long-lasting alliance. Less than a year after these friendly words, in June 1962, the Soviet leaders were harsh in their criticisms of the Chinese reaction to the formation of a Laotian government. The Soviets were furious about the fact that in press statements and public speeches the Chinese praised the peaceful solution to the Laos problem without even referring to the Soviet role during the negotiations. They strongly emphasized that internal problems in Southeast Asia should be solved by the Southeast Asian countries themselves, leaving out any reference to the Soviet involvement. More than anything this behaviour exemplifies the difference between the Chinese leaders we met during the 1954 Geneva conference, all eager to learn as much as possible from the international experience of their Soviet allies, and the self-confident Chinese representatives at the 1961–62 conference.

The absence of references to the Soviet role was of course severely criticized in Moscow. Analysts at the Soviet embassy in Beijing highlighted the statements made by the acting head of the Chinese foreign ministry's department on the USSR and Eastern Europe, who argued, in a conversation with the Czechoslovakians, that a final regulation of the Laos problem was 'hardly possible; firstly because the United States hoped that Laos would come under the guardianship of SEATO, and secondly because at the Geneva conference the Americans expected to dissolve the forces of Pathet Lao'. Moscow contended that such a reaction from the Chinese side 'on the achievement of an agreement on the formation of a Lao government, had a mission to hide the errors committed in Chinese domestic policy, and create the impression that the events referred to above was a victory for their policy line, as if it confirmed the correctness of the Chinese leadership's evaluations of strategy questions and tactics in the struggle with imperialism'.[53]

Assistance to Laos

Parallel to the negotiations in Geneva, Moscow continued the assistance to Laos initiated in December 1960. There were two main aspects of this assistance which had an impact not only on relations between the Soviet Union and Laos but also on Soviet–Vietnamese and Soviet–Chinese relations. Since the Vietnamese were partly in charge of the practical transport of this aid, Hanoi wanted to discuss the conditions for delivering these supplies. One part of that was the condition of the roads leading from the DRV into Laos. Both the roads going from Vietnam into Laos and, especially, the roads inside Laos were in a generally bad condition. The second aspect was the question of the airborne support, the so-called airbridge between Hanoi and Vientiane.

In May 1961, when the Geneva conference was already in session, Vietnamese Premier Pham Van Dong approached Soviet Ambassador Suren Tovmasyan to discuss the state of Laotian roads. He emphasized that Vietnam depended on roads, both within Laos and from Vietnam to Laos, that could be used all year and in all kinds of weather. At the time the Vietnamese did, according to the premier, all that was in their power to build this kind of roads but were unable to complete the task alone. They now hoped to get some assistance from the Soviet Union, China and the other Socialist countries. Prince Souvanna Phouma had already requested assistance from the DRV. In an effort to convince the ambassador of the usefulness of such a road, Pham Van Dong argued that it would tie Laos closer to the DRV, and therefore also the rest of the Socialist camp. He also added that Souvanna Phouma had also asked Hanoi for assistance in building a new residence for the Laotian government, a request that he would also present to the Soviet Union. A positive answer to these requests could, according to the Vietnamese premier, draw Souvanna Phouma 'closer to us'.[54]

The assistance to Laos created difficulties in the Soviet–Vietnamese relationship as well as in relations between Moscow and Beijing. In the autumn of 1961 Soviet ambassador Tovmasyan asked DRV Foreign Minister Ung Van Khiem whether discussions about military assistance to Laos and the Pathet Lao should rather be held separately with the Soviet and the Chinese, or 'if the Vietnamese preferred with the two ambassadors together'. Tovmasyan also pointed to several problems with regard to how Soviet aid was transported to Laos. He said that Vietnam and Laos together should plan exactly what was needed in Laos and make sure that those Soviet products that had already been sent to Laos, but were stuck in the DRV, immediately reach Laos. The Soviet ambassador left no doubt that he was dissatisfied with the slow speed in transporting aid into Laos.[55] By mid-1962 the Soviets advised the Vietnamese to discuss with the Chinese when aid for Laos passed through Chinese territory and added that Moscow no longer was willing to cover all expenses related to the transport of this aid. The Vietnamese were now told to arrange those parts of the operation going through China directly with the Chinese. Hanoi expressed its dissatisfaction with this new Soviet attitude and claimed that this new set-up was very unclear.[56]

The discussion about transportation continued even after the participants reached a conclusion in Geneva, but now the situation had become more delicate for the Soviet leadership. During the early autumn of 1962 the Vietnamese kept complaining about their limited possibilities to transport the necessary goods into Laos. They reminded the Soviets that from the very beginning aid to Laos was supposed to be a collaboration between the Soviet Union, the PRC, the DRV and other Socialist countries. Moreover, the Soviet Union had taken on a certain responsibility in helping out with the transportation of these goods. The Vietnamese argued that this could be done by using Soviet airplanes already stationed in Hanoi and Vinh, but Moscow was reluctant to agree to the proposal.

The Soviet Union did not have the authority to negotiate the issue of continued flights to secure the transport of goods from DRV to Laos. The Soviet government decided that, in order to meet the request from the DRV government, they would hand over to the Vietnamese side all Soviet airplanes that were transporting aid from the DRV to Laos. Furthermore, Moscow was worried that, under the current circumstances and with the fresh Soviet signature to the agreement in Geneva, the use of Soviet-owned airplanes flying into Laos could be used by their opponents, primarily the United States, to accuse the Soviets of violating the Geneva agreement. They feared that if that happened, Washington would be free to openly violate the agreement and threaten the patriotic forces in Laos.[57]

At that point Moscow was determined that Soviet planes and pilots should not be involved in a situation in which they could be accused of violating the terms of the recently signed Geneva agreement. DRV Acting Premier Le Than Ngi acknowledged the difficulty of the situation but added that without support it would be impossible to keep the Royal Army in check. If the Soviet Union could hand over the airplanes in Hanoi fairly quickly, the DRV could put them into use. There was, however, another problem, Le Than Ngi added, since the North Vietnamese did not have enough well-prepared pilots, who would be capable of replacing the Soviet pilots on these flights.[58] It was therefore necessary to delay the transfer of the aircraft for a period of two months to give the Vietnamese crews a chance to prepare themselves. In September 1962 DRV Premier Pham Van Dong asked the Soviet ambassador whether the Soviet Union would consider establishing an air bridge between Hanoi and Laos for a longer period, whereupon the Soviet ambassador asked why the Vietnamese could not do this on their own initiative. According to Pham Van Dong, a Vietnamese air bridge would only have been misunderstood by the Laotians and would be regarded in a very negative way.[59]

By September 1962 Soviet officials seemed tired of both the Vietnamese and the Chinese positions on assistance to Laos. The Chinese had now turned around and no longer approved of the continued use of Soviet airplanes for transportation into Laos. That decision was highly unpopular with the Vietnamese leaders, who, according to Pham Van Dong, were very dissatisfied with the Chinese position. The Vietnamese kept arguing that Soviet assistance remained the best solution.[60] Acknowledging the necessity of Soviet assistance, Ambassador Tovmasyan was still somewhat intrigued by the exclusive focus on the need for Soviet assistance, in comparison with assistance from other countries of the Socialist camp. He was curious as to why Pham Van Dong did not say a single word about the necessity of aid from either the PRC or the DRV itself. According to the ambassador, Dong's statements gave him the impression that the whole future of Laos depended only on the transfer of cargo on Soviet airplanes stationed in the DRV, and that the actual work should be done by the Soviet Union.[61]

Moscow no longer wanted to be the sole party providing practical assistance to Laos and demanded increased assistance from the other Socialist states involved.

In a larger context this could lead to problems in Soviet relations with the United States. The Soviet dissatisfaction with Chinese and Vietnamese attitudes was obvious in the continuous discussions of the practical part of assistance to Laos. While the Soviet Union took care of the economics in the operations, Hanoi and Beijing seem to have done nothing but complain over insufficient Soviet assistance. The Vietnamese were annoyed by the Soviet wish to use others, such as themselves, to support Laos, especially because it also signalled Soviet reluctance in assisting Hanoi in similar situations in the near future.

Geneva: A power struggle?

Towards the end of the 1950s, Laos came to play an increasingly important role as a part of the Soviet relationship with North Vietnam. Before, during and after the Geneva conference Moscow's policies towards Laos became regularly intertwined with their policies towards Vietnam, and no less with their relationship to China in Southeast Asia. In many respects, cooperation in Geneva was one of the last highlights of Sino-Soviet cooperation before the relationship broke down.[62]

From the point of view of an outsider, the union between the Socialist countries in Geneva would have seemed rather solid. However, a closer examination of intra-bloc relations during the conference shows that, although the Socialists managed to gather around common answers when facing the West, there was often a long fight to reach this common ground. As pointed out earlier, these countries came to Geneva with their own special agendas in mind, agendas that often conflicted.

The internal discussion within the Communist bloc's delegation to the Geneva conference on Laos clearly showed the Soviet dissatisfaction with the Chinese and the role they played at the conference. The Laos conference became a kind of second Geneva, where the mistakes of 1954 were not to be repeated. Analysis and comments by the Soviet side show that Moscow was seriously irritated with how the Chinese acted. However, it also shows that despite this discomfort, the Soviets insisted on continued Sino-Soviet cooperation with regard to both Laos and Vietnam. Moscow most certainly depended on a continued cooperation with a strong Chinese state in Asia.

By the Chinese, the Geneva conference on Laos was seen as the perfect opportunity to gain more international acceptance as the unquestionable leader in Asia. However, just as Moscow was dissatisfied with Beijing's behaviour in Geneva, the Chinese criticized the Soviet Union for what they characterized as 'attempts to "freeze" the situation in Laos and establish a permanent neutrality in the country on the model of Austria or Switzerland'.[63] That was not the kind of neutrality the Chinese could agree to. Together with the Vietnamese they were in favour of an independent and neutralized Laos recognized by other countries but not requiring any international guarantees. Both China and Vietnam believed that such a neutralization could help the Pathet Lao gain the necessary strength. According to Chinese analysts at the conference, Moscow's main aim was to reach a compromise with the West and prove the success of its peaceful coexistence policy. Such a policy stood in stark contrast to the Chinese aim in Laos, namely to ensure that the Pathet Lao was in a strong military position before sitting down at the negotiating table.[64]

The negotiations over Laos seriously tested the strength of the Soviet–Vietnamese relationship, Soviet–Chinese relationship and the relations between Hanoi and Beijing. One author has even argued that the competition between the Vietnamese and the Chinese with regard to Laos was one of the reasons for the eventual breakdown in cooperation between Hanoi and Beijing.[65] The Sino-Soviet relationship also suffered from the events in Geneva. The distrust that had been built up on both sides made it difficult to reconcile their views on what constituted a successful conference. More than anything, the problem of Laos showed the difference between the foreign policy doctrines of the two regimes. However, at the same time the Soviet Union and China shared one vital common goal: to prevent a stepped-up American interference in Indochina. And to achieve that, Moscow needed some measure of Chinese cooperation, and thus still hoped that China could act as an ally in areas of peripheral interest to Soviet foreign policy such as Indochina.

7 From disinterest to active support, 1962–1965

By late 1960 the Soviet leaders had expressed clearly to the Vietnamese Communists that they would not support an armed struggle for reunification of Vietnam. Moreover, Moscow expected the Lao Dong leaders to respect its opinion and proceed with the political struggle. Decision makers in Hanoi, however, did not feel committed to follow the Soviet line. They continued to build up its military force in South Vietnam, and by 1961 the situation had changed significantly. The rapid escalation of the South Vietnamese struggle worried the Soviet leaders, who felt that the situation, if not contained, 'could lead to a significant complication of the political situation in the region and transform South Vietnam into a critical centre of international tension'.[1]

After the conclusion of the Geneva conference on Laos in the summer of 1962 Chinese influence on the Lao Dong leadership became gradually more visible. This was not least due to Mao's insistence that China 'must support the armed struggles in South Vietnam and Laos without conditions', at the Tenth Plenum of the CCP's Central Committee in September 1962.[2] The increased Chinese influence in North Vietnam affected Soviet relations with the Vietnamese, and especially how Soviet policy makers perceived relations between China and the DRV. During this period the Soviets also became very dependent on other Socialist countries to obtain information on developments in the Lao Dong leadership.

By the end of 1963 the Chinese influence in Vietnam reached its highest peak, and during the winter and spring of 1964, in spite of regular diplomatic contact, relations between Soviet officials in Hanoi and the Vietnamese leadership became very tense. One purpose of this chapter is to analyse the Soviet view of Beijing's growing influence in Hanoi and evaluate the impact of Chinese policies on Soviet decision-making with regard to Vietnam. A second purpose is to explain why Moscow's interest in Vietnam increased from the summer of 1964. By the end of that year the Soviet Union had replaced the Chinese as Vietnam's major ally in the war against the United States. This chapter will aim to discuss in some depth the reasons for this change.

Soviet perceptions of China in Vietnam

We have already seen how, during the last years of the 1950s, the Lao Dong leadership was divided into two factions: one consisting of those in favour of continuing a policy of diplomacy and peaceful reunification along the lines of the Geneva agreements, and another, consisting mainly of persons with a southern origin advocating a more aggressive policy to obtain reunification. By the early 1960s the main divide was between the so-called pro-Soviet and pro-Chinese factions in the Lao Dong. Policy makers in Moscow, or at least the Southeast Asia Department in the Foreign Ministry, were well aware of these factions and their pro-Soviet versus pro-Chinese preferences. Ho Chi Minh found the division within the party particularly difficult. While most of the other Lao Dong leaders were characterized by the Soviets as either pro-Soviet or pro-Chinese, Ho was primarily referred to as being in a middle position. Individuals within the leadership even argued that it was only due to Ho Chi Minh's position that the Lao Dong Central Committee refrained from publicly supporting the Chinese point of view.[3] However, Ho's continuous attempts to mediate between the two parties and his attempts to solicit support for the Vietnamese case from both of them proved to be a very difficult task.[4]

In the early 1960s the Vietnamese stressed the need to mend the split between Moscow and Beijing. Although several signs indicated that they leaned increasingly towards the Chinese, Hanoi was determined to keep a reasonably good relationship with Moscow. However, the growing Chinese influence in North Vietnam and the close relationship between the two countries could, according to the Soviet embassy in Hanoi, be seen in a number of different contexts. One example was Vietnamese travelling arrangements and the habit of stopping over in Beijing. Delegations from the DRV always travelled via the Chinese capital en route to other destinations for meeting with the CCP leadership. The Soviet embassy assumed that these meetings were set up to instruct, as well as debrief, the Vietnamese delegations after their travels abroad. The North Vietnamese were also using increasingly more Chinese materials and documents in the training of cadres within Vietnam. The Chinese importance was further emphasized in how the Vietnamese treated different celebrations and memorial days.[5]

The Soviet embassy closely followed all the signs, even the smallest, of a closer Sino-Vietnamese relationship. The smaller issues notwithstanding, the most important reason for the development in the relationship was Hanoi and Beijing's increasingly coinciding views on the problems of the present international situation. It was their views on the situation within the international Communist movement which constituted the foundation for the continuing strong links between the Lao Dong and the CCP. The growing presence of pro-Chinese elements within the Lao Dong leadership, and also 'the active foreign policy support the Chinese has shown the Lao Dong in the question of reunification of the country', increased Chinese influence in Vietnam.[6] By the spring of 1962 China had become, in Soviet eyes, a most complicating factor within the Soviet–Vietnamese relationship.[7]

The intensification of Chinese propaganda further convinced the Soviet embassy that Beijing was seeking to maximize its influence within Vietnam. Over the previous year the Chinese had significantly intensified their propaganda effort in Vietnam. Numerous articles in newspapers and magazines had focused on the successes of the People's Republic. The propaganda was accompanied by a sizeable amount of economic assistance from China. According to Soviet numbers, Chinese economic assistance to North Vietnam, in the period from 1955 to 1962, even exceeded Soviet assistance in the same period.[8] Put together these factors contributed to a closer relationship and increased the Chinese popularity among the Vietnamese population.

However, in Soviet eyes the picture was not only grim. Moscow still had devoted friends and followers within the Vietnamese leadership. As a contrast to those within the Lao Dong who wanted an even closer cooperation with the CCP, it was also possible to detect certain reservations in these pro-Chinese attitudes. Arguing that there is 'not necessarily a contradiction between a good Soviet–Vietnamese relationship and these pro-Chinese attitudes', the Soviet embassy concluded that by April 1962 Chinese influence on Lao Dong policies was not yet decisive. With emphasis on the fact that 'what characterized these people, and their pro-Chinese moods, was a certain limit in their pro-Chinese sympathies', the Soviets contented that among the Vietnamese leaders there still existed those who did not exclude the option of closer contact with the Soviet Union. These individuals did not see the friendship with China as a hindrance to strengthened ties between the Soviet Union and Vietnam.[9]

The embassy analysts clearly supported the idea of a possibly stronger relationship between Moscow and Hanoi. In an attempt to diminish the importance of the strong Chinese influence, the Soviet embassy underlined how the Lao Dong leaders were forced to take into consideration the latent anti-Chinese feelings that up till now had existed among the Vietnamese population, and how that could be explained by 'the historical century-long enmity of the Vietnamese working class toward the Chinese feudal invaders (aggressors)'.[10] At a time when the Vietnamese were slowly tilting towards Beijing, officials at the Soviet embassy in Hanoi were eager to attract attention to those signs coming from the Lao Dong leaders that could be interpreted as a stronger interest in the Soviet side of the table.

To Moscow, the visit of a Chinese military delegation to North Vietnam from 15 to 31 December 1961 in honour of the seventeenth anniversary celebration of the founding of the PAVN was yet another illustration of the closeness in Sino-Vietnamese relations. According to Soviet embassy analysts the aim of the visit was to show both the Vietnamese leaders and the people that China was ready to give decisive support in the case of a military conflict, even war, in South Vietnam. The Chinese readiness to assist, the embassy underlined, did impress the Vietnamese friends, but they still knew that the Soviet attitude was very important in terms of 'determining the practical steps with regard to South Vietnam'.[11] However, in a Chinese account of the same visit, Marshal Ye Jianying, who was leading the delegation, urged caution in his conversations with Hanoi's leaders. The Chinese leaders allegedly feared that the Vietnamese

Communists' preference for large-scale battles might drag them into an unwanted war with the United States. Accordingly, the visitors told Hanoi that the correct way to defeat the South Vietnamese regime was to engage in guerrilla warfare in the mountains rather than to launch large-scale operations.[12] Thus, the Embassy was right about the Chinese advice to the Vietnamese but seems to have exaggerated the actual content of discussions. Although the Chinese influence was strong, there were many areas of friction between the two states.

In the end of May 1962 Ho Chi Minh told Soviet ambassador Tovmasyan that he wanted to travel to the Soviet Union to talk with Khrushchev but that he wanted to make the trip 'absolutely incognito'.[13] Ho's wish to travel without any publicity was not at all an attempt to trick the Chinese. As usual he travelled through Beijing. Arriving in Moscow he met with, among others, Deputy Foreign Minister Pushkin, with a plea for medicine and medical equipment for the South Vietnamese patriots. He wanted this assistance to go through the Soviet Red Cross to the DRV, and from there to South Vietnam. Ho also used the opportunity to thank the Soviet Union for its support in the fight against the American aggression and the South Vietnamese government of Ngo Dinh Diem.[14]

In a June 1962 memo from the Southeast Asia department to the heads of the foreign ministry it was emphasized that after the 22nd Congress of the Communist Party of the Soviet Union, a group had emerged among the Vietnamese leaders that primarily endorsed the Chinese view of foreign policies. This group distanced itself from the Soviet Union and its allies within the Communist camp. Nonetheless, several of the veteran leaders in Hanoi, such as Ho Chi Minh and Pham Van Dong, still underlined the necessity to strengthen the relationship with the Soviet Union. The fact that the Vietnamese invited cosmonaut Gennadi Titov (while China did not) was seen by the Southeast Asia Department as a confirmation that Hanoi was intent on a good relationship with Moscow. At the same time the number of Vietnamese students in the Soviet Union was steadily increasing, a situation that, according to SEAD, was a sign of a good future relationship between the two countries.[15]

But in 1962 the Soviet Union was not at all ready to support a struggle in Vietnam. Throughout that year Soviet analysts reemphasized the increasing Chinese influence in all spheres of North Vietnamese society. Political, economic and cultural relations between the DRV and the PRC, and not least relations between the Vietnamese and Chinese Communist parties played an increasingly important role. This was particularly true within the foreign policy sphere, where Hanoi's stand diverged from the Soviet foreign policy line on several issues. Among these were the personality cult, the attitude towards Albania, problems of war and peace, the role of national liberation movements, and, finally, the road from capitalism to socialism.[16] There is no doubt that the numerous reports from the embassy describing the ever-increasing Chinese influence in Hanoi must have made an impression on policy makers in Moscow. We shall see later how individuals within the Soviet foreign ministry bureaucracy, in the autumn of 1962, suggested how Moscow could improve relations between the Soviet Union and the Vietnamese and reduce the ever-growing Chinese influence.[17]

In 1962 Soviet embassy officials in Hanoi were determined to show that Moscow still had a role to play in Vietnam. They emphasized that the Vietnamese, in spite of the fact that the Chinese provided more aid to the DRV than the Soviet Union, always referred to the Soviet Union before China, when talking about assistance from fraternal countries. Likewise, they emphasized that the Vietnamese friends had lately refrained from mentioning interrelations between the DRV and China, Chinese aid and specialists, as well as the usual statistics of Chinese contributions to the Vietnamese, in conversations with Soviet embassy officials.[18] As the Chinese influence in the North Vietnamese society and leadership grew, Soviet officials increasingly spoke to those favouring Soviet influence in Vietnam over Chinese. The pleas for assistance from pro-Soviet elements within the Lao Dong obviously made an impression on Soviet officials in Vietnam and then again made them advance pleas to the Soviet leadership on behalf of the Vietnamese. Moscow's lack of interest in support for the Vietnamese must have been frustrating for the officials working in Vietnam, who witnessed how the Chinese influence increased without having any means to counter such a development. In spite of the numerous accounts of the possibilities of increasing Soviet influence in Vietnam, the message did not get through in Moscow, as the Soviet leaders had their minds set on other foreign policy problems far away from the worsening situation in Vietnam.[19]

While Moscow's policies towards Vietnam might have seemed passive, and at best reluctant, that was not the case with regard to Soviet engagement in other parts of the world. In late May 1962 members of the Soviet Politburo and the Secretariat of the Soviet Communist Party were informed of Nikita Khrushchev's plans to install missiles in Cuba, and during the summer and autumn of 1962 the Soviet leadership was fully preoccupied with what would be known as the Cuban Missile Crisis in October that year.[20] The Soviet effort to install missiles in the United States' backyard and thereby pose a much more potent threat to US security overshadowed developments in Vietnam.

Parallel to the Soviet engagement in the Caribbean, the United States increased its involvement in both Vietnam and Laos. In the spring of 1962 the United States launched, together with the Republic of Vietnam, a joint programme aimed at building the so-called Strategic Hamlets in the South Vietnamese countryside. The aim of the programme was to cut the enemy off from the rural population and fortify villages in order to keep people safe from what Washington viewed as Vietcong intimidation. However, the system was based on the idea that the peasants were the victims of such terror and thus underestimated the Southern peasants' support for the National Liberation Front. The programme was never successful and only further alienated the peasants from the Saigon government, although the main idea had been to foster loyalty towards the Ngo Dinh Diem administration.[21] In Laos the Kennedy administration decided to turn the country into a pro-American bastion in late 1962. The American move helped destroy the recent Geneva agreements that Washington had signed in midsummer that year, which stated that all foreign troops should be withdrawn from Laos and that the Pathet Lao should join the Neutralist Souvanna Phouma's coalition government.

Although the Americans withdrew their military advisors, the Central Intelligence Agency stepped up their supply to the Meo tribesmen, a guerrilla army that worked behind Pathet Lao lines.[22]

So while the United States and the People's Republic of China in their separate ways increased their involvement and influence in Vietnam and Southeast Asia, the Soviet Union was more worried about developments in other regions of the world, and their interest in Vietnam was limited to the question of how to best avoid a possibly dangerous international situation in the area. This in spite of the fears expressed in late 1961 that the situation in Vietnam could get out of control and seriously threaten world peace. Moscow did not change its view on Vietnam until the aggressive attitude of the Chinese and their readiness to support a full-scale war in Vietnam made the Soviets realize the dangers of a Sino-Vietnamese war alliance facing the full military powers of the United States.

From the Vietnamese side the emphasis on maintaining a good relationship with Moscow is an interesting aspect of the so-called triangular relationship between Moscow, Hanoi and Beijing in this period. In reports from the embassies in both Hanoi and Beijing, as well as in several analyses made by the Southeast Asia Department in the Soviet Foreign Ministry, this behaviour was often dwelt upon. Was it possible that the Vietnamese could lean increasingly on the Chinese and allow a high degree of indirect, as well as direct, Chinese influence in politics and military affairs, while still keeping a good working relationship with the Soviet Union? In spite of the growing tension between Moscow and Beijing, and the rapprochement between Hanoi and Beijing in the first half of the 1960s, several of the Vietnamese leaders, and in particular Ho Chi Minh and Pham Van Dong, often seized the opportunity to praise Soviet assistance and dedication to the Vietnamese cause. Thus, it is possible that even in 1962 there existed a more general understanding among the Vietnamese leaders that in the long run, in spite of Chinese propaganda, the Soviet Union was the only country able to provide the large amount of economic and military assistance needed in case of an all-out war between the Vietnamese Communists and the United States.

Tougher frontlines within the Communist camp

Soviet perceptions of the Chinese influence in Vietnam depended not only on reports from the Hanoi embassy but as much on information obtained by embassy officials in China and conversations with official representatives from other fraternal countries. As the relationship between Moscow and Beijing was deteriorating, Soviet officials became increasingly dependent on other sources than the Chinese and Vietnamese to determine the degree of Chinese influence in Vietnam, and even to obtain information on the actual developments, especially within South Vietnam and relations between the North and the South.

This dependence began in the autumn of 1962, when several signs indicated that Soviet embassy officials in Vietnam were increasingly isolated from the leadership in the VWP, and lasted until the autumn of 1964, when full contact between Soviet and Vietnamese officials was re-established.[23] However, in spite of the growing dependence on information from other Socialist countries, contact between the Soviets and Vietnamese in Hanoi did not come to a full stop. Employees at the embassy still had meetings with Lao Dong officials, but much of the vital information concerning issues such as the developments in the Sino-Vietnamese relationship came through other Socialist representatives. The Vietnamese now seemed much more cautious with regard to what they revealed to the Soviets and were reluctant to take a stand with regard to the escalating Sino-Soviet conflict. As a result, during this period Moscow became steadily more dependent on representatives from other Socialist countries to keep up to date on developments within South Vietnam, and not least on the relationship between Vietnam and China. This also meant that Moscow to a much larger degree would have to rely on information gathered by, and interpretations made by, their closest Socialist allies – and in effect they now often dealt with second-hand information only.

While Moscow knew the preferences of most Vietnamese leaders in the Soviet versus China question, the Soviet leaders were also influenced by the views of other Socialist countries. In conversations with representatives from other Socialist countries they often discussed the question of pro-Chinese or pro-Soviet tendencies among the Lao Dong leaders. The Polish Ambassador to the DRV, Findinski, commented on the fact that Truong Chinh spent his vacation in the Soviet Union, while Pham Van Dong had left for China, and added that he (Findinski) would not even guess what that could mean. However, this was most probably a calculated political decision made in the Lao Dong Politburo. As far as Findinski was concerned, Truong Chinh should not be trusted, since he was considered to be the most prominent pro-Chinese figure in the DRV, but with Pham Van Dong the situation was different. Findinski also suggested to Tovmasyan that it would be a good idea to 'bring Le Duan closer to us and give him more attention'.[24] The Czechoslovak ambassador in the DRV, Gerold, supported Findinski's view of Truong Chinh as 'the most manifest pro-Chinese' among the members of the Politburo of the Lao Dong CC. On the pro-Soviet side he placed Pham Van Dong, Vo Nguyen Giap and Nguyen Duy Trinh, while he characterized the position of Ho Chi Minh himself as 'centrist'.[25]

In his attempts to explain the Vietnamese position with regard to their relations with both Moscow and Beijing, Gerold argued that in their foreign policies the Lao Dong leaders 'basically supported the Chinese Communist Party without regard for the interests of the DRV. [...] They fear the Chinese and do not want to put themselves in opposition to them.' One example of Chinese influence surfaced in relation to the Comecon meeting in 1962, when the Vietnamese only were present only as observers, and not participants. The Chinese did not participate, and the Vietnamese were reluctant to go against the Chinese in this matter. However, at the very same time Ho Chi Minh went to Moscow during the meeting in order to show the Central Committee of the Soviet Communist Party and the other fraternal countries that they 'wanted to participate at the Comecon meeting, but were unable to do so'.[26]

In spite of such behaviour, according to Gerold, the Lao Dong leadership was actually to a much larger degree reaching out for the Soviet Communist Party than for the CCP. The main reason for that was that the Vietnamese leaders were convinced that the DRV could not count on much assistance from China but in contrast could in the future receive much economic aid from the Soviet Union. Thus, he added, it was no coincidence that for the negotiations about renewed economic aid from the Soviet Union to the DRV, it was Politburo member Nguyen Duy Trinh who travelled to Moscow to conduct the negotiations, and nobody else. Duy Trinh was considered to be pro-Soviet.[27] Gerold also accused the Vietnamese leaders of not being aware of China's great power-manoeuvring towards Vietnam, as well as other countries, which should have put them on guard. What the Vietnamese feared was that the Chinese would eventually lead the situation into a total split and the founding of a second centre within the international Communist movement. With such a situation they were threatened by the danger of losing the independence of both the Lao Dong and the DRV.[28]

In response to the Czechoslovak ambassador's description of the current situation within the Lao Dong, Soviet ambassador Tovmasyan emphasized that the DRV leaders did not expect much economic aid from China but talked about how they could rationalize the assistance they had already received from the Soviet Union and other Socialist countries. That attitude was a result of the implementation of the Chinese slogan 'Depend on one's own forces', introduced as a part of the Lao Dong strategy.[29] The slogan came from Chinese, but in the Vietnamese setting the meaning was more neutral because Hanoi was reluctant to follow the Chinese policies with regard to production. Therefore, he argued, in the Vietnamese sense the slogan was very different from the Chinese equivalent and gave it a character of striving for independence, perhaps first of all from the Chinese.[30]

In 1962 the image of China's role in Vietnam was influenced both by the Soviets' own contact with the Vietnamese and the Chinese and by the information provided by other trusted Socialist officials. Information provided by representatives from other Socialist countries became increasingly important during the early 1960s. The mood in Vietnam was slowly changing, as the Vietnamese put increasingly more trust in the Chinese. To keep updated, the Soviets used all sources available. In that setting the Poles played an important role. The country was represented in the ICC, a body that had first been established for all three Indochinese countries during the 1954 Geneva conference and which in 1962 existed for Laos and Vietnam only.

According to the Chinese the ICC for Vietnam had outplayed its role by late 1962, because it was now to a much larger degree serving the interests of the United States. The Chinese therefore suggested that the ICC for Vietnam should be isolated and terminated. Both Moscow and Hanoi disagreed with the Chinese on this and wanted to maintain its presence in Vietnam. The difference in views over the need for the ICC was a result of how these states pictured the future development in Vietnam. In 1962 Moscow wanted a political struggle and finally a reunification through peaceful means, whereas Beijing encouraged the

Vietnamese friends to activate and increase the armed struggle in South Vietnam and to immediately interfere militarily in the affairs of South Vietnam.[31]

The behaviour of the North Vietnamese leadership, especially in the first period after the Geneva conference on Laos, gave room for both hope and disillusionment for the Soviet representatives in Hanoi. On the one hand, it was rather clear that the overall majority of the Lao Dong leadership were in favour of a closer relationship with the CCP, but at the same time many signs from the inner circles of the leadership indicated that many still wished for a deeper Soviet engagement in Vietnam. Thus, on the eve of Chinese dominance in Hanoi, Soviet officials in Vietnam kept looking for signs that could indicate the possibility for a stronger Soviet influence there in the future, while at the same time their superiors in Moscow had other things they considered more important than Vietnam on their foreign policy agenda. However, before looking at what probably seemed a point of no return in Soviet–Vietnamese relations in 1963, it is worth mentioning that there were forces within the Soviet foreign ministry bureaucracy that were willing to once again take measures to improve the Soviet–Vietnamese relationship.

Attempts to improve Soviet–Vietnamese relations

In September 1962 analysts in the Southeast Asia Department of the Soviet foreign ministry suggested several new measures that, according to their view, would contribute to an improvement of the relationship between the Soviet Union and the DRV, as well as put a stop to the increasing isolation of the Soviet ambassador and other Soviet officials in Hanoi. It is very likely that this initiative was partly a result of Mao's declaration that he would support armed struggle in Vietnam, combined with the increased American interest in both Vietnam and Laos. The basic idea put forward by the analysts was that, to regain influence in Vietnam, the Soviet Union would have to show the Vietnamese that the Soviet leaders were committed to their cause. Two main issues were on the agenda. The first was the importance of a high-level Soviet visit to the DRV. SEAD suggested that Nikita Khrushchev visit North Vietnam in order to develop closer and more personal ties between Soviet and Vietnamese leaders. During such a visit Khrushchev should further elaborate on the decisions of the 22nd Congress of the CPSU and provide the Vietnamese with a better understanding of the decisions of that meeting.

In addition to a visit by Khrushchev, the Soviet Union should devote more attention to Vietnamese reunification. Moscow should offer political support in the question of South Vietnam and keep in mind the importance of reunification in the minds of the Vietnamese people. Their first priority should be to put a stop to the American intervention in Vietnam, isolate the United States and provide international support for the NLF. Further, the Soviet Union should contribute to a withdrawal of support for American policies in South Vietnam on the part of the British, Australians and US satellites. On that issue there existed differences in opinion between the imperialist countries that could be used to the advantage of the NLF. Another effective measure would, according to the SEAD, be to contribute to an increase in the authority of the NLF in both Vietnam and abroad. After defining the core tasks of the South Vietnamese patriots' fight, 'it will be necessary to discuss the question of a more official form of assistance from the Soviet Union to the Front'. Soviet leaders were also advised to support the establishment of a neutral South Vietnam, which according to analysts in the SEAD, was a realistic way towards a peaceful solution in the country. And, finally, they were advised to invite members of the NLF to the Soviet Union.[32]

Moscow's lack of active participation in Vietnam could be explained by what may seem like an overextension of Soviet foreign policy capabilities during 1962. Their extended involvement in the Third World, and Cuba in particular, could explain the attitude towards Vietnam. With the increased American interest in Southeast Asia the Soviet leaders did not want to risk confrontation with Washington on two fronts – both in the Caribbean and in Vietnam. Notwithstanding, the above policy suggestions show that there were probably different opinions within the Soviet foreign policy bureaucracy on how to deal with the situation in Vietnam. However, few of these suggestions were actually implemented. Most important, Khrushchev did not visit Vietnam, and even though Moscow strengthened its verbal support for the Vietnamese cause, they did not provide the practical assistance required by the Vietnamese in their preparations for a war against the Americans. Even though they spoke out in solidarity with the Vietnamese fight for reunification, in 1962 the Soviet leadership did little to convince their Vietnamese comrades that they could depend on Soviet assistance in times of trouble. The absence of a state visit illustrates Soviet interest in Vietnam at the time. There was no room for a visit to the DRV on Nikita Khrushchev's schedule in late 1962, or early 1963. In retrospective, it would probably have been a good idea.

From the Vietnamese side there were, in spite of numerous accounts of Hanoi's preference for the Chinese way with regard to reunification, indications that many in Hanoi were still open to Soviet policies. Preferences of the Lao Dong leaders was also a popular subject of conversation with representatives from other Socialist countries. For the Soviet embassy the Polish representatives in Hanoi were valuable sources because they had good access to both the Vietnamese and the Chinese. In October 1962 Polish ambassador Findinski argued that the Vietnamese friends did not follow the Chinese blindly, and that even though they were making use of Chinese tactics, it was only to a certain limit. They were still developing and strengthening the political line within the NLF. That was, according to Findinski, an indication that the Vietnamese still aspired to take the Soviet point of view into account. Therefore, he argued, they were still using both forms of struggle but using them in such a way that they would not have to 'take an unnecessary step in the direction of either China or the Soviet Union'.[33]

According to the Poles, the North Vietnamese were still striving to hold a middle position between the Soviet and Chinese Communist parties. To some degree the Soviets had even been able to lessen the degree of Chinese influence among the Vietnamese leadership, and the Polish Ambassador claimed that this policy had been a success and that the pro-Chinese group led by Le Duan had weakened its position. The group itself was not extinct as such, but its influence in the higher echelons of the party had decreased, and its opinion did not count for as much as it once did. Findinski further added that during a visit to the DRV a Chinese parliamentary delegation tried to push the Vietnamese friends to activate military struggle in the South. However, according to one of the Vietnamese leaders, the Vietnamese friends did not agree with the Chinese in this matter.[34]

As a result the Chinese delegation's visit to the DRV did not produce any significant results. The Soviet embassy described the visit as taking place in

> circumstances of a struggle between two distinct tendencies: on the one hand, the tendency to keep the close, friendly relations between the DRV and China, and on the other hand, the aspiration of the Vietnamese to secure a certain distance between the Lao Dong and the CCP, and to follow a middle line, manoeuvring between the CPSU and the CCP; moreover, the second tendency from our point of view, is gradually getting the upper hand.[35]

To judge by these comments, Moscow seemed quite content with the Lao Dong's effort to stay somewhere in the middle between themselves and the Chinese. Soviet embassy analysts explained the great attention attached to the timing of the visit and argued that the Chinese had picked the 13th anniversary of the PRC in order to get as much publicity as possible. The facts that the meetings between the Vietnamese and Chinese 'were colder than one should have expected', and that the Vietnamese speeches were less overwhelming than the ones held by the Chinese, and not least what Moscow saw as Ung Van Khiem's attempts to show his friendly feelings towards the Soviet Union during the Chinese visit were all taken as signs that the Vietnamese were not yet completely incorporated into the Chinese sphere.[36] When comparing the visit to a similar event in North Korea, Moscow underlined that during that visit the Chinese delegation was much warmer towards its host.[37]

According to the Vietnamese, 'the Chinese delegation came to the DRV to consolidate China's position in the country, [...] but we told them that Vietnam supports and is ready to support relations not only with China, but also with the Soviet Union and other countries in the Socialist camp'.[38] Apparently, Vietnamese and Soviet views on the visit of the Chinese parliamentary delegation concurred. The delegation did not make a strong impact either on DRV public opinion or on the Lao Dong leaders. That was underlined by the fact that the Vietnamese leaders supposedly told the Chinese that they wanted to keep a certain distance to the CCP and rather follow a course in between the CCP and the CPSU. The Soviet embassy was, of course, satisfied with such an attitude and added that the Chinese leadership, apparently, did not completely disapprove of the Lao Dong policy in the current situation.[39]

The Polish ambassador's analysis of the Vietnamese situation was further confirmed in Tovmasyan's conversations with Duong Bac Mai. Duong was a member of the Political Committee of the DRV National Assembly and deputy director of the Department in the Central Committee of the Lao Dong on questions related to the Home Front, but in this context his most important role was that of deputy leader of the Soviet–Vietnamese Friendship Society. He was among the pro-Soviet elements within the Lao Dong and until he passed away in 1964 Duong had regular contact with the Soviet ambassadors in Hanoi. In meetings with the Soviet ambassador Duong talked about how the whole leadership of the Lao Dong, with only a few exceptions, were pro-China. Those who supported China were among the most powerful members of the Central Committee of the Politburo and included figures such as Le Duan, Le Duc Tho, Hoang Van Hoan, Xuan Thuy, and, not least, Truong Chinh.[40]

In contrast, those who supported the Soviet Union did not hold as prominent positions. Within the Politburo nobody except Ho Chi Minh openly supported the Soviet Union. Of the members Pham Van Dong, Vo Nguyen Giap and Nguyen Duy Trinh were considered to be on friendly terms with the Soviets, but they all preferred to keep their sympathies quiet. According to Duong, it was only thanks to the position of President Ho Chi Minh that the Lao Dong CC did not overtly support the Chinese point of view. A short while earlier Ho had stopped an attempt to begin public criticisms of the Soviet Union based on a Chinese pattern. However, comrade Ho Chi Minh was already an old man, and many questions were decided above his head. His weak theoretical education made him lack the necessary focus in certain situations.[41]

Eager to turn around the pro-Chinese trend, Duong Bac Mai suggested that the Soviet Union increase its economic assistance to the DRV. He underlined that he now talked as a friend of the Soviet Union and the CPSU and that 'he, and many others, did not want to see relations between the DRV and the Soviet Union, or between the Lao Dong and the CPSU, deteriorate, and therefore they would do everything in their power to avert the current development of events'. At the same time 'we begged', Mai emphasized, 'that the CPSU would give us "all possible support in this regard" '.[42]

The different views on the future of Vietnam would soon change the relationship between Moscow, Hanoi and Beijing. In spite of both the internal Soviet suggestions to give more active assistance to the Vietnamese and the pleas from Soviet-friendly elements within the Lao Dong, Moscow was not willing to engage itself deeper in the Vietnamese situation in late 1962. The strong Chinese presence was probably one reason. Although it was important to Moscow to keep updated on developments in the Sino-Vietnamese relationship, the Soviet Union apparently did not view the increasing Chinese influence in Vietnam as an acute threat to future good relations between themselves and the Vietnamese. Nor did they seem to look at the division of the Vietnamese into distinct pro-Soviet and pro-Chinese factions as an opportunity for increased influence. Whether that was a result of Moscow's pure ignorance of the ongoing developments in Vietnam, a belief that it would be correct to allow the Chinese the main influence in the country, or simply a result of extensive Soviet engagement in other parts of the world during the autumn of 1962 is difficult to say. However, it is plausible that the combination of Soviet foreign policy challenges during the autumn of 1962, such as the Cuba crisis, and the lack of proper understanding of the situation in Vietnam steered Soviet attention away from the Indochina peninsula.

During 1963 and early 1964, Moscow's dependence on other Socialist countries in Hanoi became even stronger. The main reason for this was that from the spring of 1963 Hanoi took another large step towards China, and in December that year the Vietnamese Communists had completely abandoned Soviet ideas on reunification and sought the full support of the PRC. The Soviet dependence on the other Socialist countries adds an interesting aspect to the overall analysis of the Soviet–Vietnamese relationship. It shows that from this time onwards the Soviet Union's policy towards Vietnam was strongly influenced by the Vietnamese reluctance to provide information, and Moscow found itself in a reactive, rather than in an active, role vis-à-vis the Hanoi leadership. The Soviet Union was now more of a spectator to events in Vietnam.

Hanoi's turn to China

The new Vietnamese foreign policy line changed the nature of the relationship between Moscow and Hanoi, which is best reflected in the changing circumstances for Soviet embassy officials, especially to those stationed in Hanoi and Beijing. In Beijing meetings with both Vietnamese and Chinese officials now became both short and rare, and the Soviets depended even more on the accounts of other Socialist countries' ambassadors to obtain the necessary information on developments in Vietnam. In Hanoi the Soviet ambassador had regular meetings with top North Vietnamese officials with about the same frequency as in previous years. Meetings with Chinese representatives, however, seem to have ceased completely during 1963.

During 1963, pro-Chinese members of the North Vietnamese leadership increased their influence in both domestic and foreign policy-making, and by early 1964 the Soviet embassy could only conclude that the leaders in Hanoi were now mainly pro-Chinese.[43] At the same time the ideological conflict between Moscow and Beijing further intensified, and from China Soviet embassy officials reported an increasing number of Soviet criticisms coming through representatives of other Socialist countries. But although the relationship with Beijing deteriorated, this apparently did not have an immediate influence on practical relations between Moscow and Hanoi. In both 1962 and 1963 several Soviet delegations visited the DRV and were well received by the Vietnamese. During such visits the Vietnamese always emphasized that they intended to reunify their country through peaceful means while giving the delegates the impression that apart from the Soviet Union, no other country could assist them in fulfilling that goal.[44]

The attitudes and impressions brought back to Moscow by different delegations visiting the DRV during these years bear witness of a Vietnamese leadership eager to hold on to the Soviet link in spite of their intimate relationship with China. But were these perceptions based on Vietnamese propaganda, or did they represent a more ambivalent attitude indicating Vietnamese difficulties with regard to the growing Sino-Soviet differences? Although little is so far known about discussions between the pro-Chinese and pro-Soviet factions in Vietnam, reports from the Soviet embassy in Hanoi show that many of the Vietnamese pronounced their continued belief in the Soviet Union and encouraged the Soviet ambassador to advance pleas for more Soviet assistance to the DRV.[45] Clearly, with the possibility of a large-scale war with the Americans lurking in the shadows, the Lao Dong leaders were bound to evaluate which of the larger Communist powers could give them the necessary wartime assistance.

With the obvious changes in Vietnamese policies it is necessary to ask why Hanoi went from a middle position to a complete adherence to Beijing during 1963 and early 1964. The change did not occur from one day to another but developed in stages. In January 1963 the Czechoslovak President, Antonin Novotny, visited the DRV. During his stay he issued a joint statement together with Ho Chi Minh that endorsed peaceful coexistence. The Soviet embassy viewed the visit as an important event that drew the Vietnamese Worker's Party closer to the CPSU.[46] However, almost a year later, after the Ninth Plenum in December 1963, the pro-Chinese elements within the Lao Dong Politburo eased Ung Van Khiem out of office because he had endorsed the statement after Novotny's visit.[47] Shortly after the conclusion of the visit, influential pro-Chinese forces in the Lao Dong had, according to the Polish embassy in Hanoi, started an active campaign to decrease the political significance of the DRV–Czechoslovak communiqué.[48] This, along with several other examples, shows how the climate between the Soviet Union and the DRV was worsening as relations between China and the Soviet Union declined. The negative effect of the Novotny visit was the first stage in the Vietnamese turn to Beijing.

Liu Shaoqi's state visit to the DRV in May 1963 represents the second stage in Hanoi's turn to China. Shortly before Liu's visit, in late April, Ung Van Khiem was expelled from the DRV leadership. According to Soviet ambassador Tovmasyan, Khiem was expelled owing to his known sympathies with the CPSU. It happened quite fast and just in time for the Chinese visit. Tovmasyan characterized it as a 'present' for the Chinese.[49] Analysing the official communiqué issued after the visit, the Soviet ambassador argued that the Lao Dong had now taken large steps towards the CCP on several issues and had even contradicted some of their previous positions. However, the communiqué did not represent anything fundamentally new in the position of the Lao Dong. Moreover, the absence of a statement of full agreement between the Lao Dong and the CCP suggested that there were still disagreements between the two on several issues. In an analysis of the visit, Soviet diplomats, in spite of the obvious pro-Chinese attitudes in Vietnam, claimed to see possibilities for a continued good relationship between Moscow and Hanoi.[50]

In an assessment of the results of Liu Shaoqi's discussions in Vietnam the embassy primarily underlined the Lao Dong's further deviation from the 'middle' position between the Soviet and the Chinese Communist parties and its slipping over to the Chinese position within the international Communist movement. The fact that the Lao Dong now accepted the open polemic between Communist parties and allowed the Chinese and 'pro-Chinese' to conduct a widespread campaign among the Vietnamese people against the CPSU and Soviet views was a source of great concern. Tovmasyan also emphasized the strengthened position of the 'pro-Chinese' elements within both the Lao Dong and the DRV leadership and the further advancement of Le Duan's role. However, he concluded his report saying that 'there were still disagreements between the Lao Dong leadership and the Chinese, and that the Vietnamese even expressed limited discontent with the strong CCP attacks on us [the Soviet Union], which brought forth a limited reaction within the ranks of the Lao Dong'.[51]

On the North Vietnamese, side Liu Shaoqi's visit was only one element in a long chain of events. During the spring of 1963 the relationship between Moscow and Hanoi went through a significant change. In late February the DRV foreign ministry presented a document describing the future political course of the DRV towards South Vietnam. The document was prepared for the Politburo of the Central Committee of the Lao Dong and the DRV government by the DRV foreign ministry. It emphasized that in 1963 the NLF(SV) would have to increase and activate both its military and political forces and that one now had to relate to the possibility that 'the war in South Vietnam could be a war of the Korean type'.[52]

Such a situation also implied the need for more outside assistance, especially from the other Socialist countries. In early May 1963 the Vietnamese complained that Moscow had already turned down three requests for material assistance. In spite of the close relationship with the Chinese the Vietnamese were still dependent on Soviet assistance. The South Vietnamese forces' need for foreign currency was the background for another request to the Soviets – this time for 1 million US dollars. Holding that request up against Chinese assistance, Nguyen Van Vinh talked about how China was the main provider of weapons, and how the Chinese prepared, especially for the Vietnamese, foreign weapon models for use in the South. As a follow-up to that he wondered 'why the Soviet Union granted monopoly to one country?'[53]

These statements indicated, according to the Southeast Asia Department in the Soviet foreign ministry, that within the Lao Dong leadership there was general agreement that 'it was only China which indeed helped the South Vietnamese patriots in their struggle'. This opinion was further strengthened through the overt Chinese propaganda campaign to increase anti-Soviet emotions among the North Vietnamese population and thereby worsen Soviet–DRV relations. The strong anti-Soviet propaganda did, from Moscow's point of view, misrepresent Soviet policies with regard to South Vietnam. Moscow's policy was reunification based on the 1954 Geneva agreement; it gave the people broad moral-political support, also in economic and military terms, by strengthening the DRV as a base for reunification of the whole country.[54]

From May 1963 moral-political support was no longer enough for either Hanoi or the NLF or, for that matter, the Chinese. Throughout the summer and autumn of that year Vietnamese requests for Soviet aid become more overt, and the requests were often followed by severe criticisms for not providing enough assistance to the Vietnamese in their fight to reunify the country. Notwithstanding the accusations that Moscow only provided moral support for the Vietnamese struggle, indications in available Soviet documents suggest that the Vietnamese did receive weapons from the Soviet Union sometime in the late summer of 1963.[55] Thus, in late August 1963, when the Vietnamese ambassador to the Soviet Union, Nguyen Van Kinh, asked Soviet Deputy Foreign Minister Sergei Georgevich Lapin, 'whether the Soviet Union intended to take some measure of action in order to support the struggle of the South Vietnamese patriots', it is possible that Moscow, in military terms, already was in the process of delivering the requested supplies.[56]

While Hanoi was eager to secure more practical support from Moscow, an equally important concern was the Soviet role with regard to a possible fulfilment of the Geneva agreement. The Vietnamese ambassador handed over a message from President Ho Chi Minh with regard to the role of the Geneva co-chairmen and the deteriorating situation in South Vietnam. The Deputy Foreign Minister assured Nguyen Van Kinh that he would look at the letter from Ho Chi Minh and make sure that the Soviet press would do its best to throw light on the situation in South Vietnam. After Lapin's reassurances the ambassador said that the DRV planned to send a delegation to the Soviet Union in order to discuss the problems in the South as soon as possible.[57] The Soviets and Vietnamese had already discussed the plans for a DRV delegation to the Soviet Union several times, but the Vietnamese kept delaying the trip for different reasons. The final outcome was the delegation led by Le Duan to Moscow in January and February 1964.[58]

In the period leading up to the 9th Plenum of the Lao Dong in December 1963 Soviet diplomats in Hanoi were constantly fed information about the closeness of the Sino-Vietnamese relationship. But in spite of the tales of a watertight alliance, there were also many signs that the Vietnamese resisted full dependence on the Chinese. According to the Soviet embassy, the DRV would not necessarily follow the Chinese immediately if they should opt for a total and final break with the Soviet Union. Hanoi was still too afraid of being left alone without assistance from the Socialist camp. The fear that China would virtually absorb Vietnam was apparent – even Le Duan feared that. In a rather sarcastic comment on the Vietnamese situation, Tovmasyan said to his Czechoslovak colleague, 'They [the Vietnamese] can say no to cultural exchange with us, and thus avoid ideological influence, as some among the Vietnamese talk about, but economic assistance, on the other hand, they accept with pleasure.'[59]

And the DRV really needed economic assistance from Moscow in 1963. The Plenum had already been delayed several times, apparently because of the difficult economic situation in the country. Individuals in the party leadership were also afraid that the official course they were about to approve at the Plenum could deprive them of all future economic assistance from the Soviet Union. And as more and more Vietnamese came to understand that the increased Chinese influence on the Lao Dong had seriously worsened the economic situation in the country, they also realized that 'it would not be very wise to separate themselves from the Soviet Union'. Some comrades even wondered 'what the United States would do in South Vietnam if the DRV were to depend only on the Chinese?'[60] But in spite of these allegations that many of the Vietnamese were well aware that the only possible partner, in terms of both economic and military capacity, in case of an American invasion, was the Soviet Union, Hanoi continued on its current course and made its final step towards China in December 1963.

Moscow and the result of the 9th Plenum of the Lao Dong

According to historian King C. Chen, the Vietnamese made three major decisions that led to the eventual resumption of arms in South Vietnam. The first was the decisions of the 15th Plenum in January 1959, the second was the resolutions of the 3rd Congress in September 1960, and the third and final step towards military struggle in the South was the resolutions of the 9th Plenum held in December 1963.[61]

It was during the 9th Plenum that the Lao Dong took its last step away from Moscow's foreign policy line. In his main speech to the Plenum delegates, Le Duan dismissed the Soviet strategy for the Socialist camp as defensive and recommended Mao's theory of revolutionary war. However, in spite of his enthusiasm for Mao's concept of protracted armed struggle as a 'model strategy for many Communists in Asia, Africa, and Latin America', Le Duan did not pledge to follow the Maoist model in Vietnam itself. According to Chinese historian Qiang Zhai, Le Duan did not want an open break with the Soviet party, even if he disagreed with Moscow's international position.[62] The participants at the 9th Plenum voted unanimously in favour of its resolution. Ung Van Khiem, the only member of the Central Committee who could have voted against the resolution, was, according to one source, ill during the vote. Thus, from December 1963 the leadership in Hanoi was 100 per cent pro-China; however, the main difference between the Vietnamese and the Chinese was that Hanoi had not yet officially attacked the Soviet Union.[63]

Many in the Vietnamese leadership were sceptical of the current developments and approached the Soviets to express their concerns. One major concern was the economic situation in Vietnam, which had gradually deteriorated since Luo Shaoqi's visit in May 1963. In addition, there was much concern about the prospects for fruitful results from the upcoming meetings in Moscow between Soviet and Vietnamese leaders. The resolutions approved during the Plenum, the nationwide study of these and not least the composition of the delegation heading for Moscow did not hint at useful results coming out of the discussions in Moscow.[64]

In the midst of the Plenum, on Christmas Day 1963, Ho Chi Minh invited the Soviet ambassador to a 'friendly lunch' with himself, Le Duan, Pham Van Dong and Xuan Thuy. At the end of the meal Ho Chi Minh announced his retirement to the ambassador. Because of his high age – he claimed to have reached 74 – Ho had decided that it was time to retire. From now on he would concentrate on visiting different parts of the country, meet with children and peasants – and also occasionally visit the Soviet ambassador to keep him informed about important matters. In connection with his retirement Ho told the ambassador that Le Duan would be in charge of party-related affairs, Pham Van Dong would deal with governmental issues, Xyan Thuy would be in charge of foreign affairs, and national assembly-related issues would be the responsibility of Truong Chinh.[65] Ho Chi Minh's retirement announcement should probably be seen in connection with events during the 9th Plenum itself. Ho Chi Minh biographer William J. Duiker argues that Ho 'must have had serious reservations about the new strategy to be adopted in South Vietnam'. Because he had always argued in favour of balancing relations with Moscow and Beijing, Ho clearly rejected a policy of exclusive reliance on China. However, when the anti-Soviet tone in the speeches reached a climax, Ho, according to Duiker, 'left the conference hall quietly to smoke a cigarette'. Apparently Ho did not use his vote during the Plenum, and the question remains whether he had been intimidated into silence by the new Lao Dong leadership.[66]

Was Ho Chi Minh's so-called retirement a result of the strategy changes during the Plenum? And why did Ho announce his retirement to the Soviet ambassador in this fashion? It certainly is possible that this was Ho Chi Minh's way of warning the Soviet ambassador of his decreasing influence in Hanoi's policy-making and also a warning of what would come out of the 9th Plenum. Ho's continued emphasis on a good relationship with the Soviet Union did to some extent make him the last obstacle to those in favour of a full dependence on China. Still, Ho was not the only member of the Politburo who was reluctant to burn all bridges with Moscow. Even though the majority of Politburo members were clearly pro-Chinese in their attitudes, a large faction was still conscious of the need to avoid a complete break with Moscow.[67]

In an effort to achieve more support from the Soviet Union, the North Vietnamese sent a delegation to Moscow in February 1964. The timing for this trip had been difficult, and it had been delayed several times, most likely due to the postponement of the 9th Plenum. In addition to Le Duan, the delegation consisted of Le Duc Tho and the revolutionary poet To Huu.[68] As always, the Vietnamese delegation stopped in Beijing and held a meeting with the Chinese before heading for the Soviet capital. During the meetings with Mao, Le Duan reported that the purpose of the trip to the Soviet Union was to explain the Lao Dong's position after the 9th Plenum to the Soviet leaders and ascertain Soviet policies. He added that Ho Chi Minh had already decided not to issue a joint communiqué with the Soviets at the end of the visit. Mao did, of course, use the opportunity to disparage the Russians and warned Le Duan that Moscow's main goal was to cut some kind of political deal with the United States and therefore would put pressure on them (China) 'in order to let the United States know that they are tough toward China but friendly toward the United States'. Le Duan's meeting with Mao took place during a time when the CCP chairman directed the full force of his propaganda machine to public condemnation of the Soviet Union.[69]

At a reception hosted by the Soviet embassy in Hanoi before the delegation left for Moscow, Le Duan stated that in meetings with the Soviet leaders the DRV delegation would 'openly argue their points of view on all basic issues with regard to the international development and the international Communist movement, even on those questions where we disagree with the CPSU'.[70] By the time the delegation reached Moscow, however, Le Duan's staunch attitude had been somewhat modified, and according to Tovmasyan, who was present during the meetings, the DRV delegation and, in particular, Le Duan had been very reserved.[71]

In addition to the somewhat staunch Vietnamese attitude, Soviet behaviour during the meetings may also have contributed to a generally bad negotiating environment. In late February 1964, after the delegation had returned from Moscow, the Polish ambassador in Hanoi disclosed to the Soviet ambassador what he had heard about the Moscow meetings. Apparently Khrushchev had, in a joking manner, presented himself to the Vietnamese as 'the main revisionist', whereas Suslov had referred to himself as 'the Stalinist'. According to the Pole, Khrushchev's many jokes over this matter had not been well accepted by the Vietnamese. Judging by Tovmasyan's comments, Le Duan strove not to add to the worsening of relations between the two parties, but it was often difficult to separate his position from that of the Chinese when he expressed his views on different issues. But the meetings had, according to Tovmasyan, been useful, in spite of certain disagreements.[72]

Even on the Vietnamese side the meetings were defined as a success. In conversations with the Soviet ambassador, the Vietnamese claimed that Le Duan greatly appreciated the results of the meetings.[73] But that was not entirely true. From a Vietnamese point of view Le Duan's trip to Moscow was a failure. If the intention had been to explain the decisions reached at the 9th Plenum and then appeal to the Soviets for the necessary assistance to continue their armed struggle in the South, Le Duan left Moscow with nothing. At that point Moscow was only willing to provide moral support, but did, however, not exclude future cooperation if Hanoi's attitude towards Moscow's views changed.[74] Judged by the harsh tone in meetings between Soviet and Vietnamese officials in Hanoi after Le Duan's trip to Moscow, and the Polish account of Khrushchev's attitude, the Soviet tone towards the Vietnamese had been rather patronizing. If they tried to persuade the Vietnamese to follow the Soviet foreign policy line, they did not succeed but only made the Soviet–Vietnamese relationship deteriorate even further.

According to Ilya Gaiduk, Soviet influence in Vietnam 'fell to its post-1954 nadir' with the resolutions of the 9th Plenum and remained frozen from the visit of the North Vietnamese delegation to Moscow in January 1964 until the start of the hot war in the Tonkin Gulf six months later.[75] Judging by the lack of top-level interest from the Soviet side during this period such an observation would be correct, but in bilateral relations the local-level diplomacy – in this case the role of

Soviet diplomats in the DRV – also plays an important role. In particular, the diplomats through their interactions with Vietnamese officials and their analysis of developments in the country at large contribute to the overall perceptions of the other party. During 1963 there were many examples of how several of the Vietnamese leaders strove to maintain a working relationship with the Soviet Union; the case of Ho Chi Minh himself, and his reluctance to rely exclusively on Chinese assistance, might well be the prime example that relations were not as frozen as one could be led to believe by considering only interactions at the very top level.[76]

The tide is turning

Parallel to the decision made at the 9th Plenum to continue armed struggle in South Vietnam, the DRV leaders signalled to their Soviet and East European allies that they were willing to consider negotiations, or at least explore the possibility through the Poles, to neutralize Vietnam. On one occasion in early January 1964 Pham Van Dong expressed, 'we want South Vietnam to be liberated with the help of the Soviet Union and other Socialist countries. The DRV is positive to Vietnamese neutralization, just like we have earlier informed the Soviet and Polish government, but the conditions are "not yet ripe" '.[77]

In the period immediately following the Le Duan delegation's visit to Moscow, the climate between Soviet diplomats and Vietnamese officials in Hanoi did seem rather tense. Unfortunately, many of the conversations during the spring of 1964 remain classified, and researchers are not allowed to view these. However, from the documents available, Laos once again stands out as a major discussion topic between the Soviet and the Vietnamese. The Poles suggested a new Geneva conference on Laos, and so did the French. The North Vietnamese were ready for a new conference on Laos but rejected a Chinese proposal that the situation in all of Indochina should be the subject of discussion.[78] Moscow was positive to convene a new conference on Laos.[79]

At the same time, during the spring and early summer of 1964, the unstable situation in Indochina was a growing concern among the Soviet leaders. As long as the Vietnamese were determined to follow their policy of military struggle to reunify the country, a full-scale war with South Vietnamese and American troops remained the most likely scenario. In an attempt to warn the Vietnamese, the Soviet government issued a statement on 27 July, in which they threatened to resign as co-chairman of the Geneva conference on Laos.[80] The Vietnamese soon responded to this statement and insisted that the Soviet Union remain in the post as co-chair. Under the cover that they worried about the negative effect a Soviet withdrawal would have on the people of Laos, Le Duc Tho argued that the problems in Laos should be solved at a possibly forthcoming Geneva conference.[81] Undoubtedly, the Vietnamese worried that if the Soviets were to give up the post as co-chair, they would completely disengage from the region and leave Hanoi with no other alternatives than to further develop their alliance with China.

From mid-July it is possible to detect a more positive tone between the Soviet embassy and North Vietnamese officials. Embassy officials claimed to see an increase in articles on the Soviet Union in the DRV press, which was interpreted as a positive sign; the Lao Dong leaders also seemed gradually more relaxed in the company of Soviet officials in Vietnam.[82] The signs of improvement came shortly before the attacks in the Gulf of Tonkin. In less than a week after the Tonkin incident Pham Van Dong emphasized to Soviet chargé d'affaires Privalov the importance of exchanging opinions in the current situation. 'We really do have a war going in our country', Pham Van Dong said to Privalov.[83] Shortly after, in the second half of August, the Soviet embassy seems to have facilitated contact between UN Secretary General U Thanth, who forwarded an American proposal for negotiations between Washington and Hanoi, and Pham Van Dong. The Vietnamese were not against such a proposal but underlined that from their point of view the best solution was to meet at a conference in Geneva or in a neutral country that both agree upon.[84]

During the autumn of 1964 Moscow clearly fought back against the Chinese influence. There was much emphasis on the increase in disagreements between the Vietnamese and the Chinese, and among the Lao Dong leaders there was growing concern that the Chinese would not be able to stand up against a fully fledged American attack on Vietnam. The Vietnamese had begun to realize that without cooperation with the Soviet Union it would be impossible to guarantee the safety of Vietnam, since China did not have the necessary economic strength. Such worries had been expressed by the Vietnamese during a meeting between Communist parties from the Far East and Southeast Asia in China sometime in late August.[85]

By November Moscow's view on support to the Vietnamese had visibly changed. As we have already seen, Moscow's change of heart was the result of a long process. During the spring and summer of 1964, Soviet diplomats and Vietnamese officials in Hanoi had resumed a more normal level of contact. The most important subjects of conversation during that period were the Soviet threats to resign as co-chairman of the Geneva conference, the question of a new conference to solve the deteriorating situation in Laos and the question of whether such a conference could possibly also include sessions on South Vietnam. The climate between the Soviets and Vietnamese in Hanoi improved significantly from mid-1964 onwards.

The ultimate sign that relations had improved was the decision to establish a permanent mission of the NLV(SV) in Moscow. The invitation came on 24 December, during the visit of an NLF delegation to the Soviet Union. On the day before the invitation, the DRV ambassador to the Soviet Union, Nguyen Van Kinh, told Soviet Deputy Foreign Minister Lapin that 'the establishment of an NLFSV mission in Moscow would be very important for the strengthening of the Front's international authority'.[86]

From disinterest to active support

Since the early 1960s Soviet representatives in Hanoi and Beijing had kept reassuring themselves, and not least Moscow, that although several important figures within the Vietnamese leadership showed clearly pro-Chinese sympathies, as an overall tendency they still remained loyal to the Soviet Union as the ultimate leader of the Socialist camp. That notion was further supported through conversations with pro-Soviet elements within the Lao Dong. But after Chinese Premier Luo Shaoqi's visit to the DRV in May 1963, and the resolutions made at the 9th Plenum in December that year, it became increasingly difficult for Soviet embassy officials to keep up the image of a Vietnamese leadership that worked independently of Beijing. By the end of 1963 the last obstacle to a completely pro-Chinese attitude within the Lao Dong, namely Ho Chi Minh himself, seems to have lost most of his influence on party policies.

The incidents in the Gulf of Tonkin in August 1964 transformed the Soviet view on Vietnam's importance. The small country in Southeast Asia and its never-ending battle for reunification and independence had now become the centre of Cold War superpower rivalry. By the end of 1964 the Soviet Union had assumed the position of the DRV's main provider of military and economic aid and advice and had made a complete turnaround from their previous position with sole emphasis on diplomacy and negotiations. Within less than a year Moscow's involvement in Vietnam had changed from disillusionment and disinterest to active involvement. What was the reason behind this policy change on the Soviet side?

In the DRV a corresponding change had taken place. In February 1964, while Le Duan was meeting with Soviet leaders in Moscow, the distrust between the Soviets and the Vietnamese was obvious to all participants, especially due to the Soviet reluctance to assist the Vietnamese in their military strategies. Le Duan's position during the Moscow meetings further emphasized the strong Chinese influence in DRV politics. So why did the leaders in Hanoi, shortly after such a strong declaration of alliance with the Chinese, turn away from Beijing and towards Moscow? To some extent the change of heart that took place in Hanoi and Moscow during the summer and autumn of 1964 were the result of longer processes within the two parties, but more importantly, it was a response to the deteriorating security situation in Vietnam, more precisely the threat of an immediate US intervention.

Hanoi's main reason for reigniting its alliance with the Soviet Union was twofold: first, the Vietnamese leaders had realized that the Americans were now about to escalate their involvement in Vietnam to an extent that would most likely develop into a full-scale war. The only possible and reliable ally in such a situation would be the Soviet Union. China had the manpower but not the sophisticated weapons necessary to fight the Americans. Second, leaders in Hanoi were afraid that sole dependence on the Chinese would provide fewer alternatives in a time of war. Leaders in Beijing completely refused to even consider any form of negotiations, whereas the Soviet Union had already signalled that it was positive to, and even could contribute to, a negotiated solution to the situation in Vietnam if that proved possible. Thus, it might have been Moscow's more positive attitude towards future negotiations, combined with a growing willingness to provide the Vietnamese with supplies for the war, that turned the tide from Beijing to Moscow.

The background for the Soviet change of mind consists of three major issues that to a large degree coincide with Hanoi's state of mind: first, the gradual realization that the Americans really were about to invade Vietnam, and that the Vietnamese leaders now needed large amounts of outside support to counter the American invasion. Moscow realized that no one but the Soviet Union could provide that kind of assistance. Second, the Sino-Soviet relationship had now fully collapsed and, with it, the cooperation in support for Vietnam. If the Soviets wanted to retain any control over developments in Vietnam, they would have to engage themselves in the country in spite of the possible damage to their relationship with the West. Third, China's political strategy was significantly radicalized through 1963 and 1964, and Moscow was afraid that the strategy Beijing recommended to the Vietnamese could seriously hurt any chances of a reasonable outcome in the conflict in Vietnam.

Together, these three factors played a significant role in Moscow's decision to support the Vietnamese struggle against the American aggressors. However, it is important to keep in mind that the changes in strategy and priorities taking place in both Moscow and Hanoi constituted a gradual process that began sometime during the summer of 1964 and was due as much to Vietnamese initiatives as to a more sudden change of mind among the Soviet leaders. Even though relations between Moscow and Hanoi cooled for a period lasting a little less than a year, channels of contact were soon reopened once the two states realized that they were fighting to reach a common goal.

Conclusions: Changing alliances

The DRV will have to deal with the American imperialists on their own.[1]
Chinese official to Kosygin, Spring 1965

Hanoi's change of heart starting in mid-1964, and its newfound preference for Moscow over Beijing, must have been a severe disappointment to the Chinese leaders. For more than fifteen years, even before the establishment of the PRC in October 1949, and the subsequent Chinese recognition of the DRV, the CCP provided assistance to the Vietnamese Communists in their struggle against the French. In 1949–50 Stalin encouraged Mao to take particular responsibility for developments in Vietnam. Beijing's central role as the provider of practical aid and advice to the DRV continued after the temporary division of Vietnam in late 1954 and was an important part of Soviet foreign policy strategy towards the region. Sino-Soviet cooperation in Vietnam continued well into the early 1960s but broke down as a result of the deterioration in the Sino-Soviet relationship. Until the spring of 1963 leaders in Moscow believed that Soviet relations with Hanoi were in reasonably good shape. That assumption was wrong. The DRV leaders had already been tilting towards China for a while, and by the end of the year the leadership in Hanoi was fully integrated into the Chinese sphere of interest. However, Hanoi's full China orientation lasted only for a short period of the year at most, and when the Lao Dong leadership, from the early autumn of 1964, began moving towards Moscow, it was Beijing's turn to worry, especially about its own future role in Vietnam.

The new Soviet approach to Hanoi's struggle, and Moscow's decision to actively support Hanoi in its military struggle for reunification, soon created new problems in the triangular relationship between Moscow, Hanoi and Beijing. The source of Beijing's concern was the ongoing rapprochement between Moscow and Hanoi. While on the one hand the Chinese were satisfied with Moscow's turnabout and their decision to support Vietnam, on the other they were reluctant to accommodate the Soviets in their efforts to ship supplies to the DRV.

The Chinese attitude was illustrated by Beijing's behaviour during the spring of 1965, when Beijing's reluctance to assist the Soviets in their new strategy for Vietnam became particularly obvious. The Soviet leaders were clearly frustrated by Beijing's lack of cooperation with regard to the transportation of Soviet military supplies over Chinese territory. The disagreements began already in February 1965 when a load of Soviet weapons meant for the DRV was held back at the Sino-Soviet border. To solve the problem Soviet ambassador Shcherbakov raised the issue with Prime Minister Pham Van Dong, who then promised to 'take the necessary measures'.[2] It was, however, unlikely that Pham Van Dong, in spite of his promises, would be able to solve this issue with the Chinese. The DRV leaders were in a difficult situation. On the one hand, they desperately needed the support of the Soviet Union, but on the other, Sino-Soviet disagreements over this support complicated their relationship with the Chinese, and prevented vital Soviet assistance from reaching Vietnam.

On the surface, the Chinese problem was the Beijing leaders' need to control all supplies sent to the DRV via Chinese territory. It was a clear demand from Beijing that they had a right to know what kind of supplies were transported on their soil. The Chinese demands primarily contributed to numerous delays in the arrival of Soviet supplies to the DRV. These delays became particularly obvious in March 1965 when the DRV leaders, to expedite the transfer of military supplies to Vietnam, specifically asked for the use of aircraft. Moscow agreed, but Beijing rejected the proposal. In his talks with the Soviet ambassador, Pham Van Dong was not able to explain the Chinese position. He argued that the Chinese in principle agreed with the Soviets helping the DRV but that they 'might not approve of the methods of the Soviet assistance'. He also added that he had urged the military to negotiate with both the Soviet Union and China on how to solve the problem of shipping weapons by rail.[3] Thus, only one year after Le Duan's fruitless trip to the Soviet capital in February 1964, Moscow had made a complete turnabout in its view on the need to support the DRV against the American aggressors. The main problem now was how to arrange the necessary support to the DRV while at the same time keeping a reasonable balance in the relationship with the Chinese.

In 1965 Moscow still depended on Beijing's assistance to fulfil its promises of aid to the DRV. The transport controversy illustrates that. Moscow's intention to fully support the DRV could only be undertaken with a minimum of cooperation from the PRC. At the same time Moscow might still have wanted to include China as a partner in assisting the Vietnamese, both to simplify its own task and to present the Communist movement as a tight ship working together to support the Vietnamese fight for reunification. By implicitly including the Chinese in their plans for assistance, Moscow could also reduce US attention to its own role in Vietnam.

However, if Moscow's intention was to encourage Chinese participation and cooperation in Vietnam, the plan did not have an immediate effect. The Chinese were clearly offended by Soviet claims that they hindered the swift transport of Soviet aid to Vietnam. Deputy Foreign Minister Liu Zhao emphasized that China wanted to have an important role in bringing Soviet aid fast to Vietnam and now felt accused of withholding aid. In spite of the significant increase in assistance from Moscow to Hanoi the Chinese were still sharp in their criticisms. In Beijing in late March the Chinese deputy foreign minister repeatedly asked Soviet ambassador Chervonenko why Moscow did not provide more assistance to the DRV, and whether they planned to increase this assistance. However, on his direct questions on whether the Soviet government intended to send armed forces and staff to the DRV, and whether they intended to build an airfield in China and establish an air bridge, the Soviet ambassador replied that in that case such measures would be presented in a statement from the Soviet government.[4]

Beijing's need for control was not the only reason behind the Sino-Soviet controversies over aid to the DRV. Most of all the Chinese leaders feared that Moscow was ready to enter into negotiations with the United States in Vietnam, and thereby use Vietnam to retain a certain amount of control over China. As a result, they did not understand why the Soviets were in such a rush to prepare military measures, if what they really wanted was to negotiate a peaceful solution to the Vietnamese situation. The Chinese deputy foreign minister asked,

> Why, at a time when the American imperialists continue to bomb Vietnam, keep intensifying the war and the aggressiveness against the DRV, and threaten us and demand that we surrender, cannot the Socialist countries take a strong line against the enemy?[5]

He further added that the Chinese position was not to give in to the enemy, and that since the morale amongst the Vietnamese was high, the assistance of the Soviet Union and China was extremely valuable. Therefore negotiations should, according to the Chinese, be avoided at all costs.[6] The reluctance towards negotiations was a result of the duality in Beijing's position. On the one hand, they wanted the war in Vietnam to intensify. On the other, they were inherently suspicious of all Soviet motives, not least the initiative to negotiate, and viewed them as being targeted against China.

The duality in the Chinese position was also a problem to the Vietnamese. In Hanoi the DRV leaders were eager to prevent Sino-Soviet problems from interfering with their struggle against the United States. In mid-April 1965, when Gromyko asked DRV Foreign Minister Nguyen Duy Trinh about his view on a possible future top-level meeting between the DRV, PRC and the Soviet Union, the foreign minister replied that the Chinese wanted two-way meetings between the Soviet Union and the DRV, and between China and the DRV. According to Nguyen Duy Trinh, the Chinese argued that due to the existence of different positions within the Communist camp the Vietnamese friends should discuss their problems separately with the Soviet Union and China.[7] The Vietnamese seem to have been content with such an arrangement, hoping that, by keeping the rivals separated, the conflict would not interfere with Hanoi's war against the United States.

Sino-Soviet disagreements over how to support the Vietnamese in their struggle for reunification in the 1963–65 period was part of the reason for Vietnam's ascendancy on Moscow's list of foreign policy priorities. During the 1950s and first half of the 1960s, the circumstances in Asia in general, and Indochina in particular, changed considerably, and so did the Soviet view on Vietnam's significance. Three main factors were particularly central in shaping Soviet policies towards Vietnam during this period: Vietnamese policies; Soviet relations with the West and in particular the Americans and, as a part of that, the increased US engagement in Vietnam; and last, but not least, developments in the Sino-Soviet relationship. By early 1964 Sino-Soviet relations had collapsed, and with the possibility of a direct US invasion in Vietnam, Moscow could no longer count on the Chinese to provide the necessary assistance to Vietnam. The threat of a full-scale war in Vietnam, making it a 'hot-spot' of the Cold War superpower rivalry, increased Vietnam's importance in Soviet foreign policies and led to active Soviet involvement starting at the end of 1964.

Thus, by 1964–65 Moscow had reclaimed its role as the strongest member of the triangle, and the Soviet–Vietnamese–Chinese relationship had come full circle. From late 1964 Hanoi received full support from the Soviet Union both financially and in terms of weapons and military advice. Although China still retained an important role due to its proximity to Vietnam, it was no longer in a position to outbid the Soviets in terms of assistance, especially if the Vietnamese decided to combine military struggle with negotiations. Moscow now acted as Hanoi's main partner in the fight for Vietnamese unification after a downfall during the strong pro-Chinese era within the Vietnamese Communist leadership.

Establishing a relationship: Moscow and Hanoi's struggle

While attending a Soviet state banquet in honour of Mao and the signing of the new Sino-Soviet treaty on 16 February 1950, Ho Chi Minh is reported to have asked Stalin, albeit in a joking manner, whether Moscow might consider to sign a treaty along the same lines with the Democratic Republic of Vietnam. Stalin's response was negative, and Ho left Moscow together with the Chinese delegation the day after.[8] Ho Chi Minh's suggestion, as well as Stalin's answer, tell a lot about the different visions about the future relationship between the Soviet Union and the DRV at the beginning of the 1950s. While Ho Chi Minh had clear ambitions of obtaining Stalin's assistance for his struggling country, the Soviet leader had little interest in the situation in Vietnam. The DRV leadership was, in spite of its active pursuit of Soviet aid and advice, not able to secure Moscow's support for a military struggle to reunify Vietnam in the latter part of the 1950s and during the first few years of the 1960s.

The core of the Soviet–Vietnamese relationship began with the settlements in Geneva in the summer of 1954. In classical interpretations, Moscow viewed the Geneva settlements as a major success. The conference had enabled Moscow to further international détente and removed the threat of escalation in Indochina through American military intervention. In addition, the conference provided Moscow with the perfect occasion to introduce China as one of the great powers and possibly also reduce the tensions in China's relationship with the West, especially the United States. More specifically, the conference promoted Soviet objectives in Europe, as it served as an opportunity to undermine the plans for the rearmament of Germany within the planned EDC.[9]

In the first years after Geneva, Soviet policy makers focused on two particular issues in Vietnam: first, the reconstruction of the DRV economy and society and, with it, the development of Socialism in the northern part of Vietnam, and second, the future reunification of the two zones. The Vietnamese were convinced that the Soviet Union, and also China, possessed the models Vietnam needed to develop their country and economy. At the same time it was possible to trace a certain amount of distrust on the Vietnamese side based on a feeling that neither of the two large powers really understood the reality of the situation in Vietnam. The Soviet attitude, on the other hand, was that the Vietnamese, being a younger member of the Socialist camp, should learn from the more experienced members (in particular the Soviet Union). These attitudes might serve as one example of how ideology would come to play a role as part of the Soviet–Vietnamese relationship.

While the DRV leaders looked to the Soviet Union for inspiration in the reconstruction of the country, the Soviets encouraged the DRV government to introduce three- and five-year plans for the DRV economy based on a Soviet model. To develop DRV industry, Moscow provided advisors and skilled labourers who would educate factory workers and government officials to better contribute to the reconstruction of the country. In addition. there were also exchange programmes through which North Vietnamese received training in different Soviet educational facilities and party schools. Thus, from the mid-1950s the Soviets made modest attempts to replicate their domestic system in the DRV. Although this practice took place on a rather small scale, especially due to the different circumstances in the Soviet Union and the DRV, its very existence justifies an image of Soviet expansion in the DRV as geo-ideological.[10]

A new phase in the Soviet–Vietnamese relationship began in the spring of 1956. The Twentieth Congress of the Soviet Communist Party had both a direct and an indirect effect on Soviet–DRV relations. The most visible direct effect was reflected in the introduction of the new Soviet foreign policy line. Introduced in 1955 but reemphasized during the Twentieth Congress, the new foreign policy line with its emphasis on peaceful coexistence was probably one of the main reasons behind the Soviet decision not to insist on the implementation of the political provisions of the Geneva agreement. A more indirect effect was the ideological implications of the revelations of Stalin's mistakes during the congress and its reflections on Sino-Soviet relations. Especially with regard to land reform and the rectification of errors campaign, comments from Lao Dong leaders indicate that Khrushchev's denunciation of Stalinism inspired the Vietnamese Communists to re-examine some of their practices.

The interests of Soviet leaders and Vietnamese Communists with regard to the future development of Vietnam also diverged. Moscow was satisfied with having a Socialist regime in North Vietnam and would not assist the Lao Dong if such assistance could hamper the improvement of Soviet–American relations. Hanoi, on the other hand, considered national reunification its main goal and was slowly realizing that to achieve this goal, Moscow would not be the place to seek support.

One of the major foundations for the Soviet–Vietnamese relationship was a well-functioning Sino-Soviet economic and military cooperation. Even with the signing of several agreements on economic and military cooperation between the Soviet Union and the DRV, Soviet policy makers were inclined to leave most of the practical assistance to the Chinese. The close cooperation between the Soviets and the Chinese in Vietnam during the second half of the 1950s was not without problems, but it was largely successful. Not even the failure to hold the promised all-Vietnamese elections reduced Sino-Soviet cooperation in Vietnam. From a DRV point of view this was clearly a beneficial situation, as it had more to gain from cooperation than competition between the two Communist powers.

In May 1959 Moscow reached a crossroads in its Vietnam policy when the Hanoi leadership announced its decision to complement the diplomatic struggle for reunification with a limited military struggle. The change of strategy in Hanoi was a challenge to Moscow.[11] The decision to authorize, and subsequently expand, an armed insurgency in South Vietnam was made by the Vietnamese Communists without any active involvement from the Soviet Union and in the autumn of 1959 provoked serious Soviet concern. Hanoi's new policies contradicted the Soviet principle of peaceful coexistence, and together with the Chinese leaders the Soviets reacted. After conversations with the DRV leaders during 1959 and 1960, in which the Soviets recommended to Hanoi that they maintain a policy of seeking peaceful reunification of the country, they were under the impression that the Lao Dong had accepted their advice. Leaders in Moscow were content that a possibly dangerous situation in Vietnam had been avoided through cooperation between Moscow and Beijing, who, even at a point when Sino-Soviet disagreements had become quite acute on other matters, agreed on the need to contain the impatient Vietnamese and stop their plans for armed struggle.

Thus, by late 1960 the Soviet leaders had several times made known to the Vietnamese Communists in no uncertain terms that Moscow would not support an armed struggle for reunification of Vietnam. Moreover, it expected the Lao Dong leaders to 'follow' its opinion and proceed with the political struggle. But the Vietnamese Communists had no intention to follow the Soviet line. They continued to build up their military force in the South, and by 1961 the situation had changed significantly. The Vietnamese reluctance to follow Soviet and Chinese advice worried the Soviet leaders, who feared that the aggressiveness of the Vietnamese could trigger a deeper US involvement in Vietnam. This in turn could force the Soviets into a situation in which they would have to reconsider their own position in and strategy towards Vietnam.

Cooperation and coordination: The China factor

From the very beginning of the relationship, Stalin emphasized the important role of China as the link between the Soviet Union and Vietnam. In Stalin's eyes China would be responsible for guiding the Vietnamese revolution. The fact that the PRC, less than three months after its own establishment, recognized the DRV and began to support the Viet Minh in its fight against the French, illustrates how important the Vietnamese revolution was in the eyes of Chinese leaders. To the leaders in Hanoi, however, a direct alliance with the Soviet Union would have been preferable. An alliance with Moscow without the Chinese as intermediaries would have been advantageous from a North Vietnamese point of view, because it would satisfy Hanoi's need for independence from China. In Moscow, however, the geographical distance and Vietnam's lack of strategic importance to the Soviet Union was a good enough argument to leave responsibility in the area in the hands of the Chinese.

Communist China's entrance onto the scene of international politics in 1954 was a significant event within the Communist camp and contributed to a change in Moscow's view of the situation in Vietnam. During Mao's first visit to Moscow in 1950 Stalin had underlined China's important role as the leading Communist power in Asia, reemphasizing the division of labour he had discussed with Liu Shaoqi in July 1949. However, Stalin's division of labour proposal should be viewed with some suspicion. It could have been a sincere description of how Moscow viewed its future position in Asia, with China taking the lead in that part of the world and the Soviets being content with such a division of labour. Another possible explanation could be that Stalin, through such a proposal, wanted to show his trust in the Chinese, while at the same time keeping a certain amount of control of developments in Asia, through his agent China. An equally likely explanation, however, is that Stalin wanted to avoid controlling countries so far away, to minimize Soviet foreign policy risks. Regardless of the reasons behind Stalin's logic in the late 1940s, his thoughts on the respective roles of Beijing and Moscow would come to have serious implications for the future relationship between the Soviet Union, China and the Democratic Republic of Vietnam.

During the first few years of the 1950s the triangular relationship between Moscow, Hanoi and Beijing functioned satisfactorily in the view of all three countries. The DRV received large amounts of assistance through China in the form of equipment, officers and advice. The Soviet Union could follow the situation in Vietnam from a distance, content with the fact that the aid they provided through China was well applied and did not harm Moscow's relations with more important Western countries such as France. The PRC secured itself a leading role in the Communist movement in Asia, acting as provider of equipment, advice and troops to struggles not only in Korea and Indochina but in several other countries as well. In the period leading up to the Geneva conference in 1954 the PRC played a much more active role in Vietnam than the Soviet Union did. Beijing's involvement was important to Hanoi because it secured the DRV's northern border, and to the Soviet Union because it took on responsibilities that were beyond Soviet capacity, or even choices.

During the Geneva conference itself China played an important role, and the results of the conference bear witness to a successful Sino-Soviet cooperation. While the Chinese representatives used their participation at the conference to learn as much as possible about international diplomacy, the Soviet delegation, and Molotov in particular, were full of praise with regard to the role of Chinese chief negotiator Zhou Enlai. Through their quick learning during the conference, and their ability to influence the Vietnamese, the Chinese had shown themselves as invaluable partners to Moscow in dealing with Vietnam. This new situation to some extent enhanced Chinese influence on Soviet policies towards Vietnam and gave the Chinese more leverage in future Soviet decisions regarding Vietnam.

Hanoi accepted the result of the Geneva conference due to considerable pressure from both Moscow and Beijing. Although they were not completely satisfied with the agreement reached at Geneva, the future leaders in North Vietnam accepted its provisions because a ceasefire and temporary partition of Vietnam offered several advantages to the Vietminh. One was the possibility of economic assistance from the Socialist camp, necessary to build Socialism in North Vietnam. Another was that a ceasefire might contribute to achieving international recognition also from non-Communist countries. Third, control of the rice-producing Red River Delta would make the Vietminh able to establish solid state power in the North and build a base for further revolutionary activities if that should prove necessary. However, when discussing the 1954 Geneva conference on later occasions, the Vietnamese and Chinese would jointly accuse the Soviets of having sold out the Vietnamese national interest for their own benefit.[12]

Hanoi's decision from May 1959 to complement the political and diplomatic efforts for reunification with a military struggle evoked a joint negative response in Moscow and Beijing. At the time, and well into the early parts of the 1960s, when disagreements between the Soviets and the Chinese increased, the two governments agreed on the principle of containing the Vietnamese. Notwithstanding the common Sino-Soviet interest in avoiding an international crisis in Vietnam, Khrushchev and Mao had disparate reasons for wanting to contain the Vietnamese. Moscow was concerned with developments in Europe and anxious not to destroy a fragile relationship with the West, whereas Beijing was mostly concerned with its own problematic domestic situation. In the beginning of the 1960s neither of Hanoi's two major allies wanted to deal with a potentially dangerous situation in Vietnam. As a result, they set their differences aside and jointly advised the Vietnamese to hold on to the strategy of diplomatic struggle to reunify their country.

The 1961–62 Geneva conference on Laos was where Soviet and Chinese willingness to put ideological differences aside was most evident. The balance of power between the Soviet Union and China had changed significantly, and so had the situation in Indochina. In the seven years since the last Geneva conference China had strengthened its position within the international Communist movement, and Hanoi had repeatedly displayed its independence from its two large allies. From the point of view of an outsider, the union between the Socialist countries in Geneva would have seemed rather solid. Comments in Soviet documents show that Moscow was irritated with the way the Chinese acted, but at the same time they also show that despite this discomfort, the Soviets insisted on continued Sino-Soviet cooperation with regard to both Laos and Vietnam. Moscow most certainly wanted to continue its cooperation with a strong Chinese state in Asia.

The negotiations over Laos tested the Soviet–Vietnamese relationship, the Soviet–Chinese relationship and the Sino-Vietnamese relationship.[13] In the Sino-Soviet case the distrust that had built up on both sides made it difficult to reconcile views on what constituted a successful conference. However, just like during the one in 1954, the Soviet Union and China shared one vital common goal: to prevent further American interference in Indochina. In 1962 there was only one way to do that, namely to prevent Vietnamese attempts to manipulate the triangular relationship. That, however, could only be done if Moscow and Beijing kept their ideological conflict away from mutual relations in Southeast Asia and worked together to contain the Vietnamese. Soviet policy makers realized that this could only be achieved in cooperation with the Chinese.

By the end of 1963 the Soviet leaders had to acknowledge that the Hanoi leadership had been completely absorbed into the Chinese sphere. Although Moscow initially had wanted the Chinese to take on the major responsibility for developments in Vietnam, the Soviets had still expected to retain a minimum of leverage in Hanoi. The increased Chinese influence in the Lao Dong, and with it the absence of Soviet influence, combined with the growing American engagement in South Vietnam, was of great concern to the Soviet leadership. The first decisive step on the 'road to Beijing' came with Chinese Premier Liu Shaoqi's visit to the DRV in May 1963. The second and final step was the resolution adopted by the Lao Dong Central Committee at its 9th Plenum in December that year. Both events signalled Hanoi's readiness to continue armed struggle to reunify Vietnam with the aid of China, and hence its closeness to the Chinese foreign policy doctrine. With these developments it became increasingly difficult for Soviet embassy officials to keep up the image of a Vietnamese leadership that worked independent of Beijing. By Christmas 1963 the split within the Socialist camp completely dominated relations between Moscow and Hanoi. The pro-Chinese Vietnamese leaders were now in charge of Lao Dong policies, while the neutral and pro-Soviet leaders, and among them Ho Chi Minh, gradually lost influence.

During 1963 and early 1964, Chinese influence in Hanoi reached its highest level during the almost 15-year-long relationship, and Moscow's position was at a low ebb. This situation was a result of Moscow's frustrations with regard to the Soviet–Vietnamese relationship, the troubles with China and the current international situation. The Cuban crisis in October 1962 had shaken those in charge of Soviet foreign policy and made them even more reluctant to involve themselves in Vietnam. All these factors combined with an overall feeling of resignation made Moscow decide that for the time being there was nothing it could do with regard to the Vietnamese situation.

However, while the pro-Chinese Vietnamese gained the upper hand in the Lao Dong Politburo the Soviets did not withdraw from Vietnam. Officials at the Soviet embassy in Vietnam continued to work hard to keep the relationship alive. Such work was welcomed by several Vietnamese Lao Dong leaders who worried that a total dependence on the Chinese would, in time, hurt the Vietnamese cause and emphasized to Soviet officials the need for a stronger Soviet involvement in Vietnam. The problem in 1963 and early 1964 was the discrepancy between the ideas of those working in Vietnam and those in charge of Soviet policies in Moscow. In spite of reports that the Soviet Union had many supporters in Vietnam, Soviet foreign policy makers were reluctant to sacrifice their fragile relationship with the West for the sake of Vietnam. The Vietnamese leaders had now clearly chosen the Chinese as their primary allies, and it was now up to China to provide the necessary assistance.

The change in Soviet policies towards Vietnam came in 1964. From the end of that year the change was visible to everyone, as Hanoi began receiving large amounts of Soviet financial and military assistance. However, it is important to keep in mind that the Soviet change from what might be described as a passive onlooker to an active participant in the Vietnamese struggle for reunification began sometime in early summer 1964, with the Tonkin Gulf incident as the final catalyst. Three main causes can be singled out in an attempt to explain this change in Soviet policies: first, both Hanoi and Moscow from mid-1964 realized that the Americans were about to launch a full-scale invasion of Vietnam. The increased American involvement in Vietnam, represented by the November 1963 assassination of South Vietnamese President Ngo Dinh Diem, the increasing number of American advisors in South Vietnam and the fact that from early 1964 the Americans virtually ruled South Vietnam as a colony, forced the Soviet Union to take the situation in Vietnam much more seriously. By mid-1964 Vietnam had become a focal point in the superpower rivalry. Second, cooperation between the Soviet Union and the PRC had come to a complete stop in all fields, and Moscow had only limited possibilities for supporting the Vietnamese through China. Thus, to retain any influence on developments in Vietnam, the Soviets were forced to engage themselves directly without China serving as an intermediary. The third and final cause is linked to the internal developments in China and the Vietnamese' understanding of these. In 1964 the radicalization of Beijing's political orientation had reached a point at which it would be impossible for Hanoi to rely on Chinese assistance exclusively. As a result, by the end of the year, leaders in Moscow feared that without Soviet assistance and a more active Soviet involvement, it could become impossible to keep a certain amount of control over the situation in Vietnam.

One of the Vietnamese reasons for replacing Beijing with Moscow as main partner was a wish for as many alternatives as possible now that war was coming. The only partner that could offer several different policy options was the Soviet Union. Beijing's harsh refusal to even consider any form of negotiations only added to Hanoi's wish for the Soviet Union as its main ally. Obviously, the possibility of negotiations with the United States as a means to solve the situation in both Laos and Vietnam was a much-debated issue between Soviet and Vietnamese officials in the spring and summer of 1964. Moscow signalled its readiness to support the DRV in case there were to be negotiations.[14] The shift from Beijing to Moscow was a gradual process that began sometime in mid-1964 and was due as much to Vietnamese initiatives as to a change of heart among the Soviet leaders.

Explaining changes: Leverage and ideology

In the 15-year period from 1949 to 1964 the Soviet–Vietnamese relationship went through different stages or phases. These were to a large degree linked to developments in the Sino-Soviet relationship and Soviet perceptions of the

Chinese role in Vietnam. The changes in relations between these three countries must be explained through the use of two different, but related approaches: first, a detailed account based on the basic questions 'what' and 'why', and second, a more theoretical analysis accentuating, for instance, the degree of smaller states' leverage on superpower decisions and the validity of ideology as a useful concept for analysis of international politics.

Hanoi's active and independent policies in its relations with larger allies give substance to the idea that during the Cold War a small, or the so-called peripheral, state could have a significant impact on superpower decisions. Smaller states could act relatively independently of the superpowers and still obtain support. The key term in this regard is *leverage*. The triangular relationship between Moscow, Hanoi and Beijing is particularly intriguing in that regard because of the many possible constellations it included. Until the Chinese began questioning the leading role of the Soviets, the triangle followed the pattern of a hierarchy, with the Soviet Union on the top, China coming second and Vietnam third, but with the Soviets leaving the formulation of policies towards Indochina in the hands of the Chinese. However, as the Chinese gained a more important role internationally, and post-Stalin leaders began to deviate from what Mao considered to be the right course, the Chinese began to see themselves on the same level as the Soviets. As a result the hierarchy between the three states was disturbed, and the Vietnamese were forced – or allowed – to deal with two competing patrons. The Vietnamese initially saw the split as damaging but gradually realized that the Sino-Soviet rivalry could open up possibilities, allowing them to pursue their own independent policies.

Before the change in Moscow's policy towards Vietnam in 1964 the American ideas of a strong Soviet influence on the DRV had little basis.[15] What neither of the superpowers realized was the strength in Hanoi's policies vis-à-vis both its allies and its opponents. New sources show that Hanoi had much impact on the decisions made in Moscow (as well as in Beijing). Lao Dong leaders made their own decisions and often ignored allied advice that stood in contrast to their own plans. That approach, however, was not always displayed in active policy-making but more often through a strategy of withholding essential information that at a later stage would force the Soviet Union (and occasionally China) to go along with plans that they would normally not agree to. Hanoi was able to follow this strategy primarily because Soviet leaders expected the Vietnamese to follow their lead and take their advice and did not pay necessary attention to information suggesting otherwise.

While the issue of smaller states' leverage on the superpowers' policy decisions can explain the impact of Hanoi's independence of it allies, the role of ideology can help explain the changes in alliance partners that took place between the three states during these years. In the classical interpretations of Cold War history ideology was often seen in contrast to realism. The basic idea was that states either pursued ideological goals or were concerned with their security. With regard to Soviet decision-making during the Cold War, strong evidence suggests that concerns for expanding state power (security) and promoting

Communist ideology were merged into one body of thinking in which it was difficult to distinguish one from the other. Ideology became an integrated part of the Soviet perception of security, and vice versa. The two concepts became mutually dependent, hence security and ideology defined the framework of Soviet decision-making. There could, sometimes, be tension between goals derived from real politik and ideology, but usually both considerations had to be reconciled before decisive action could be approved.[16]

Thus ideological beliefs and national interests would not normally stand in opposition to one another, and the political actor did not have to choose one or the other way of thinking. Ideologists could differentiate between conduct based on principles and pragmatic behaviour based on rational calculations, at a given historical moment. Whereas the first would be aimed at achieving the long-term goal of a particular order, the second would be more directly concerned with the short-term survival of a polity. Ideologists would base their final decision on the opportunities and constraints presented by material reality during the pursuit of ideologically defined goals, and ideologists in power would know, or quickly learn, that to obtain the final, long-term goal, ideologies must include technical prescriptions for their realization. Ideology 'does not necessarily exclude the use of reason to determine policies, as many analysts insist'.[17]

In several settings, the 1954 Geneva conference perhaps being the most prominent example, Moscow sincerely thought that the policy it conducted was in the best interests of the Vietnamese Communists themselves. As a result, Soviet policy makers were indifferent to information that suggested the Vietnamese were not as happy with Soviet decisions as they should have been. It is therefore possible to view Soviet actions in Vietnam from a different perspective of success, namely measured on the basis of the current situation in Vietnam, and the Soviet view of what would benefit the Vietnamese struggle the most at the time. In the case of Geneva, one should not discard the possibility that Soviet policy makers reasoned that the results of the conference were appropriate for the current conditions in the DRV and would, in the long term, from a strategic point of view benefit both the development of Socialism in Vietnam and the Vietnamese party. However, such an analysis demands a stronger emphasis on ideology as an explanatory factor in the Soviet–Vietnamese relationship. It also requires us to view Soviet policies towards Vietnam as based not only on evaluations of how this policy would affect Soviet relations with for instance the West but also on a deeper policy level echoing the basic ideological values of the Soviet state.

However, a major problem when using ideological approaches is to explain why ideology sometimes matters, while at other times it does not.[18] This is also a problem when using ideology to analyse the triangular relationship between Moscow, Hanoi and Beijing. Based on the above definition of ideology it is possible to argue that this was one of the engines pushing forward the triangular relationship between Moscow, Hanoi and Beijing in the mid-1950s. The Soviet leaders were convinced that the Vietnamese should learn from their experience, and in many areas Soviet advisors attempted to transmit Soviet ideas and plans to the Vietnamese leadership. Parallel to this there was a strong conviction among the Vietnamese leaders that the Soviet Union and China possessed the models necessary to build and strengthen Vietnamese society. These mechanisms explain why practical cooperation between the Soviets and the Chinese with regard to Vietnam lasted longer than suggested by existing literature and the growing ideological differences at the time. Even during the early years of the 1960s when the polemic between Beijing and Moscow was rather strong and the Soviets had withdrawn their advisors from China, Moscow and Beijing continued to cooperate in Vietnam and Laos. Regardless of the growing distance between the Soviet Union and China, their representatives in Vietnam and Laos agreed to set ideological differences aside to cooperate in supporting the Communist forces in another country.

If Hanoi had been under the influence of only one ideological centre, the case would have been rather straightforward. But the DRV's main problem was that it had close relations with two centres, and both came with the label 'ideological'. At the outset they all shared the same set of beliefs and ideological principles, and we have seen that these principles were compatible during the 1950s and first few years of the 1960s. However, the radicalization of China's Communism combined with the split between Moscow and Beijing seriously complicated Hanoi's situation, and eventually forced it to take sides in the conflict. While Hanoi's decision to authorize the South-based Communists to take up armed struggle in 1959 against Moscow's wishes can be seen as an example of how a relatively small state can act independently of the superpowers, the Soviet decision to give full military, economic and political support to the North Vietnamese from 1964 could be understood on the basis of ideology as a useful concept in international politics.

Soviet polices towards Vietnam in the 15-year period from 1949 until 1964 cannot be properly characterized under one single label. It followed several different tracks: One driven by considerations for the relationship with the United States and Western Europe, another by the fundamental ideological dynamics inherent in the Soviet foreign policy doctrine, and, on yet other occasions, it was influenced by the strong and independent policies of the Vietnamese Communist leadership. If we contend that in the eyes of Soviet policy makers there was not a question of choosing between an interest-based and an ideological position when making decisions regarding Vietnam, we may argue that there was a foreign policy strategy based on a combination of both positions, a concept labelled *ideological realism*. In addition, Moscow was continuously subjected to the strongly independent policies of the Vietnamese communists which functioned as a *pull* factor, showing how this small state at times had a significant impact by forcing Moscow's hand. The combination of these two factors shaped the Soviet–Vietnamese relationship from the very first contact between the two states in 1945–47, until they became close partners in war in late 1964.

Examples of Moscow's *ideological realist* approach include the similarities between Stalin's decision in 1950 to grant China the main responsibility for Vietnam and the Soviet decision of 1964 to support the Vietnamese Communists in their fight against the United States. Stalin's decision in 1950 was based on the assumption that a division of labour would be beneficial to the relationship between Moscow and Beijing. By 1964 the situation had changed completely, and Moscow had experienced a long period of serious problems in its relations with Vietnam. The main cause of these problems was the strong Chinese influence within the North Vietnamese leadership. As an ideologically defined state, the Soviet Union saw threat in terms of the expansion of its adversaries' domestic system. China had now become a hindrance to good Soviet–Vietnamese relations, and to counter the US escalation of warfare in Vietnam, Moscow offered both practical and ideological support. In 1964 China was as much an adversary as the United States.

Soviet policies towards Vietnam were influenced by the moves made in Beijing. Moscow's relations with the West, the American involvement in South Vietnam, the fall of the Diem government and the first bombing raids over North Vietnam – all these factors played important roles in Soviet policy considerations. However, when looking at the Soviet–Vietnamese relationship in the 15-year perspective from the proclamation of the People's Republic of China in October 1949 until the autumn of 1964, the role of China remained a constant and central factor in Moscow's relations with Hanoi. The ups and downs of the Sino-Soviet relationship made a profound impact on the Soviet perception of its role in Vietnam, both in terms of active and more passive support. It was the Chinese Communist victory and the subsequent Chinese recognition of the DRV in January 1950 that forced Stalin to take a more active interest in the country; it was the Vietnamese turn to Beijing that made Moscow scale down its interest in the early 1960s, and finally, the total breakdown of Sino-Soviet relations and the radicalization of Beijing's policies played a vital role when the Soviet leaders in late 1964 decided to give full support to Hanoi in its military struggle against the United States.

Appendix 1: Politburo and Secretariat of the Lao Dong Central Committee

Overview based on information passed on to Soviet officials in Vietnam and Moscow from 1954 to 1964.

1954 (pr. 11 June 1954)[1]

Politburo

Ho Chi Minh
Truong Chinh
Le Duan
Hoang Quoc Viet
Pham Van Dong
Vo Nguyen Giap
Nguyen Chi Thanh
Le Van Luong

Members of the Central Committee

Ton Duc Thang
Phan Ding Khai
Nguyen Long Bang (DRV Ambassador to the Soviet Union 1954–1957)
Chu Van Tang
Hoang Van Hoan
Tran Dang Ninh
Tran Quoc Hoan
Le Thanh Nghi
Nguyen Duy Trinh
Pham Thien Hung
Ung Van Khiem

Candidates for membership in the CC

Nguyen Khang
Nguyen Van Tran
Ha Huy Giap
Ho Viet Thang
Van Dien Dung
Nguyen Van Kinh (DRV Ambassador to the Soviet Union 1957–)
To Huu
Nguyen Chanh
Hoang Anh

1956

Politburo: (pr. 7 September 1956)[2]

Ho Chi Minh (President, Chairman, General Secretary)
Pham Van Dong
Truong Chinh
Vo Nguyen Giap (Commander General PAVN, and Deputy General Secretary)
Hoang Quoc Viet
Le Duc Tho
Nguyen Chi Thanh
'the comrades working in South Vietnam'

Politburo: (pr. 10 December 1956)[3]

Ho Chi Minh
Truong Chinh
Pham Van Dong
Vo Nguyen Giap
Nguyen Chi Thanh
Le Duan (working in South Vietnam)
Le Duc Tho
Hoang Van Hoan
Pham Hung
Nguyen Duy Trinh
Le Thanh Nghi

1957

Politburo: (pr. June 1957)[4]

Ho Chi Minh – president/chairman of the party and general secretary
Truong Chinh – in charge of rectification of errors campaign, ideological
   questions, and the agitation and propaganda department of the CC Lao Dong

Pham Van Dong – the work of the government and economic questions

Vo Nguyen Giap – military questions, assisting Ho Chi Minh in his work

Nguyen Duy Trinh – permanent secretary of the Secretariat, together with Vo Nguyen Giap assisted Ho Chi Minh in his work

Pham Hung – occupied with questions concerning South Vietnam, allocating and organizing people in the South, and also with the leadership's questions regarding the fight for reunification of the country

Le Thanh Nghi – Pham Van Dong's aid in the CC's economic committee

Hoang Van Hoan – currently recovering in Moscow, but normally in charge of work in the National Assembly

Nguyen Chi Thanh – assisting Vo Nguyen Giap in the CC's military committee. In charge of political work within the PAVN

Le Duan – recently back from South Vietnam. Currently preparing a report on the situation and work in Nam Bo

Pham Van Dong, Pham Hung and Nguyen Duy Trinh also part of a commission within the CC working with questions regarding the organization of the government's work.

Members of the Secretariat

Ho Chi Minh
Truong Chinh
Pham Van Dong
Vo Nguyen Giap
Nguyen Duy Trinh

1959

31 members of the Central Committe of the Lao Dong (including those abroad and in South Vietnam)[5]

Politburo

Ho Chi Minh
Pham Van Dong
Vo Nguyen Giap
Le Duan
Truong Chinh
Pham Hung
Hoang Van Hoan
Le Duc Tho
Le Thanh Ngi
Nguyen Chi Thanh

Secretariat

Le Duan
Nguyen Duy Trinh
Pham Hung
Hoan Anh
To Huu

The Committe of South Vietnam (COSVN)

Le Duan (Chairman)

1963

Changes in the leadership according to Ho Chi Minh (25 December 1963)[6]

Ho Chi Minh – retired (according to himself)
Le Duan – party related affairs
Pham Van Dong – governmental issues
Truong Chinh – national assembly-related issues
Xuan Thuy – foreign affairs

Appendix 2: Economic assistance and specialists from the Socialist camp to the DRV, 1955–1962[1]

Year	Received	Used	in %	Aid (non-refundable)
16.07.1955	6.75	6.75	100.0	–
18.07.1955	–	–	–	90.0
01.12.1956	6.75	6.66	98.6	–
07.03.1959	22.5	19.3	85.7	–
14.06.1960	78.75	21.8	27.6	–
23.12.1960	96.75	60.715	62.7	4.5
30.12.1961	3.5	3.6	102.9	–
15.09.1962	10.0	–	0	–
Total	**225.10**	**118.825**	**52.8**	**94.5**

Source: Soviet assistance (p. 60)

Note
* A total of 8 agreements concluded from 1955–1962.

Country	Total amount credit/aid	Non-refundable aid	Long-term credits
Total amount	829.0	328.4	500.6
Soviet part	319.6	94.5	225.1
PRC	411.8	202.5	209.3
GDR	13.5	13.5	–
Poland	15.7	4.2	11.5
Checkoslovakia	15.9	8.0	7.9
Rumenia	39.4	3.4	36.0
Hungary	10.9	1.9	9.0
Bulgaria	2.3	–	2.3

Source: Other Socialist countries' assistance (p. 66)

Note
* Also some minor sums from Mongolia.

Year	Soviet specialists in the DRV	DRV specialists in the Soviet Union
1955	279	–
1956	394	235
1957	165	13
1958	122	11
1959	110	14
1960	181	121
1961	513	121
1962	236	72
1963 (01.09)	195	–

Source: Soviet–DRV exchange of specialists (pp. 65–66)

Appendix 3: Soviet ambassadors to Vietnam, 1954–1965

1954–56: Lavrishchev, Aleksandr Andreevich
1956–57: Zimyanin, Mikhail Vassiljevich
1957–61: Sokolov, Leonid Ivanovitsj (advisor, Soviet embassy DRV, 1954–56)
1961–64: Tovmasyan, Suren Akopovitsj
1964–74: Shcherbakov, Ilya Sergeevich (advisor, Soviet embassy Beijing, 1963–64)

Archives in Moscow, Russia

AVP RF – Arkhiv Vneshnei Politiki Rossiiskoy Federatsii (Foreign Policy Archive of the Russian Federation)

'Fund' is the equivalent to 'collection' in Western archives.

Fund 079	Referentura on Vietnam, 1947–1965
Fund 0100	Referentura on China, 1949–1965
Fund 0445	The Geneva Conference
	1954 (Indochina)
	1961/1962 (Laos)
Fund 0570	Referentura on Laos
Fund 06	Secretariat of Foreign Minister Vyacheslav M. Molotov
Fund 021	Secretariat of Deputy Foreign Minister Valerian A. Zorin
Fund 022	Secretariat of Deputy Foreign Minister Andrey A. Gromyko
Fund 026	Secretariat of Deputy Foreign Minister Vasiliy V. Kuznetsov
Fund 0531	Secretariat of Deputy Foreign Minister Nikolay T. Fedorenko
Fund 0536	Secretariat of Foreign Minister Dimitriy T. Shepilov

RGASPI – Rossiiskii Gosudarstvennyi Arkhiv Sotsial' no-Politicheskoi Istorii (Russian State Archive of Social-Political History)

Fund 74	Kliment Y. Voroshilov, Chairman of the Presidium of the Supreme Council of the Soviet Union
Fund 84	Anastas I. Mikoyan, First Deputy Premier
Fund 17	The Central Committe of the CPSU
* opis 128	Foreign Policy
* opis 3	Decisions of the Politburo, 1919–1952
Fund 558	Josef Stalin

RGANI – Rossiiskii Gosudarstvennyi Arkhiv Noveishei Istorii (Russian State Archive of Contemporary History)

Fund 2   Plenums of the Central Committee of the CPSU
Fund 5   Central Committee of the Communist Party of the Soviet Union
Fund 6   The Committee for Party Control, 1934–1966
Fund 11   Protocol meetings of the commissions of the Central Committee of the CPSU on questions about ideology, culture and international party contacts, 1939–1966
Fund 89   The Communist Party of the Soviet Union on Trial, 1918–1992

Notes

Introduction

1 Quoted in John L. Gaddis, *We Now Know. Rethinking Cold War History*, Oxford: Clarendon Press, 1997, p. 67.
2 Norwegian masters thesis.
3 Mari Olsen, 'Solidarity and National Revolution. The Soviet Union and the Vietnamese Communists, 1954–1960', *Defence Studies 4/97*, Norwegian Institute for Defence Studies: Oslo, 1997.
4 Adam B. Ulam, *Expantion and Coexistence. Soviet Foreign Policy, 1917–1973*, Fort Worth, 1974, p. 699.
5 See also Douglas Pike, *Vietnam and the Soviet Union: Anatomy of an Alliance*, Boulder and London: Westview Press, 1987; Allan W. Cameron, 'The Soviet Union and Vietnam: The Origins of Involvement' in W. Raymond Duncan (ed.), *Soviet Policy in Developing Countries*, Waltham: Ginn-Blaisdell, 1970.
6 An attempt at a different perspective can be found, as the title indicates, in William R. Smyser, 'The Independent Vietnamese: Vietnamese Communism Between Russia and China, 1956–1969', *Southeast Asia Series (55)*, Athens, Ohio: Papers in International Studies, 1980.
7 Olsen, 'Solidarity'; Ilya V. Gaiduk, *Confronting Vietnam. Soviet Policy toward the Indochina Conflict, 1954–1963*, Stanford: Stanford University Press, 2003; and *The Soviet Union and the Vietnam War*, Chicago: Ivan R. Dee, 1996.
8 Olsen, 'Solidarity' especially Chapters 4 & 5.
9 Gaiduk, *Confronting Vietnam*.
10 Gaiduk, *The Soviet Union and the Vietnam War*.
11 The Soviet involvement in Afghanistan will be the most appropriate example in this regard.
12 Benoit de Treglode, 'Premiers contacts entre le Viet Nam et l'Union Sovietique (1947–1948). Nouveaux documents des archives russes', in *Approches – Asie*, No. 19. 1999.
13 Qiang Zhai, *China and the Vietnam Wars, 1950–1975*, Chapel Hill: University of North Carolina Press, 2000; see for example the two articles by Chen Jian, 'China and the First Indochina War, 1950–1954' and 'China's Involvement in the Vietnam War, 1964–1969' in *Mao's China and the Cold War*, Chapel Hill: University of North Carolina Press, 2001; and Ang Cheng Guan, *Vietnamese Communists' Relations with China and the Second Indochina Conflict, 1956–1962*, Jefferson, NC: McFarland & Company, Inc., 1997; and *The Vietnam War from the Other side. The Vietnamese Communists' Perspective*, London: RoutledgeCurzon, 2002.
14 For the dominant view of this conflict before the new sources were released, see John Gitting's *Survey of the Sino-Soviet Dispute, 1963–1967*, London, 1968; Donald S. Zagoria, *The Sino-Soviet Conflict 1956–1961*, Princeton, NJ: Princeton University Press, 1962; Donald S. Zagoria, *Vietnam Triangle: Moscow, Peking, Hanoi*, New York:

Pegasus, 1967; Peter Jones and Sian Kevill (comps.), Alan J. Day (ed.), *China and the Soviet Union, 1949–1984*, Harlow, 1985.

15 Of more recent works, see Vladislav Zubok and Constantine Pleshakov, *Inside the Kremlin's Cold War. From Stalin to Khrushchev*, Cambridge, Mass: Harvard University Press, 1996 and Odd Arne Westad (ed.), *Brothers in Arms: The Rise and Fall of the Sino-Soviet Alliance, 1945–1963*, Washington, D.C: Woodrow Wilson Center Press, 1998. The largest collection of articles and documents related to the Sino-Soviet relationship can be found in the Cold War International History Project Bulletin, published from the Woodrow Wilson Center in Washington, D.C. See in particular issues 6–7 and 8–9 on the Cold War in Asia.

16 Recent examples are Yang Kuisong, 'Changes in Mao Zedong's Attitude toward the Indochina War, 1949–1973', *CWIHP Working Paper No. 34*; Odd Arne Westad, Chen Jian, Stein Tønnesson, Nguyen Vu Tung and James G. Hershberg (eds), '77 Conversations between Chinese and Foreign Leaders on the Wars in Indochina, 1964–1977', *CWIHP Working Paper No. 22*; Stephen J. Morris, 'The Soviet–Chinese–Vietnamese Triangle in the 1970's: The View from Moscow', *CWIHP Working Paper No. 25*; see also 'The Cold War in Asia', *CWIHP Bulletin 6/7* – Winter 1995.

17 Mark Philip Bradley, *Imagining Vietnam and America. The Making of Post-Colonial Vietnam, 1919–1950*, Chapel Hill: University of North Carolina Press, 2000.

18 Robert K. Brigham, *Guerrilla Diplomacy: The NLF's Foreign Relations and the Viet Nam War*, Itacha: Cornell University Press, 1999.

19 Until 1999 this archive was called the Russian Center for the Preservation and Study of Documents on Recent History (Rossiyskiy tsentr khraneniya i izucheniya dokumentov noveishey istorii (RTsKhIDNI))

20 Until 1999 this archive was called the Storage Center for Contemporary Documents (Tsentr khraneniya sovremennoy dokumentatsii (TsKhSD)).

21 Unfortunately, large sections of the International Department of the RGANI have been closed for researchers during most of the 1990s.

22 Since I first came to work in the Moscow archives in May 1994 there have been many changes in the rules for access. For the AVP RF, several categories of documents that were available in the first years, such as the conversations of the Soviet embassy employees, have since been reclassified. Also, it has been increasingly difficult to obtain photocopies from the archives, especially in the later years.

23 With the term 'classical schools of interpretation' I mean 'traditionalism', 'revisionism' and 'post-revisionism'.

24 Olsen, 'Solidarity'; Gaiduk, *Confronting Vietnam*.

25 The leverage of smaller states in international politics has been labelled 'pericentrism', and was introduced as a supplementary approach to the study of the Cold War by Tony Smith in the article 'New Bottles for New Wine: A Pericentric Framework for the Study of the Cold War', *Diplomatic History*, Vol. 24, No. 4 (Fall 2000). 'Pericentrism' has its origin from periphery and emphasises the junior actors of the international system, and their role as 'pull factors' – dragging the Great Powers into new areas of conflict. I will argue that pericentrism might also work as a suitable common heading for explanatory factors labelled, for example, 'Third World' in O.A. Westad's Bernath Lecture in 2000, in which he uses the superpower involvement and alliance building in, for example, the Third World as one possible paradigm or means to understad the Cold War as an international system; see, O.A. Westad, 'The New International History of the Cold War: Three (Possible) Paradigms', *Diplomatic History*, Vol. 24, No. 4 (Fall 2000), 2000a. A similar argument, under the heading 'alliances', can be found in Westad's 'Secrets of the Second World: The Russian Archives and the Reinterpretation of Cold War History', *Diplomatic History*, Vol. 21, No. 2 (Spring 1997). A similar concept, however, is Geir Lundestad's 'Empire by Invitation', explaining the role of the West European states as pull factors when the United States engaged itself

in Europe after the Second World War; in Geir Lundestad, *The American 'Empire' and Other Studies of U.S. Foreign Policy in a Comparative Perspective*, New York, 1990.

26 Both archive-based monographs on the Cold War and the numerous attempts to conceptualize new trends in Cold War research emphasize the rebirth of ideology as an interpretative tool. See, for example, Gaddis, *We Now Know*; Zubok and Pleshakov, *Inside the Kremlins Cold War*; Vojtech Mastny, *The Cold War and Soviet Insecurity: The Stalin Years*, Oxford: Oxford University Press, 1996; Sergei Goncharov, John Wilson Lewis and LitaiXue, *Uncertain Partners: Stalin, Mao, and the Korean War*, Stanford, CA: Stanford University Press, 1993; on theoretical interpretations of the Cold War and the impact of ideology, see, for example, Douglas J. Macdonald, 'Formal Ideologies in the Cold War: Toward a Framework for Empirical Analysis' in O. A. Westad (ed.), *Reviewing the Cold War: Approaches, Interpretations, Theory*, London: Frank Cass Publishers, 2000b; Westad, 'Secrets of the Second World' and 'The New International History of the Cold War: Three (Possible) Paradigms'.

27 Mastny, *The Cold War and Soviet Insecurity*, p. 9.

28 Nigel Gould-Davies, 'Rethinking the Role of Ideology in International Politics during the Cold War', *Journal of Cold War Studies*, Vol. 1, No. 1 (Winter 1999), p. 92.

29 William C. Wohlforth, 'A Certain Idea of Science. How International Relations Theory Avoids the New Cold War History', *Journal of Cold War Studies*, Vol. 1, No. 2 (Spring 1999), p. 52.

1 Choosing sides: The Democratic Republic of Vietnam and the World, 1945–1949

1 The full Vietnamese name for this organization was Viet Nam Doc Lap Dong Minh, or Vietminh for short (League for National Independence).

2 For a detailed account of the events in Vietnam in the fall of 1945, see David Marr, *Vietnam 1945: The Quest for Power*, Berkeley: University of California Press, 1995 and Stein Tønnesson, *The Vietnamese Revolution of 1945. Roosevelt, Ho Chi Minh and de Gaulle in a World at War*, London: Sage, 1991.

3 See Goscha, Christopher E., *Thailand and the Southeast Asian Networks of the Vietnamese Revolution 1885–1954*, London: Curzon Press, 1999, p. 236.

4 Ho Chi Minh sent a series of cables to Truman in the period from 29 September 1945 to 28 February 1946, see Bradley, Mark Philip, *Imagining Vietnam and America. The Making of Post-Colonial Vietnam, 1919–1950*, Chapel Hill: University of North Carolina Press, 2000, p. 237, n. 56; also Igor V. Bukharkin has identified a telegram from Ho to Stalin dated 22 September 1945, see Igor V. Bukharkin, 'Moscow and Ho Chi Minh, 1946–1969', paper presented at the *CWIHP conference* 'New Evidence on the Cold War in Asia', Hong Kong, January 1996.

5 Goscha, *Thailand and the Southeast Asian Networks*, pp. 249–251.

6 Ibid., pp. 236–238.

7 According to Bradley, *Imagining Vietnam*, p. 153, the office opened in late summer 1946, where as others have argued that it was established as early as 1945. See Goscha, *Thailand and the Southeast Asian Networks*, pp. 236; for the notion that the office was in operation from April 1947 see Luu Van Loi, *50 Years of Vietnamese diplomacy, 1945–1995, Vol. 1 (1945–1975)*, Hanoi: The Gioi Publishers, 2000, p. 94.

8 Bradley, *Imagining Vietnam*, pp. 123–125.

9 Ibid., p. 146.

10 Ibid., p. 129.

11 The archival collection *Referentura po V'etnamu* in the AVP RF (Foreign Policy Archive of the Russian Federation) was established in 1947, which may serve as an indication that relations became more frequent from this year onwards. Also in the party archive RGASPI (now the Russian State Archive of Socio-Political History) the

first mention of Vietnam is in 1947, when the Soviet delegation at the Asian Relations Conference in New Delhi brought back information conveyed by Tran Van Giau, a member of the Central Committee of the Vietnamese Communist Party. See 'Short Report on the Soviet Delegations' Participation at the Asian Relations Conference in India', written by comrades Zhukov and Plishevskii, 14 May 1947, RGASPI, Fund (f.) 17, Opis (op.) 128, delo (d.) 405, p. 26.

12 The lack of an initial before the last name Zhukov allows for some speculation as to which Zhukov we are talking about. There were several Zhukov's within the foreign ministry bureaucracy in the late 1940s, but none of these seem to have been working with Asian affairs at this time. I therefore suggest that the person in question was Evgenii Michailovich Zhukov. He was an acknowledged historian specializing on Asia and his role during the Asian conference in mid-November 1947 (which has been established in the literature), as well as several articles on the role of the October Revolution in the East, indicates that he might very well have been trusted with the position as head of the Soviet delegation to the conference in New Delhi. Although no one has placed him as a participant at the New Delhi conference, he did, according to Charles B. Mclane, visit India in the spring of 1947. He has also been referred to as the leading Soviet spokesman on colonial affairs in the immediate postwar period. See Charles B. Mclane, *Soviet Strategies in Southeast Asia. An Exploration of Eastern Policies under Lenin and Stalin*, Princeton, NJ: Princeton University Press, 1966, pp. 251 and 256.

13 'Short Report on the Soviet Delegation's Participation at the Asian Relations Conference in India' written by comrades Zhukov and Plishevskii, 14 May 1947, RGASPI, f. 17, op. 128, d. 405, pp. 17–27.

14 Ibid., p. 26.

15 According to William J. Duiker the Soviet Union recognized Indonesia in 1947. See W.J. Duiker, *Ho Chi Minh: A Life*, New York: Hyperion, 2000, p. 421. However, according to the findings in German historian Ragna Boden's ongoing Ph.D. project on 'Soviet policy towards Indonesia, 1945–65' (Philipps-Universität Marburg) the Soviet Union recognized Indonesia (then in the form of the USI: United States of Indonesia) on 25 January 1950. This is documented in a letter from Gromyko to Indonesian foreign minister Mohammed Hatta. They agreed to exchange ambassadors, although only by the end of 1953, and the exchange took place in 1954.

16 Pike, *Vietnam and the Soviet Union*, p. 31.

17 Mclane, *Soviet Strategies*, p. 367.

18 Ibid., p. 274.

19 Ulam, *Expantion and Coexistence*, p. 449.

20 Pike, *Vietnam and the Soviet Union*, p. 32. Quotation marks in the original text.

21 Mclane, *Soviet Strategies*, pp. 351–353.

22 Walter LaFeber, *America, Russia, and the Cold War, 1945–1996*, New York: McGraw-Hill, 1997, pp. 70–71.

23 Mclane, *Soviet Strategies*, pp. 354–355. The nine nations that established the Communist Information Bureau were all European, and throughout its existence the Cominform had no formal members from either Asia, Africa or the Americas.

24 Duiker, William J., *Ho Chi Minh: A Life*, New York: Hyperion, 2000, pp. 420–423.

25 Record of conversation, A.G. Kylazhenkov – Pham Ngoc Thach, 9 September 1947, Arkhiv Vnesjnei Politiki Rossiskoi Federatsii [Foreign Policy Archive of the Russian Federation] (AVP RF), Fund (f.) 079 (Vietnam), Opis (op.) 1, Papka (pa.) 1, delo (d. 1), pp. 33–36.

26 Ibid., pp. 34. I have found no confirmation of support in the literature on Chinese assistance to the Vietminh of support as early as 1947. It is, however, possible that this support could have been offered through the Hong Kong branch of the CCP or by Chinese Communist guerrilla forces in the Chinese–Vietnamese border areas as early as 1947, although there is no concrete evidence of this. See Chen Jian, *Mao's*

China and the Cold War, Chapel Hill: University of North Carolina Press, 2001, pp. 119–120.

27 In several different contexts during 1947 and 1948, the Russians and their Vietnamese contacts use the name Vietnamese Communist Party (VCP) – 'Kompartii Vietnama' – when communicating in Russian. In Vietnamese history books the official name is Indochinese Communist Party (Dang Cong San Dong Duong) until the name was changed to Vietnamese Workers Party (VWP) or Lao Dong in 1951. The name 'Vietnamese Communist Party' did not become the official party name until 1976.

28 Ibid. AVP RF, f. 079, op. 1, pa. 1, d. 1, pp. 35–36.

29 Mclane, *Soviet Strategies*, p. 273. According to a report from the Southeast Asia Department in the Soviet foreign ministry in January 1947, French domestic policies were partly to blame for the situation France was dealing with in Vietnam. The Soviet analysts argue that the only thing worse than France's own problems in Vietnam was the possibility of mediation between the Chinese (in this case the Guomindang) and the United States with regard to Vietnam. See SEAD report 'About the latest events in Viet Nam' – 10 January 1947, AVP RF, f. 079, op. 1, pa. 1, d. 1, pp. 2–9.

30 Record of conversation, A.G. Kylazhenkov – Pham Ngoc Thach, 9 September 1947, AVP RF, f. 079, op. 1, pa. 1, d. 1, pp. 35–36. Pham Ngoc Thach refers to the Vietnamese Communist Party (in Russian – 'Kompartii Vietnama').

31 Ibid., p. 36. Pham Ngoc Thach played an important role in setting up DRV relations with non-Communist countries in Asia. He had been a close associate of Tran Van Giau in Saigon and was a close confidant of Ho Chi Minh. For more bibliographical data see: Goscha, *Thailand and the Southeast Asian Networks*, p. 388.

32 Mclane, *Soviet Strategies*, p. 432.

33 Ibid., pp. 357–358.

34 Ibid., p. 359.

35 I have not been able to find any documentation on the Calcutta conference among available materials in either the RGASPI or the AVP RF, but that does not exclude the possibility that such records exist in still restricted materials or in yet to be explored archives such as the archive of the youth organization Komsomol. According to German historian Ragna Boden, documents on Calcutta in RGASPI (f. 17, op. 128, d. 1069, No. 36: On sending a Soviet youth delegation to Calcutta) were still classified in 2002.

36 Mclane, *Soviet Strategies*, pp. 359–360.

37 Le Hy did not refer to the DRV.

38 Record of conversation, M.Sh. Bakhitov – Le Hy, 31 August 1948, AVP RF, f. 079, op. 2, pa. 1, d. 1, pp. 1–2

39 Ibid., p. 2. Once again Le Hy refers to the 'Vietnamese Republic' rather than the DRV. and in Communist circles is referred to as 'partijnikh kommunisticheskikh krugov' – in the Russian original.

40 Ibid., p. 3.

41 Record of conversation, S.S. Nemtchin – Nguyen Duc Quy, 21 September 1948, AVP RF, f. 079, op. 2, pa. 1, d. 2, p. 25.

42 Tréglodé, Benoît de, 'Premier contacts entre le Viet Nam et l'Union Sovietique (1947–1948). Noveaux documents des archives russes', *Approches – Asie*, No. 19, 1999, p. 134.

43 Goscha, *Thailand and the Southeast Asian Networks*, p. 295.

44 Record of conversation, Soviet envoy to Thailand, Sergei Sergeevitch Nemtchin – Head of the Vietnamese delegation in Southeast Asia Nguyen Duc Quy, 21 September 1948, AVP RF, f. 079, op. 2, pa. 1, d. 2, pp. 23–26.

45 Goscha, *Thailand and the Southeast Asian Networks*, pp. 298–299 refers to a V. Chuong that most probably was a highly trusted Communist cadre who worked with shifting the ICP's network from Thailand to China in 1948.

46 Record of conversation, S.S. Nemtchin – Nguyen Dyc Quy, 21 September 1948, AVP RF, f. 079, op. 2, pa. 1, d. 2, p. 24.

47 Ibid., p. 25.

48 Record of conversation, Soviet Attache in Thailand I.G. Ysatchov – Nguyen Duc Quy, 28 September 1948, AVP RF, f. 079, op. 2, pa. 1, d. 2, pp. 27–28.
49 Qiang Zhai, *China and the Vietnam Wars, 1950–1975*, Chapel Hill: University of North Carolina Press, 2000, p. 10; Sophie Quinn-Judge, *Ho Chi Minh: The Missing Years, 1919–1941*, Berkeley: University of California Press, 2003, Chapter 2.
50 Qiang Zhai, *China and the Vietnam Wars*, pp. 11–12; according to Chen Jian, *Mao's China*, technical difficulties and the lack of reliable telegraphic communications prevented contact between the Chinese and Vietnamese Communist leaderships in the period from 1946 to 1949. However, the ICP and the CCP had established telegraphic communication late in 1947, but, for technological reasons, this channel of communication had never been stable (pp. 120, 328 n. 8); for the Vietnamese claim that the CCP had offered assistance as early as 1947, see record of conversation, A.G. Kylazhenkov – Pham Ngoc Thach, 9 September 1947, AVP RF, f. 079, op. 1, pa. 1, d. 1, p. 34.
51 Record of conversation, S.S. Nemtchin – Nguyen Duc Quy, 3 October 1948, AVP RF, f. 079, op. 2, pa. 1, d. 2, p. 30.
52 Ibid.
53 de Tréglodé, 'Premier contacts', p. 135; de Tréglodé's study has later been complemented by Christopher Goscha's article 'La survie diplomatique de la RDVN: Le doute sovietique efface par la confiance chinoise (1945–1950)?', in *Approches – Asie*, No. 18, 2003. In this article, Goscha argues that the road to recognition of the DRV was significantly more difficult on the Communist side than what has previously been known. He further argues that it was the victory of the Chinese Communists in October 1949 that reintegrated revolutionary Vietnam into a European Communist setting as the European Communists initially distrusted the Vietnamese Communists and Ho Chi Minh. Thus, Communist China's confidence in the Vietnamese Communists reduced (or even eliminated) the initial Soviet doubt.
54 Memorandum 'The establishment and activities of the marionette government in Vietnam', by the Southeast Asia Department, 20 September 1949, AVP RF, f. 079, op. 3, pa. 2, d. 5, p. 111.
55 Yang Kuisong, 'Changes in Mao Zedong's Attitude toward the Indochina War, 1949–1973', *CWIHP Working Paper No. 34*, p. 4.

2 Setting the stage: The Soviet Union, China and the First Indochina War, 1949–1953

1 Yang Kuisong, 'Changes in Mao Zedong's Attitude toward the Indochina War, 1949–1973', *CWIHP Working Paper No. 34*, Washington, D.C., February 2002, p. 4.
2 Niu Jun, 'The Origins of the Sino-Soviet Alliance' in O.A. Westad (ed.) *Brothers in Arms. The Rise and Fall of the Sino-Soviet Alliance, 1945–1963*, Washington, D.C.: Woodrow Wilson Center Press, 1998, p. 71.
3 Jonathan D. Spence, *The Search for Modern China*, New York and London: W.W. Norton & Company, 1990, pp. 514–533.
4 Spence, *The Search for Modern China*, p. 524; Duiker, William J., *Ho Chi Minh: A Life*, New York: Hyperion, 2000, p. 419.
5 Niu Jun, 'The Origins of the Sino-Soviet Alliance' in Westad (ed.) *Brothers in Arms*, p. 73.
6 Duiker, *Ho Chi Minh*, pp. 420–422.
7 When working with the early years and especially in 1949–50 one has to be very careful as the international events that took place in that period were extremely complicated, particularly concerning relations between the Soviet Union, the PRC and Vietnam. Available sources contain plenty of contradictory and clearly false information concerning events and dates.
8 Luu Van Loi, *50 Years of Vietnamese Diplomacy, 1945–1995, Vol. 1 (1945–1975)*, Hanoi: The Gioi Publishers, 2000, p. 97.

9 Luu Van Loi, 50 *Years of Vietnamese Diplomacy*, pp. 97–98. The region allegedly mentioned by Stalin is the area bordering Laos that was later used to establish the Ho Chi Minh trail. However, Stalin probably could not distinguish Vietnam from Indochina, thus the comment sounds strange.

10 Soviet embassy in Beijing to MID. Memorandum on the politico-economic situation in DRV, 18 January 1952, AVP RF, f. 079, op. 7, pa. 4, d. 14, p. 96.

11 The first Vietnamese ambassador to the Soviet Union, Nguyen Long Bang, arrived in Moscow in April 1952. The first Soviet ambassador to the DRV, Aleksandr Andreevich Lavrishchev, arrived shortly after the conclusion of the Geneva conference in July/August 1954.

12 Qiang Zhai, *China and the Vietnam Wars, 1950–1975*, Chapel Hill: University of North Carolina Press, 2000, pp. 14–15.

13 Ibid., p. 15.

14 Ibid.; Duiker, *Ho Chi Minh*, p. 422.

15 Goncharov, Sergei N., John W. Lewis, and Xue Litai, *Uncertain Partners: Stalin, Mao, and the Korean War*, Stanford, 1993, p. 107.

16 For a Russian article about the history of Vietnamese studies in Russia, see Anatolii A. Sokolov, 'From the History of Vietnam Studies in Russia', in *Traditional Vietnam. A Collection of Articles* (Moscow, 1996). This historiographical article presents the different stages and themes within the study of Vietnam and Indochina in Russia from the earliest times up to 1996. The increase in Soviet scholarly work on Vietnam is also decribed by Mclane, Charles B., *Soviet Strategies in Southeast Asia. An Exploration of Eastern Policies under Lenin and Stalin*, Princeton, NJ: Princeton University Press, 1966, pp. 435–437. Mclane underlines the emphasis put on the Chinese Communist victory in the Soviet scholarly works.

17 K. Michailov to Zorin, 12 February 1950, AVP RF, f. 079, op. 4, pa. 2, d. 2, pp. 1–2.

18 Qiang Zhai, *China and the Vietnam Wars*, p. 17; Chen Jian, *Mao's China*, p. 120; for an account of Ho's meeting with Stalin in Moscow see Luu Van Loi, *50 Years of Vietnamese Diplomacy*, pp. 97–98. The dates of Ho's arrival and departure from Moscow differ significantly in the sources; for this account I have chosen to rely on the above dates for his visit to Moscow.

19 Vyshinski's diary. Reception for the ambassador of the DRV, Nguyen Long Bang, 22 April 1952, AVP RF, f. 079, op. 7, pa. 3, d. 4, pp. 1–2.

20 The Indochina Communist Party (ICP) was established in 1930. After February 1951 its name was changed to Vietnamese Worker's Party (VWP or Dang Lao Dong Viet Nam – Lao Dong for short). Although ICP was the official name of the party until 1951, we have already seen how, in communication with Soviet representatives during the latter part of the 1940s and early 1950s, the Vietnamese used the name Vietnamese Communist Party ('Kompartii Vietnama') instead of the correct title ICP.

21 Chen Jian, *Mao's China*, pp. 121, 123–124; Qiang Zhai, *China and the Vietnam Wars*, pp. 15, 19–20. The Vietnamese would have accepted Luo as ambassador as early as 1950, but the Chinese wanted to delay his official appointment because the ongoing fighting in Vietnam made it inappropriate for the DRV to receive formal representatives from foreign countries.

22 When he arrived in Moscow in April 1952, the first DRV ambassador, Nguyen Long Bang, provided first-hand information on the unstable situation in the DRV capital at that time. The same situation applied for the two years between 1950 and 1952 and prevented the establishment of a Soviet or Chinese embassy. See Vyshinski's diary. Reception for the ambassador of the DRV, Nguyen Long Bang, 22 April 1952, AVP RF, f. 079, op. 7, pa. 3, d. 4, pp. 1–2. However, it should be emphasized that the Chinese found a way around this and established separate military and political missions in the DRV in the early 1950s. See Qiang Zhai, *China and the Vietnam Wars*, Chapter 1.

23 Record of conversation, Andrei Gromyko – PRC ambassador to the Soviet Union, Wang Jiaxiang, 22 February 1950, AVP RF, f. 079, op. 4, p. 2, d. 2, pp. 36–37. A copy

of this conversation was sent to all members of the Politburo. See also Decisions of the Politburo, 17 March 1950, RGASPI, f. 17, op. 3, d. 1080, p. 55, pkt. 256. 'Accept the suggestion of MID USSR to agree with the proposition that the PRC embassy in the USSR represent the interests of the DRV in the Soviet Union.'

24 Michailov and G. Tynkin to Vyshinsky, 1 April 1950, AVP RF, f. 079, op. 4, pa. 2, d. 2, p. 42.

25 S. Mhitarjan to MID. Annotation to the information given by the unofficial DRV representative in Canton, Gao Hyn Lin, on the situation in Vietnam in April 1951, 28 July 1951, AVP RF, f. 079, op. 6, pa. 3, d. 4, pp. 32–34.

26 The Soviet foreign ministry archive set up a separate fund for Vietnam in 1947. Until after the Geneva conference in the summer of 1954 the fund mainly consists of materials gathered by Soviet representatives in China and materials produced by MID in Moscow. First-hand reports on conditions in Vietnam were rare until the first Soviet Ambassador, Aleksandr Andreevich Lavrishchev, arrived in Hanoi in late September 1954.

27 Telegram from M. Bakhitov (Beijing) to V.A. Zorin, 2 June 1950, AVP RF, f. 079, op. 4, pa. 2, d. 2, pp. 66–67. See also Decisions of the Politburo, letter from Vyshinski to Hoang Minh Giam, 30 January 1950, RGASPI, f. 17, op. 3, d. 1079, pkt. 372, addendum No. 1, l. 206. In the letter Vyshinski confirmed that he had received the letter of 14 January about recognition from Ho Chi Minh. After looking through the proposal from the DRV government, and taking into account that the DRV represented the majority of the Vietnamese population, the Soviet Union made the decision to establish diplomatic relations between the Soviet Union and the DRV and 'exchange envoys' (obmenjat'sja poslannikami). Notwithstanding the Soviet decision to exchange envoys the Vietnamese continued to want an ambassador but could not push it yet.

28 Duiker, *Sacred War*, pp. 70–71.

29 Extracts from the French press on the issue of recognition, 1950, AVP RF, f. 079, op. 4, pa. 2, d. 2, p. 33.

30 S. Mkhitarian (2nd secretary Southeast Asia Department). Extracts from the international press regarding Soviet recognition of the DRV, 10 March 1950, AVP RF, f. 079, op. 4, pa. 2, d. 2, pp. 44–59.

31 Soviet embassy in Beijing to MID. Memorandum on the politico-economic situation in the DRV, 18 January 1952, AVP RF, f. 079, op. 7, pa. 4, d. 14, pp. 30–97 (conclusion, pp. 95–97).

32 GRU – the Soviet acronym for the Soviet military intelligence (foreign and domestic); in English the Main Intelligence Directorate.

33 The date on the document indicating when it was originally written, and the filing date set by the foreign ministry archivists, could be weeks, and sometimes even months, apart. This does not necessarily mean that the document did not reach its recipient in due time, but it indicates that Moscow, particularly in the early period, considered this only one of several sources on the topic. There is of course also a possibility that excerpts of the document had been delivered earlier alone or together with oral information.

34 Soviet Consulate in Canton to MID, 'The situation in Vietnam in April 1951' (a report presented to the consulate by DRV representatives in Canton), 15 June 1951, AVP RF, f. 0100, op. 44, pa. 338, d. 148, p. 6.

35 Ibid., p. 7.

36 This was the name that the Vietminh army adopted in 1950.

37 Chen Jian, *Mao's China*, pp. 123–124; Qiang Zhai, *China and the Vietnam Wars*, p. 19.

38 Qiang Zhai, *China and the Vietnam Wars*, p. 26; Chen Jian, *Mao's China*, pp. 124–127.

39 Chen Jian, *Mao's China*, p. 128; Qiang Zhai, *China and the Vietnam Wars*, pp. 33–34.

40 Soviet embassy Beijing to MID. Memorandum on the politico-economic situation in DRV, 18 January 1952, AVP RF, f. 079, op. 7, pa. 4, d. 14, p. 95.

41 Ibid., AVP RF, f. 079, op. 7, pa. 4, d. 14, p. 95.

42 Qiang Zhai, *China and the Vietnam Wars*, p. 35.

43 Ibid., pp. 36–37.
44 Ibid., p. 37.
45 Diplomaticheskii Slovar', Vol. I – III, Moskva: Izdatel'stvo 'Nauka', 1986, p. 269.
46 Vyshinski's diary. Reception for the ambassador of the DRV, Nguyen Long Bang, 22 April 1952, AVP RF, f. 079, op. 7, pa. 3, d. 4, pp. 1–2.
47 Light infantry weapons are handweapons, smaller cannons, but not larger cannons and anti-air artillery.
48 'PRC and DRV', report, 8 June 1954, AVP RF, f. 079, op. 9, pa. 8, d. 19, pp. 38–39.
49 According to Duiker, *Ho Chi Minh*, pp. 420–422, Stalin had harboured doubts about Ho Chi Minh's own ideological orthodoxy for many years and became especially suspicious when Ho sought to establish a relationship with the United States in the months immediately following the Pacific War. Stalin also disliked how the ICP formally abolished itself in November 1945. According to Duiker, Stalin's suspicion became particularly obvious in 1947 when the Soviet Union granted recognition to Indonesia, but not the DRV, perhaps because he doubted that the Vietminh would be victorious against the French. (However, as shown in Chapter 1 of this study, the Soviet Union did not recognize Indonesia until January 1950). During Ho's visit to Moscow in early 1950, Stalin's dislike of him was clearly on display, and it was only due to Chinese pressure that Stalin agreed to recognize the DRV. Apparently one of the reasons why Stalin changed his mind on this issue, and proclaimed his readiness to support the DRV, was to prevent a possible Beijing – Washington alliance.
50 The only reference to this trip in the Russian archives can be found in correspondence between Ho and Stalin before and immediately after Ho's stay in Moscow. See letters from Ho Chi Minh to Stalin (Filippov) and letters from Stalin to Ho Chi Minh, 30 September, 17 October and 19 November 1952, RGASPI, f. 558 (Stalin), op. 11, d. 295.
51 Chinese historian Qiang Zhai, *China and the Vietnam Wars*, p. 38, has not been able to find any details on these talks in Chinese archives.
52 Ho Chi Minh to Stalin (Filippov) and letters from Stalin to Ho Chi Minh, 30 September, 17 October and 19 November 1952, RGASPI, f. 558 (Stalin), op. 11, d. 295.
53 From March until November 1953, V.V. Kuznetsov held the position as Soviet ambassador to the PRC parallel to his post as deputy foreign minister. He remained in his post as first deputy foreign minister until 1977.
54 Record of conversation, V.V. Kuznetsov – Zhou Enlai, 16 June 1953, AVP RF, f. 0100, op. 46, pa. 362, d. 12, pp. 112–113.
55 Qiang Zhai, *China and the Vietnam Wars*, pp. 38–42. The results of the land reform and its implications for the Sino-Vietnamese relationship will be discussed in Chapter 4.

3 The end of the war and the Geneva conference, 1953–1954

1 Chen Jian, *Mao's China and the Cold War*, Chapel Hill: University of North Carolina Press, 2001, p. 131.
2 Stanley Karnow, *Vietnam: A History*, London: Pimlico, 1991, pp. 207–208.
3 See e.g. Chen Jian, 'China and the Indochina Settlement at the Geneva Conference of 1954'. Paper presented at the Symposium on 'The First Indochina War: Nationalism, Colonialism, and the Cold War', 1–3 November 2002, at the Lyndon B. Johnson Library and Museum, Austin, Texas, p. 31. [Cited with the written permission of the author, Ang 2002]. According to Chen Jian, Zhou Enlai made a particularly important independent decision during the last days of the conference when he persuaded both the Soviets and especially the Vietnamese to change the Communist demand on the demarcation line from the 16th to the 17th parallel.
4 Qiang Zhai, 'China and the Geneva Conference of 1954', *The China Quarterly* (129), 1992, p. 121.

5 Gaiduk, Ilya V., *Confronting Vietnam. Soviet Policy toward the Indochina Conflict, 1954–1963*, Stanford: Stanford University Press, 2003, pp. 49–50, argues that Moscow threw the Vietnamese over in 1954. The Geneva Conference and the use of the DRV as a pawn in a Great Power game serves as a perfect example of this.

6 Chen Jian, *Mao's China*, pp. 133–134.

7 The abbreviation SVN (State of Vietnam) will be used for South Vietnam until the referendum and proclamation of the Republic of Vietnam (RVN) on 23 October 1955.

8 In a later account of the Geneva conference, Soviet analysts underlined that 'the first days in Geneva showed that the People's Republic of China, as a great power, was not only interested in deciding the urgent international problems in Asia and other parts of the world, but also ready to actively take part in solving these problems'. See 'The Geneva Conference and PRC', SEAD report, 11 February 1955, AVP RF, f. 0100, op. 48, pa. 408, d. 136, p. 4.

9 Record of conversation, Molotov – John Foster Dulles (US Secretary of State), 13 February 1954, AVP RF, f. 06, op. 13a, pa. 25, d. 7, pp. 31–32.

10 Record of conversation, V.V. Kuznetsov (Soviet Deputy Foreign Minister) – Charles Bohlen (U.S. ambassador), 17 March 1954, AVP RF, f. 026, op. 2, pa. 4, d. 2, p. 42.

11 Ibid.

12 Foreign Minister Molotov's report to the CPSU Central Committee Plenum on the Geneva Conference, 24 June 1954, see RGANI, f. 2, op. 1, d. 94; or download from: http://www.fas.harvard.edu/~hpcws/index_f.htm (Harvard Project on Cold War Studies).

13 Record of conversation, V.V. Kuznetsov – Charles Bohlen, 19 March 1954, AVP RF, f. 026, op. 2, pa. 4, d. 2, pp. 49–50.

14 They based their reports and recommendations on conversations between the Soviet ambassador in Beijing and Chinese officials, as well as on reports and analytical documents written by Soviet embassy officials in China.

15 Chen Jian, *Mao's China*, p. 140.

16 Many states had recognized the PRC, including the UK, India and Norway, but not France or the United States. In addition, the PRC had not yet got access to the United Nations, as ROC (Taiwan) represented China in that forum.

17 Chen Jian, 'China and the Indochina Settlement', pp. 4–5. In his speeches, Zhou used the carrot and stick analogy, arguing that the carrot should be used to tempt the French, while the stick should be used to deal with the Americans.

18 Qiang Zhai, *China and the Vietnam Wars*, p. 50; Chen Jian, 'China and the Indochina Settlement', pp. 4–5.

19 Qiang Zhai, *China and the Vietnam Wars*, pp. 50–51.

20 Excerpts from Molotov's diary: Reception for Chinese Ambassador Zhang Wentien, 6 March 1954, AVP RF, f. 0100, op. 47, pa. 379, d. 5, pp. 10–15; see also Qiang Zhai, *China and the Vietnam Wars*, pp. 51–52.

21 SEAD memorandum to Molotov, Gromyko, Zorin, Novikov, Federenko, Sobolov, Soldatov and Lavrishchev , 17 March 1954, AVP RF, f. 0100, op. 47, pa. 389, d. 107, p. 5.

22 Ibid., pp. 5–6.

23 Ibid., p. 6.

24 Ibid., pp. 6–7. The perceptive reader has probably already wondered about my use of the terms 'Vietnam' and 'Indochina' in the last few paragraphs. My use of the territorial names here reflects the Soviet background document for these arguments.

25 Ibid., AVP RF, f. 0100, op. 47, pa. 389, d. 107, p. 7.

26 The International Control Commission was set up during the Geneva conference. It consisted of members from Poland, Canada and India, with India holding the chairmanship. Its task was to supervise the fulfilment of the Geneva Conference and a separate commission was set up for each of the three Indochinese countries – Vietnam, Laos and Cambodia.

27 Before, during and after the conference, the Chinese perceived the Soviets as somewhat pessimistic with regard to what could be achieved in Geneva. See Qiang

Zhai's argument that in contrast to the Chinese the Soviets expected rather little from the final outcome of the conference. Qiang Zhai, 'China and the Geneva Conference of 1954', p. 121.

28 MID USSR – Plans for discussions with Zhou Enlai and Ho Chi Minh, 4 April 1954, AVP RF, f. 022, op. 7b, pa. 106, d. 7, pp. 23–26. These plans contained among other things references on how to relate to France, the question of Vietnamese partition, as well as the necessity to include the clause demanding the end to US interference. However, by early April the Soviet position seems clearer and more articulated.

29 Komitet Informatisii report to Kirill Novikov from N. Solodovnik, 16 July 1954, AVP RF, f. 079, op. 9, pa. 8, d. 19, pp. 120–121.

30 MID USSR – Plans for discussions with Zhou Enlai and Ho Chi Minh, 4 April 1954, AVP RF, f. 022, op. 7b, pa. 106, d. 7, pp. 23–24.

31 Ibid.

32 Ibid.

33 Ibid.

34 Record of conversation, General-Lieutenant Petruschevskii – a Chinese official, top secret – one copy only, 30 March 1954, AVP RF, f. 079, op. 9, pa. 7, d. 15, p. 61.

35 Ibid.

36 Deputy foreign minister V. Zorin to Foreign Minister Molotov, 16 January 1954, AVP RF, f. 06, op. 13a, pa. 35, d. 159, p. 3.

37 The contents of ambassador Nguyen Long Bang's report was used in background materials for the Geneva conference, but the report was first handed in to the Soviet foreign ministry on 14 May 1952. Komitet Informatsii report 'The People's Republic and the Democratic Republic of Vietnam', 8 June 1954, AVP RF, f. 079, op. 9, pa. 8, d. 19, pp. 28–48. For a more detailed discussion of the report, see Chapter 2.

38 William J. Duiker, *The Communist Road to Power in Vietnam*, Boulder, CO: Westview, 1981, pp. 154–160; Young, Marilyn B., *The Vietnam Wars, 1945–1990*, New York: HarperPerennial, 1991, pp. 30–33; Qiang Zhai, *China and the Vietnam Wars*, pp. 43–44.

39 For a detailed account of Chinese preparations for Dien Bien Phu, see Chen Jian, *Mao's China*, pp. 131–138 and Qiang Zhai, *China and the Vietnam Wars*, pp. 43–49.

40 The classic work on Dien Bien Phu is Bernhard Fall's, Hell in a Very Small Place: the Siege of Dien Bien Phu, London, 1967; see also Duiker, *The Communist Road*, pp. 160–162.

41 Qiang Zhai, *China and the Vietnam Wars*, p. 46

42 Ibid., p. 49. During the first part of the conference from 26 April to 7 May 1954, the participants tried to solve the problems in Korea. Randle 1969: 157–168.

43 On the Chinese stand, see e.g. Qiang Zhai, *China and the Vietnam Wars*, p. 52.

44 On the question of Chinese, Korean and DRV participation, we have seen that the Soviets took a much tougher stand. From the very beginning, they argued that China should play an important role during the conference. Soviet preparatory materials for the conference also clearly state that DRV participation was self-evident. See SEAD memorandum to Molotov, Gromyko, Zorin, Novikov, Federenko, Sobolov, Soldatov and Lavrishchev, 17 March 1954, AVP RF, f. 0100, op. 47, pa. 389, d. 107, p. 5; and also MID USSR – Plans for discussions with Zhou Enlai and Ho Chi Minh, 4 April 1954, AVP RF, f. 022, op. 7b, pa. 106, d. 7, pp. 23–26.

45 Robert F. Randle, *Geneva 1954. The Settlement of the Indochinese War*, Princeton, NJ: Princeton University Press, 1969, p. 8.

46 Chen Jian, 'China and the Indochina Settlement', pp. 11–12.

47 Chen Jian, *Mao's China*, pp. 140–141.

48 Foreign Minister Molotov's report to the CPSU Central Committee Plenum on the Geneva Conference, 24 June 1954, RGANI, f. 2, op. 1, d. 94, p. 21.

49 Qiang Zhai, *China and the Vietnam Wars*, p. 57.

50 Foreign Minister Molotov's report to the CPSU Central Committee Plenum on the Geneva Conference, 24 June 1954, RGANI, f. 2, op. 1, d. 94, p. 19.

51 Chen Jian, 'China and the Indochina Settlement', p. 12.
52 The citation is taken from Qiang Zhai, *China and the Vietnam Wars*, p. 55.
53 Qiang Zhai, *China and the Vietnam Wars*, pp. 52–53.
54 Ibid., p. 52.
55 'The Geneva Conference and PRC', 11 February 1955, AVP RF, f. 0100, op. 48, pa. 408, d. 136, pp. 13–27; and Foreign Minister Molotov's report to the CPSU Central Committee Plenum on the Geneva Conference, 24 June 1954, RGANI, f. 2, op. 1, d. 94.
56 Qiang Zhai, *China and the Vietnam Wars*, pp. 60–61.
57 Chen Jian, *Mao's China*, pp. 142–143; Qiang Zhai, *China and the Vietnam Wars*, p. 60.
58 Qiang Zhai, *China and the Vietnam Wars*, pp. 60–61.
59 Komitet Informatisii report to Kirill Novikov from N. Solodovnik, 16 July 1954, AVP RF, f. 079, op. 9, pa. 8, d. 19, p. 123.
60 Chen Jian, 'China and the Indochina Settlement', p. 16.
61 Qiang Zhai, *China and the Vietnam Wars*, p. 61; Christopher E. Goscha, 'Vietnam or Indochina? Contesting Concepts of Space in Vietnamese Nationalism, 1887–1954', Nias Reports, No. 28, Nordic Institute for Asian Studies, 1995, pp. 145–146.
62 'The Geneva Conference and the PRC', 11 February 1955, AVP RF, f. 0100, op. 48, pa. 408, d. 136, p. 14.
63 Ibid., p. 16.
64 Record of conversation, V.V. Vaskov – Mao Zedong, 5 July 1954, AVP RF, f. 0100, op. 47, pa. 397, d. 7, pp. 69–70.
65 Chen Jian, 'China and the Indochina Settlement', pp. 22–25.
66 Luu Van Loi, *50 Years of Vietnamese Diplomacy, 1945–1995, Vol. 1 (1945–1975)*, Hanoi: The Gioi Publishers, 2000, p. 122.
67 Chen Jian, 'China and the Indochina Settlement', pp. 26–27.
68 Foreign Minister Molotov's report to the CPSU Central Committee Plenum on the Geneva Conference, 24 June 1954, RGANI, f. 2, op. 1, d. 94.
69 Ibid., pp. 25–27.
70 'The Geneva Conference and the PRC', 11 February 1955, AVP RF, f. 0100, op. 48, pa. 408, d. 136, p. 21.
71 Ibid., pp. 25–27.
72 Rumours say that delegates to the conference stopped the clock in the Palais de Nations to help Mendès-France keep his deadline.
73 Vietminh was the name of the Vietnamese patriots fighting the French from 1946 to 1954, which were in effect the Communist armed forces. After the Geneva conference the armed forces of the DRV were organized into the People's Army of Vietnam (PAVN). In 1960, when the National Liberation Front of South Vietnam was founded, many of its founding members were former Vietminh soldiers. Stanley I. Kutler (ed.) Encyclopedia of the Vietnam War, New York: Charles Scribner's Sons, 1996, p. 565.
74 Randle, *Geneva 1954*, p. 596. Article 14 (a) in the Agreement on the Cessation of Hostilities in Viet Nam.
75 Randle, *Geneva 1954*, pp. 570–571. Article 6 and 7 in the Final Declaration.
76 The Final Declaration was positively agreed to by four out of the nine participants at the conference, Great Britain, France, the Soviet Union and China.
77 Young, *The Vietnam Wars*, pp. 41–42.
78 Randle, *Geneva 1954*; J.L. Nogee and R.H. Donaldson, *Soviet Foreign Policy since World War II* (3rd edn), New York: Pergamon Press, 1988, pp. 110–111; Cameron, Allan W., 'The Soviet Union and Vietnam: The Origins of Involvement' in W. Raymond Duncan (ed.), *Soviet Policy in Developing Countries*, Waltham: Ginn-Blaisdell, 1970, pp. 189–196; Qiang Zhai, 'China and the Geneva Conference of 1954', p. 113.
79 Westad, Odd Arne, Chen Jian, Stein Tønnesson, Nguyen Vu Tung and James G. Hershberg (eds), '77 Conversations between Chinese and Foreign Leaders on the Wars in Indochina, 1964–1977', *CWIHP Working Paper No. 22*, 1998, p. 42.

4 Together for Communism? Sino-Soviet cooperation and the rebuilding of North Vietnam, 1954–1957

1 Record of conversation, Zimyanin – Li Zhimin, June/July 1956, AVP RF, f. 079, op. 11, pa. 13, d. 5, p. 149.
2 Joseph Buttinger, *Vietnam. A Political History*, London: Andre Deutch, 1969, pp. 415–429; Gabriel Kolko, *Anatomy of a War*, New York: Pantheon Books, 1985, pp. 22–71. According to a report from the Komitet Informatsii in late December 1954 Ho Chi Minh had many supporters in the South. Information gathered from different news correspondents reporting from Saigon and foreign press releases indicated that Ho would receive 90 per cent of the votes in South Vietnam if there were to be general elections at that time. Komitet Informatsii to Novikov, 29 December 1954, AVP RF, f. 079, op. 9, pa. 7, d. 16, pp. 117–130.
3 Young, Marilyn B., *The Vietnam Wars, 1945–1990*, New York: HarperPerennial, 1991, p. 45.
4 Ambassador Lavrishchev was already well acquainted with the situation in Vietnam, as well as with its leaders, from his participation at the Geneva Conference.
5 Molotov to Lavrishchev, 30 September 1954, AVP RF, f. 079, op. 9, pa. 6, d. 8, pp. 23–26.
6 Ibid.
7 The Lien Viet (Unified National Front) was founded in 1946, reorganized in 1951, and in 1955 renamed the Vietnam Fatherland Front (VNFF). Ralph B. Smith, *An International History of the Vietnam War: Vol. 1, Revolution versus Containment, 1955–61*, New York: St. Martin's Press, 1983, pp. 62–64. The development of the VNFF is described in Carlyle A. Thayer, *War By Other Means. National Liberation and Revolution in Viet-nam 1954–60*, Sydney: Allen and Unwin, 1992, pp. 27–32, 40–43, 46–48.
8 Molotov to Lavrishchev, 30 September 1954, AVP RF, f. 079, op. 9, pa. 6, d. 8, pp. 23–26.
9 Ibid.
10 Herring, George C., *America's Longest War: The United States and Vietnam, 1950–1975*, New York: John Wiley & Sons, 1979, pp. 47–48.
11 Herring, *America's Longest War*, p. 48.
12 In South Vietnam there were three large religious sects: the Binh Xuyen, whose armed elements were in control of Cholon, in the area nearby Saigon, and the Cao Dai and the Hoa Hao, both of whom literally ran states within the state. It was the American decision of 31 December 1954, to support South Vietnam directly rather than channelling the aid via France, that enabled Diem to take control over the sects. The shift in American policies strengthened Diem and weakened the sects, as it deprived them of the financial support they had received through the French. Herring, *America's Longest War*, p. 51; Thayer, *War By Other Means*, pp. 21–22.
13 Novikov to Molotov, 29 July 1954, AVP RF, f. 06, op. 13a, pa. 35, d. 156, pp. 1–2.
14 When the government in Hanoi feared that serious famine was about to hit the country in late 1954 and early 1955, it turned to Moscow and Beijing for assistance. The October harvest had failed, and since partition the DRV was deprived of the important food supplies from southern Vietnam. The critical situation was eventually solved by shipping rice from China on Soviet ships to the DRV; see record of conversation, Novikov – DRV Ambassador to the Soviet Union Nguyen Long Bang, 28 October 1954, AVP RF, f. 079, op. 9, pa. 6, d. 5, p. 78; and MID to the CC CPSU, 29 October 1954, AVP RF, f. 079, op. 9, pa. 6, d. 8, p. 10.
15 Record of conversation, Novikov – Pham Van Dong, AVP RF, 27 July 1954, f. 06, op. 13a, pa. 35, d. 158, p. 46.
16 Novikov to Molotov, 29 July 1954, AVP RF, f. 06, op. 13a, pa. 35, d. 156, p. 2.
17 Ibid.; Molotov to Lavrishchev, 30 September 1954, AVP RF, f. 079, op. 9, pa. 6, d. 8, pp. 23–26.

18 V.V. Kuznetsov to Molotov, 11 January 1955, AVP RF, f. 079, op. 10, pa. 10, d. 15, pp. 1–2.
19 Instructions for negotiations with the governmental delegation from the DRV, June/July 1955, AVP RF, f. 022, op. 8, pa. 117, d. 30, pp. 12–21 [Hereafter Instructions June/July 1955].
20 Instructions June/July 1955: 12.
21 For estimates of Soviet assistance to India, see Ramesh Thakur and Carlyle A. Thayer, *Soviet Relations with India and Vietnam*, London: MacMillan, 1992.
22 A total of eight agreements on long-term credits and non-refundable aid were signed in the years from 1955 to 1962. For Soviet overviews of assistance to the DRV both from the Soviet Union and other Socialist countries see, 'Economical, trade and cultural relations between the Soviet Union and the Democratic Republic of Vietnam', SEAD memorandum, 3 December 1963, AVP RF, f. 079, op. 18, pa. 39, d. 24, pp. 58–79. For the main figures in this document, see Appendix; an earlier estimate of Soviet assistance to the DRV can be found in Thakur and Thayer, *Soviet Relations with India and Vietnam*, pp. 189–192.
23 Instructions June/July 1955: 12–21; by 1955 Chinese–North Vietnamese military cooperation was already well organized. When established on April 17, 1950 the Chinese Military Advisory Group (CMAG) consisted of advisors that could assist the People's Army of Vietnam (PAVN) headquarters, three full divisions, and finally an officers training school. Altogether the CMAG would count 281 people – of which 79 were advisors and their assistants. See Qiang Zhai 2000: 19.
24 General Antonov to Deputy Foreign Minister V.A. Zorin, 10 June 1955, AVP RF, f. 079, op. 10, pa. 9, d. 8, p. 32.
25 Ibid.
26 Record of conversation between General-Lieutenant Petruschevskii – a Chinese official, top secret – one copy only, 30 March 1954, AVP RF, f. 079, op. 9, pa. 7, d. 15, p. 61.
27 Qiang Zhai, *China and the Vietnam Wars, 1950–1975*, Chapel Hill: University of North Carolina Press, 2000, p. 74.
28 Ang Cheng Guan, *Vietnamese Communists' Relations with China and the Second Indochina Conflict, 1956–1962*, Jefferson, NC: McFarland & Company, Inc., 1997, pp. 13–18.
29 V.A. Zorin to the CC CPSU, 23 September 1955, AVP RF, f. 079, op. 10, pa. 9, d. 8, p. 57. The memo to the CC CPSU only contains references to the withdrawal of political and economic advisors and does not include the military advisors. However, as the military advisors played a very important role, it is safe to assume that the ambassador was referring to these as well. Keeping the Chinese military advisors in place was even more valuable to the Soviets than keeping the other advisors. This was because the Soviets had always been cautious about introducing Soviet military advisors into Vietnam, first of all not to offend the Chinese, who had a much longer tradition of supporting the Vietnamese in that field, and second to avoid increased US focus on North Vietnam.
30 V.A. Zorin to the CC CPSU, 23 September 1955, AVP RF, f. 079, op. 10, pa. 9, d. 8, p. 57.
31 Record of conversation, L.I. Sokolov – Chinese Ambassador to the DRV, Luo Guibo, 8 December 1955, AVP RF, f. 079, op. 10, pa. 9, d. 5.
32 Chen Jian, *Mao's China and the Cold War*, Chapel Hill: University of North Carolina Press, 2001, p. 206; see also Qiang Zhai, *China and the Vietnam Wars*, p. 74.
33 Ulam, Adam B., *Expantion and Coexistence. Soviet Foreign Policy, 1917–1973* (2nd edn) Fort Worth: Holt, Rinehart and Winston, 1974, pp. 558–560.
34 Randle, Robert F., *Geneva 1954, The Settlement of the Indochinese War*, Princeton, NJ: Princeton University Press, 1969, p. 571.
35 George M. Kahin, *Intervention: How America became Involved in Vietnam*, New York: Knopf, 1986, p. 93.
36 Thayer, *War By Other Means*, pp. 21–23, 37–40, 48–49.

37 Kolko, *Anatomy of a War*, p. 85; David L. Anderson, *Trapped By Success. The Eisenhower Administration and Vietnam, 1953–61*, New York: Colombia University Press, 1991, pp. 125–128; Thayer, *War By Other Means*, pp. 48–49.
38 Thayer, *War By Other Means*, pp. 71–73.
39 Record of conversation, Zimyanin – Pham Hung, 23 March 1956, AVP RF, f. 079, op. 11, pa. 13, d. 5, pp. 36–38.
40 On the situation of fulfilling the Geneva Agreement – short information, 11 (13) August 1956, AVP RF, f. 079, op. 11, pa. 14, d. 16, p. 98.
41 Record of conversation, Soviet Deputy Foreign Minister, V.V. Kuznetsov – General Secretary of the Lao Dong, Truong Chinh, 28 February 1956, AVP RF, f. 079, op. 11, pa. 13, d. 2, p. 3.
42 Ibid.
43 Record of conversation between Zimyanin – Pham Hung and Ung Van Khiem, 20 April 1956, AVP RF, f. 079, op. 11, pa. 13, d. 5, p. 75.
44 Ibid.
45 Ibid., pp. 75–77.
46 According to Truong Chinh the Vietnamese had now realized that the chances of convening a new Geneva conference were slim. See record of conversation between Soviet Deputy Foreign Minister, V.V. Kuznetsov – General Secretary of the Lao Dong, Truong Chinh, 28 February 1956, AVP RF, f. 079, op. 11, pa. 13, d. 2, pp. 3–8.
47 Ambassador Zimyanin's thoughts were expressed in a memorandum entitled 'Some questions on the fulfillment of the Geneva agreement on Indochina', 2 April 1956, AVP RF, f. 79, op. 11, pa. 14, d. 16, p. 58.
48 'Some questions on the fulfillment of the Geneva agreement on Indochina', 2 April 1956, AVP RF, f. 79, op. 11, pa. 14, d. 16, p. 62.
49 Smith, *An International History*, pp. 64–67; see also Ang Cheng Guan, *Vietnamese Communists'*, p. 28.
50 Ang Cheng Guan, *Vietnamese Communists'*, pp. 27–28.
51 See e.g. Jonathan R. Adelman and Deborah A. Palmieri, *The Dynamics of Soviet Foreign Policy*, New York: Harper and Row Publishers, 1989, pp. 149–150; Ulam, *Expantion and Coexistence*, pp. 572–599; Nogee, J.L. and R.H. Donaldson, *Soviet Foreign Policy since World War II* (3rd edn), New York: Pergamon Press, 1988, pp. 119–126; Michael Kort, *The Soviet Colossus. A History of the USSR*, New York: Routledge, 1990, pp. 239–241.
52 According to Chen Jian and Yang Kuisong, Mao Zedong and other CCP leaders later complained repeatedly that Khrushchev's secret speech came as a surprise to the CCP and other Communist parties. See 'Chinese Politics and the Collapse of the Sino-Soviet Alliance' Westad, Odd Arne (ed.), *Brothers in Arms: The Rise and Fall of the Sino-Soviet Alliance, 1945–1963*, Stanford, 1998, p. 260 and n. 73.
53 Ambassador Suren Akopovich Tovmasyan to MID, 17 October 1961, AVP RF, f. 079, op. 12, pa. 31, d. 3, p. 44. To exemplify the Vietnamese attitude the report underlines that the Vietnamese did not want to show a Soviet film critical to Stalin. According to Politburo member Le Duc Tho showing such a film could lead to new discussions on the errors committed during land reform. Nor did the Lao Dong share the opinion of the Soviet Union and other fraternal countries with regard to Albania. According to officials at the Soviet embassy Ho Chi Minh gave the impression of feeling sorry for Enver Hoxha. The political letter is concluded by underlining that 'Ho Chi Minh is, despite his weaknesses, a friend. The embassy recommends that the contact between the two countries be strengthened in all fields.'
54 Smyser, William R., *The Independent Vietnamese: Vietnamese Communism Between Russia and China, 1956–1969*, Athens, Ohio: Papers in International Studies, Southeast Asia Series (55), 1980, p. 6.
55 Record of conversation between Soviet Ambassador Mikail Vassiljevich Zimyanin – Nguyen Duy Trinh, 27 April 1956, AVP RF, f. 079, op. 11, pa. 13, d. 5, pp. 84–95.

In this conversation Nguyen Duy Trinh presents the discussion during the 9th Plenum of the Lao Dong CC (quote from p. 93); see also Smyser, *The Independent Vietnamese*, pp. 5–12. These pages contain a discussion of Hanoi's reaction to the Twentieth Congress.

56 In 1956 Le Duan held the position of regional secretary in Nam Bo, which was the southernmost region of the Party's political apparatus in Vietnam. Brigham, Robert K., *Guerrilla Diplomacy: The NLF's Foreign Relations and the Viet Nam War*, Itacha: Cornell University Press, 1999, p. 7.

57 Thayer, *War By Other Means*, pp. 57–59.

58 Record of conversation, Soviet Ambassador Mikail Vassiljevich Zimyanin – Nguyen Duy Trinh, 27 April 1956, AVP RF, f. 079, op. 11, pa. 13, d. 5, p. 95.

59 Record of conversation, M.V. Zimyanin – Nguyen Duy Trinh, 27 April 1956, AVP RF, f. 079, op. 11, pa. 13, d. 5, pp. 90–91.

60 Ibid. p. 85.

61 According to Thayer, *War By Other Means*, pp. 67–68, parts of the proposal were approved and would allow a consolidation of the party's forces and provide a basis for 'political violence' should that ever become necessary. However, such steps were only to be undertaken by cadres in the South using their own resources in accordance with the programme of the Fatherland Front.

62 Anastas Mikoyan allegedly made full reports from all his trips abroad. I have so far not been able to localize these reports, nor have I seen other researchers refer to them.

63 According to Ang Cheng Guan the lack of a joint communiqué at the end of Mikoyan's visit suggests that the Vietnamese and the Russians could not reach a unity of views. See Ang Cheng Guan, *Vietnamese Communists*, p. 21. An explanation as just could be that the working character of the trip did not call for such communiqué.

64 Record of conversation, M.V. Zimyanin – Pham Van Dong, 18 May 1956, AVP RF, f. 079, op. 11, pa. 13, d. 5, pp. 117–118. Pham Van Dong reveals that he has not completely understood Mikoyan's ideas on the tempo of the DRV's transition into a Socialist state. According to the ambassador this would be worked out as soon as the Three-Year plan for the DRV's national economy was ready.

65 Record of conversation, M.V. Zimyanin – Nguyen Duy Trinh, 27 April 1956, AVP RF, f. 079, op. 11, pa. 13, d. 5, p. 95.

66 Record of conversation, M.V. Zimyanin – Truong Chinh and Nguyen Duy Trinh, 16 August 1956, AVP RF, f. 079, op. 11, pa. 13, d. 6, pp. 55–58.

67 Record of conversation, M.V. Zimyanin – Nguyen Duy Trinh, 27 April 1956, AVP RF, f. 079, op. 11, pa. 13, d. 5, pp. 84–95. Accounts of this situation in available Soviet documents confirm the notion that Ho's position within the party remained the same, and was not in any way endangered by the revelations during the rectification of errors campaign.

68 Record of conversation, Sulinov – representative in charge of economic and financial questions at the PM's office, Buy Kong Chung, 29 October 1956, AVP RF, f. 079, op. 11, pa. 13, d. 8, pp. 57–60. Soviet official Sulinov has no title in the document or any organisational affiliation. His inquiries into the internal affairs of the DRV, and the fact that he has no title or organization may indicate that he represents either the GRU or the CPSU.

69 Record of conversation, Zimyanin – Li Zhimin, June/July 1956, AVP RF, f. 079, op. 11, pa. 13, d. 5, p. 149.

70 Edwin E. Moise, *Land Reform in China and North Vietnam: Consolidating the Revolution at the Village Level*, Chapel Hill, NC: University of North Carolina Press, 1983, p. 4.

71 Moise, *Land Reform in China and North Vietnam*, p. 5.

72 Buttinger, *Vietnam*, pp. 418–419.

73 Young, *The Vietnam Wars*, p. 50; Karnow, Stanley, *Vietnam: A History*, London: Pimlico, 1991, pp. 240–241; Buttinger, *Vietnam*, pp. 425–437.

74 The most careful estimate indicating between 3,000 and 15,000 executions was made by Moise 1983. Fall, Bernard B., *The Two Viet-Nams. A Political and Military Analysis*,

London and Dunmow: Pall Mall Press, 1963, on the other hand, operates with a much higher figure – 50,000 executions. See also Young, *The Vietnam Wars*, p. 50.

75 Moise, *Land Reform in China and North Vietnam*, p. 237.

76 Record of conversation, Zimyanin – Ho Chi Minh, 10 August 1956, AVP RF, f. 79, op. 11, pa. 13, d. 6, pp. 38–40.

77 Land reform in North Vietnam was based much on the experiences had in China and had also to some degree been supervised by Chinese advisors. See record of conversation, Zimyanin – Nguyen Duy Trinh, 28 August 1956, AVP RF, f. 79, op. 11, pa. 13, d. 6, pp. 75–85; see also Moise, *Land Reform in China and North Vietnam*, p. 238. Moise's book compares land reform in China and Vietnam and is the most extensive study on the topic.

78 Record of conversation, Zimyanin – Ho Chi Minh, 7 September 1956, AVP RF, f. 79, op. 11, pa. 13, d. 6, p. 93.

79 His birth name was Dang Xuan Khu.

80 P.J. Honey, *Communism in North Vietnam*, Cambridge, Mass: MIT Press, 1963, pp. 43–46; Edwin Moise has modified the view that the DRV went disastrously wrong due to slavish imitation of the Chinese land reform. He argues that Chinese influence is real and that the Vietnamese reform was based on Chinese models, but the Lao Dong did not copy these models precisely/correctly and that the mistakes made were due to misconduct of the reform and not because they imitated the Chinese. See Moise, *Land Reform in China and North Vietnam*, pp. 234–236.

81 Record of conversation, Zimyanin – Ho Chi Minh, 7 September 1956, AVP RF, f. 79, op. 11, pa. 13, d. 6, p. 93. This was also about the same time as Le Duan came up north.

82 Record of conversation, Soviet chargé d'affaires A.M. Popov – Nguyen Duy Trinh, 25 October 1956, AVP RF, f. 079, op. 11, pa. 13, d. 8, p. 54.

83 Extract from the journal of Soviet chargé d'affaires, A.M. Popov, 10 December 1956, AVP RF, f. 079, op. 11, pa. 13, d. 8, pp. 93–99.

84 In a June 1957 reference to the Lao Dong Politburo members Le Duan is listed as recently back from South Vietnam, currently preparing a report on the situation in Nam Bo. Pham Hung is listed as occupied with questions concerning South Vietnam, allocating and organizing people in the South, and in charge of the leadership's questions regarding the fight for reunification of the country. See record of conversation, Zimyanin – Nguyen Duy Trinh, 12–14 June 1957, AVP RF, f. 079, op. 12, pa. 17, d. 5, pp. 220–235. Le Duc Tho's role and his strengthened position in 1956 are underlined by R.B. Smith, *An International History*, 1983: 66. Tho is, however, not mentioned as a Politburo member in 1957 but reappears in 1959.

85 The disturbances were caused by religious discrimination against the local Catholic community, which had increased during the conduct of land reform. Members of the Catholic community were advised by an ICC Fixed Team to petition for regrouping to the south. The ICC Fixed Teams were groups with members from all the three ICC countries – Poland, India and Canada – which supervised and controlled that the provisions of the Geneva agreement were followed in both zones, especially the ceasefire agreement. When villagers assembled to present their grievances to the Canadian member of the ICC FT, the local militia attempted to disperse the demonstrators. These attempts proved ineffective, and reinforcements were called in. As a result violence broke out and shots were fired. All attempts at mediation failed. Finally troops were sent in to control the demonstrators and arrest the leaders. The numbers killed and injured remain unknown, but according to the official version 'several persons were killed and many more were wounded'. Thayer, *War By Other Means*, pp. 94–95. Quote from p. 95.

86 Record of conversation, A.M. Popov – Nguyen Duy Trinh, 19 November 1956, AVP RF, f. 079, op. 11, pa. 13, d. 8, pp. 75–76.

87 A. Gromyko to the CC CPSU, 17 October 1956, AVP RF, f. 022, op. 9, pa. 134, d. 56, p. 1.

88 Copy from the Embassy's Yearly report from 1956, AVP RF, f. 079, op. 12, pa. 17, d. 19, p. 80 – found in a document dated 12 November 1960, AVP RF, f. 079, op. 15, pa. 30,

d. 20, p. 64. This is a one-page copy from the yearly report of 1956 (filed in 1957). Yearly reports are still unavailable to researchers in the AVP RF.

89 Ibid.
90 Record of conversation, Pavel Iudin, Soviet ambassador in Beijing – Van Tziao Chan (Head of the CC CCP department of relations with brotherly parties), January 1956, AVP RF, f. 0100, op. 49, pa. 410, d. 9, pp. 27–29.
91 Brigham, *Guerrilla Diplomacy*, p. 7.
92 Record of conversation, Zimyanin – Ho Chi Minh, 21 June 1956, AVP RF, f. 079, op. 11, pa. 13, d. 5, pp. 129–133.
93 Ibid., p. 129.
94 Ibid., pp. 129–133.
95 After the signing of the Geneva agreement in July 1954, DRV Prime Minister Pham Van Dong allegedly said that he did not think there would be any elections. See Honey, *Communism in North Vietnam*, p. 15; Thayer, *War By Other Means*, pp. 6–7.
96 Record of conversation, Zimyanin – Ho Chi Minh, 21 June 1956, AVP RF, f. 079, op. 11, pa. 13, d. 5, pp. 129–133.
97 Record of conversation, Zimyanin – Ung Van Khiem and Pham Hung, 23 June 1956, AVP RF, f. 079, op. 11, pa. 13, d. 5, p. 137.
98 Ibid., pp. 137–140.
99 Smith, *An International History*, p. 64.
100 *The Great Vanguard of the Vietnamese People. The History of the Communist Party of Vietnam*, Moscow: Polizdat, 1981, p. 115.
101 Thayer, *War By Other Means*, p. 92.
102 Ibid., pp. 104–106.
103 Gaiduk, Ilya V., *Confronting Vietnam. Soviet Policy toward the Indochina Conflict, 1954–1963*, Stanford: Stanford University Press, 2003, Chapters 5 and 6 argue that in 1956, as well as in 1959, the North Vietnamese leadership deliberately held back information and misled both the Soviets and the Chinese aiming to force them into supporting a military reunification struggle in Vietnam.
104 Yang Kuisong argues that Mao's conciliatory attitude in the mid-1950s was a diplomatic tactic determined by realistic policy needs, and that his endorsement of compromise and peace in Southeast Asia would begin to waver once the international situation changed. That is exactly what happened when Khrushchev denounced Stalin at the Twentieth Congress of the CPSU. Yang Kuisong (transl. Qiang Zhai), 'Changes in Mao Zedong's Attitude toward the Indochina War, 1949–1973', *CWIHP Working Paper No. 34*, Washington D.C., February 2002, pp. 15–16.
105 Record of conversation, Zimyanin – Luo Guibo, 11 August 1956, AVP RF, f. 079, op. 11, pa. 13, d. 6, pp. 41–42.

5 Reunification by revolution? The Soviet and Chinese role in Vietnamese reunification plans, 1957–1961

1 The Final Declaration of the Geneva Conference, Document 1, § 6, see Randle, Robert F., *Geneva 1954, The Settlement of the Indochinese War*, Princeton, NJ: Princeton University Press, 1969, p. 570.
2 Pham Van Dong's protest letter of 25 January 1957, AVP RF, f. 079, op. 12, pa. 17, d. 3, pp. 4–5.
3 Record of conversation, Soviet Ambassador Zimyanin – Chinese Ambassador Luo Guibo, 30 January 1957, AVP RF, f. 079, op. 12, pa. 17, d. 5, p. 48.
4 Record of conversation, Zimyanin – Li Zhimin, 18 September 1957, AVP RF, f. 079, op. 12, pa. 17, d. 6, p. 70.
5 Duiker, William J., *The Communist Road to Power in Vietnam*, Boulder, CO: Westview, 1981, p. 182; Duiker, William J., *Sacred War. Nationalism and Revolution in a*

Divided Vietnam, New York: McGraw-Hill, 1995, p. 115; Thayer, Carlyle A., *War By Other Means. National Liberation and Revolution in Viet-nam 1954–60*, Sydney: Allen and Unwin, 1989, pp. 159–160. There is no trace in available Soviet archival documents of any discussion on the topic between the Soviets and the Vietnamese prior to the announcement of the counterproposal.

6 Extract of directive from the CC CPSU to the Soviet delegation to the Second Session of the UN General Assembly, 29 January 1957, AVP RF, f. 079, op. 12, pa. 18, d. 18, p. 6.

7 Ibid.

8 Ibid.

9 Young, Marilyn B., *The Vietnam Wars, 1945–1990*, New York: HarperPerennial, 1991, p. 53.

10 Yearbook of the United Nations 1956, pp. 110–112.

11 Record of conversation, Zimyanin – Ung Van Khiem, 30 January 1957, AVP RF, f. 079, op. 12, pa. 17, d. 5, pp. 50–51.

12 Record of conversation, Zimyanin – Ho Chi Minh, 30 January 1957, AVP RF, f. 079, op. 12, pa. 17, d. 5, p. 52.

13 Ibid.

14 Thayer, *War By Other Means*, p. 160; Yearbook of the United Nations 1956, p. 112.

15 Duiker, *The Communist Road*, p. 182; Pike, Douglas, *Vietnam and the Soviet Union: Anatomy of an Alliance*, Boulder and London: Westview Press, 1987, p. 42.

16 Yearbook of the United Nations 1957, pp. 111–113.

17 Record of conversation, Zimyanin – Pham Van Dong, 18 January 1957, AVP RF, f. 079, op. 12, pa. 17, d. 5, pp. 14–15.

18 Record of conversation, Zimyanin – Pham Van Dong, 7 March 1957, AVP RF, f. 079, op. 12, pa. 17, d. 5, p. 96.

19 Ibid., pp. 91–97; Thayer, *War By Other Means*, 1989: 157.

20 The exchange of visits started with the trip of the President of the Presidium of the USSR Supreme Soviet, K.Y. Voroshilov, to Hanoi from 20 to 23 May 1957, followed by Ho Chi Minh's visit to the Soviet Union in July. Before Ho's visit, Soviet ambassador Zimyanin urged the North Vietnamese to carefully plan questions related to material aid from the Socialist countries to the DRV, see record of conversation, Zimyanin – Vo Nguyen Giap, 29 May 1957, AVP RF, f. 079, op. 12, pa. 17, d. 5, pp. 182–183; during this period Ho Chi Minh also went on a tour of Korea, China, the Soviet Union and Eastern Europe (July–August 1957), to Moscow for the 40th anniversary of the October Revolution (October–November (December) 1957) and to India and Burma (February 1958), see Thayer, *War By Other Means*, 1989: 165–166, 169–173. The main aim of these trips was to secure support for the economy of the DRV and also for the reunification of the country.

21 Said about the visit to Burma and India, see record of conversation, Soviet chargé d'affaires A.M. Popov – Ung Van Khiem, 31 January 1958, AVP RF, f. 079, op. 13, pa. 20, d. 8, pp. 18–22.

22 Record of conversation, Zimyanin – Ung Van Khiem, 27 January 1957, AVP RF, f. 079, op. 12, pa. 17, d. 5, pp. 41–43. For exact numbers on Soviet specialists in the DRV see Appendix.

23 Record of conversation, Zimyanin – Luo Guibo, 22 January 1957, AVP RF, f. 079, op. 12, pa. 17, d. 5, p. 26.

24 Record of conversation, Zimyanin – Pham Van Dong, 27 April 1957, AVP RF, f. 079, op. 12, pa. 17, d. 5, pp. 156–161

25 Ibid., p. 159, in the Russian text the words 'many obligations' had been put in quotation marks 'mnogo nagruzok'.

26 Record of conversation, Zimyanin – Vo Nguyen Giap, 29 May 1957, AVP RF, f. 079, op. 12, p. 17, d. 5, pp. 182–183.

27 When he took on the post as ambassador in 1957 Leonid Ivanovich Sokolov was well acquainted with the situation in Vietnam. He began his diplomatic career as advisor at

the Soviet embassy in Hanoi in 1954 where he stayed until 1956. In 1957 he returned to Hanoi to assume the post of Soviet ambassador, after a year's work within the central administration of the Soviet foreign ministry in Moscow. See *Diplomaticheskii slovar, tom III*, Moskva: Izdatelstvo 'Nauka', 1986, p. 383.

28 Record of conversation, Soviet ambassador Leonid Ivanovich Sokolov – Vo Nguyen Giap, 25 February 1958, AVP RF, f. 079, op. 13, pa. 20, d. 8, pp. 31–33.

29 Thayer, *War By Other Means*, 1989: 177.

30 Record of conversation, Sokolov – Pham Van Dong, 3 May 1960, AVP RF, f. 079, op. 15, pa. 28, d. 6, pp. 101–104.

31 Economic, trade and cultural relations between the Soviet Union and the DRV, memorandum by the Southeast Asia Department in MID, 3 December 1963, AVP RF, f. 079, op. 18, pa. 39, d. 24, p. 60.

32 'Questions that might be posed during conversations with the Vietnamese friends', draft, SEAD, 30 January 1959, AVP RF, f. 079, op. 14, pa. 24, d. 13, pp. 14–16.

33 Economic, trade and cultural relations between the Soviet Union and the DRV, memorandum by the Southeast Asia Department in MID, 3 December 1963, AVP RF, f. 079, op. 18, pa. 39, d. 24, pp. 58–79. Previous estimates of Soviet economic and military assistance to the DRV in the period show a stable level of assistance with only smaller variations from one year to another. For estimates, see Pike, *Vietnam and the Soviet Union*, p. 139; Thakur, Ramesh and Carlyle A. Thayer, *Soviet Relations with India and Vietnam*, London: MacMillan, 1992, p. 117.

34 According to Soviet documents, the 15th Plenum was held from December 1958 to February 1959, but the general assumption in the literature of when it was held is January. See 'On the situation in South Vietnam', an analysis by Acting Head of the SEAD in MID Nikolai Moljakov, 22 December 1961, AVP RF, f. 079, op. 16, pa. 32, d. 20, pp. 102–108. On the last page of the document was added: 'The report has been based on materials from MID, the General Staff of the Soviet Army, and KGB by the Council of Ministers.' For Le Duan's report, see Thayer, *War By Other Means*, pp. 183–185; King C. Chen, 'Hanoi's Three Decisions and the Escalation of the Vietnam War', *Political Science Quarterly*, 90 (2) 1975, pp. 244–246.

35 Record of conversation, Zimyanin – Li Zhimin, 18 September 1957, AVP RF, f. 079, op. 12, pa. 17, d. 6, p. 69.

36 Ibid.

37 Ibid.

38 Record of conversation, Zimyanin – Truong Chinh, 8 June 1957, AVP RF, f. 079, op. 12, pa. 17, d. 5, pp. 199–206.

39 Record of conversation, Zimyanin – Nguyen Duy Trinh, 12 and 14 June 1957, AVP RF, f. 079, op. 12, pa. 17, d. 5, pp. 220–235. This document contains information on the different members of the Politburo and their tasks. Compared to earlier accounts of Politburo and Central Committee members it shows that leaders known to be in favour of a new and more aggressive strategy towards the South are gaining more power in the top party leadership.

40 On 15 April 1958 Pham Van Dong informed Soviet ambassador Sokolov that the party had appointed two additional deputy prime ministers to strengthen the government. The two appointees were members of the Politburo, Truong Chinh and Pham Hung. With regard to Pham Hung's appointment Dong said: 'It has to be taken into account that the appointment of Pham Hung, who is a Southerner, and has worked for a long time in South Vietnam, calls for certain political consequences in the plans of the fight for a peaceful reunification of the country.' See record of conversation, Sokolov – Pham Van Dong, 15 April 1958, AVP RF, f. 079, op. 13, pa. 20, d. 8, p. 95.

41 The word 'Thum' is not a Vietnamese name. The closest English translation of the Vietnamese word 'thùm' is 'stinking' or 'smelling bad'.

42 Record of conversation, Second Secretary at Soviet embassy G. Kadumov – official at the DRV Ministry of State Security 'Thum', 4 April 1958, AVP RF, f. 079, op. 13, pa. 20, d. 10, pp. 202–203.
43 Ibid. AVP RF, f. 079, op. 13, pa. 20, d. 10, p. 203. The document presented above is impressive because of the frankness in the discussion. It is rare in the sense that such information was not often provided, and if so usually in a much vaguer tone. There seem to be two possible explanations as to why this Vietnamese official was so frank with a low-ranking embassy official. Thum may have been an informant or a message deliverer from the DRV internal circle, informing on the general mood among the regrouped and, by doing so, implicitly warning the Soviets that the pressure on DRV policy makers from the regrouped in favour of armed struggle was increasing. His information may also have been a test case, implying that he was a person used by the party leadership to find out how the Soviets felt about armed struggle to reunify Vietnam. He might also have been one of the Southern regroupees himself, with a preference for armed struggle. The ideas of Thum's possible role in this record of conversation originates from an e-mail correspondence with Vietnamese historian Nguyen Vu Tung on 24 September 1996. See also Olsen 1997: 104–105.
44 MID (Deputy Foreign Minister) to Soviet ambassador L.I. Sokolov, 16 April 1958, AVP RF, f. 079, op. 13, pa. 20, d. 3, pp. 15–19.
45 Young, *The Vietnam Wars*, pp. 60–61.
46 Thayer, *War By Other Means*, pp. 123, 128–129.
47 Chen Jian, 'China's Involvement in the Vietnam War, 1964–69', *The China Quarterly, 1995* (142), p. 358.
48 Chen Jian, 'China's Involvement in the Vietnam War, 1964–69', p. 358.
49 Although Mao was cautious when Hanoi decided to renew armed struggle in South Vietnam, he was also irritated by the Soviet unwillingness to carry on revolution. Yang Kuisong, 'Changes in Mao Zedong's Attitude toward the Indochina War, 1949–1973', *CWIHP Working Paper No. 34*, Washington, D.C., February 2002, p. 18.
50 Gordon H. Chang, *Friends and Enemies. The United States, China, and the Soviet Union, 1948–1972*, Stanford, CA: Stanford University Press, 1990, pp. 184, 204–205; Thayer, *War By Other Means*, p. 180.
51 Record of conversation, Sokolov – Ho Chi Minh, 16, 17, 19 January 1959, AVP RF, f. 079, op. 14, pa. 23, d. 5, p. 24.
52 Record of conversation, Soviet embassy advisor A.M. Popov – Nguyen Duy Trinh, 12 March 1959, AVP RF, f. 079, op. 14, pa. 24, d. 7, p. 168.
53 Record of conversation, Sokolov – Le Duan, 15 April 1959, AVP RF, f. 079, op. 14, pa. 23, d. 5, pp. 102–107.
54 Record of conversation, A.M. Popov – Truong Chinh, 21 May 1959, f. 079, op. 14, pa. 24, d. 7, pp. 265–268.
55 'On the situation in South Vietnam', an analysis by Acting Head of the Southeast Asia Department in MID Nikolai Moljakov, 22 December 1961, AVP RF, f. 079, op. 16, pa. 32, d. 20, pp. 102–108; for Hanoi's decisions in 1959/60 see King C. Chen, 'Hanoi's Three Decisions', pp. 244–246.
56 King C. Chen, 'Hanoi's Three Decisions', p. 240.
57 Zimyanin to Malin, 16 October 1959, AVP RF, f. 0100, op. 52, pa. 442, d. 5, p. 52. The actual contents of the discussion are not known, but a note referring to the meeting was found in Soviet files on China. The note confirms that a meeting between Khrushchev, Mao, Kim Il Sung, and Ho Chi Minh took place in Beijing on 2 October 1959, and that the discussion evolved around the future strategy in South Vietnam. See also Pravda, 1 October 1959.
58 'On the situation in South Vietnam', an analysis by Acting Head of the SEAD in MID Nikolai Moljakov, 22 December 1961, AVP RF, f. 079, op. 16, pa. 32, d. 20, p. 104.
59 Ibid.

60 Thayer, *War By Other Means*, 1989: 187–187; Smith, Ralph B., *An International History of the Vietnam War: Vol. I, Revolution versus Containment, 1955–61*, New York: St. Martin's Press, 1983, p. 168.
61 From Sokolov's journal. Record of information presented in MID DRV by deputy foreign minister Ung Van Khiem for the heads of diplomatic representation from the Socialist countries, 15 April 1960, AVP RF, f. 079, op. 15, pa. 28, d. 6, pp. 91–97.
62 Record of conversation, Chervonenko – Chan Ti Binh, 3 February 1961, AVP RF, f. 0100, op. 54, pa. 466, d. 7, p. 37.
63 Smith, *An International History*, Vol. I, p. 184.
64 Ibid., pp. 184–185.
65 Brigham, Robert K., *Guerrilla Diplomacy: The NLF's Foreign Relations and the Viet Nam War*, Itacha: Cornell University Press, 1999, p. 1.
66 'On the situation in South Vietnam', an analysis by Acting Head of the SEAD in MID Nikolai Moljakov, 22 December 1961, AVP RF, f. 079, op. 16, pa. 32, d. 20, p. 104.
67 The National Liberation Front of South Vietnam, Soviet embassy in Hanoi to MID, 14 November 1961, AVP RF, f. 079, op. 16, pa. 32, d. 20, pp. 84–92. Quote from page 84.
68 'On the si'On the situation in South Vietnam', an analysis by Acting Head of the SEAD in MID Nikolai Moljakov, 22 December 1961, AVP RF, f. 079, op. 16, pa. 32, d. 20, p. 107.
69 Chang, *Friends and Enemies*, pp. 184, 204–205; Thayer, *War By Other Means*, p. 180; Zubok, Vladislav and Constantine Pleshakov, *Inside the Kremlin's Cold War. From Stalin to Khrushev*, Cambridge, Mass: Harvard University Press, 1996, pp. 230–233; Zagoria, Donald S., *The Sino-Soviet Conflict 1956–1961*, Princeton, NJ: Princeton University Press, 1962, pp. 325–327.
70 Record of conversation, Chervonenko – Chan Ti Binh, 8 October 1960, AVP RF, f. 0100, op. 53, pa. 454, d. 9, p. 35.
71 According to Chan Ti Binh, the Chinese deputy foreign minister said that, for example, this would affect the deliverance of equipment received from the DDR and Hungary, which could not be installed and sent to Vietnam for use because of the departure of the Soviet specialists. Record of conversation, Chervonenko – Chan Ti Binh, 8 October 1960, AVP RF, f. 0100, op. 53, pa. 454, d. 9, p. 35.
72 Ibid., pp. 37–38.
73 Record of conversation, chargé d'affaires N.I. Godunov – Ho Chi Minh, 22 June 1960, AVP RF, f. 179, op. 15, pa. 28, d. 6, pp. 160–162, quote from p. 161.
74 Record of meeting, Soviet advisor Godunov – representatives from the Socialist countries, 24 August 1960, AVP RF, f. 079, op. 15, pa. 29, d. 9, pp. 179–180. The Lao Dong Four-point text was not in the file, and no further comments to the four points were made.
75 Soviet ambassador Suren Akopovich Tovmasjan to MID, 17 October 1961, AVP RF, f. 079, op. 16, pa. 31, d. 3, pp. 35–57, quote from p. 48.
76 Young, *The Vietnam Wars*, p. 82.
77 Qiang Zhai, *China and the Vietnam Wars, 1950–1975*, Chapel Hill: University of North Carolina Press, 2000, p. 112.
78 Qiang Zhai, *China and the Vietnam Wars*, pp. 112–113; Ralph B. Smith, *An International History of the Vietnam War: Vol II, The Struggle for South-East Asia, 1961–1965*, London: Macmillan, 1985, p. 38.
79 Political letter from Ambassador Tovmasian to MID. 'Some Questions on the Activities of the CC Lao Dong after the Moscow Meeting of Communist and Workers Parties in 1960', 17 October 1961, AVP RF, f. 079, op. 16, pa. 31, d. 3, p. 42.
80 Ibid., pp. 44–45.
81 Record of conversation, Councellor Soviet embassy in the DRV Nikolai I. Godunov – Le Duan, 9 May 1961, AVP RF, f. 079, op. 16, pa. 31, d. 7, p. 24.
82 Ibid. AVP RF, f. 079, op. 16, pa. 31, d. 7, pp. 24–27. Citation from p. 27.
83 Record of conversation, N.I. Godunov – Hoang Van Tien, DRV Acting Foreign Minister, 5 July 1961, AVP RF, f. 079, op. 16, pa. 31, d. 7, p. 116. For an account of

the NLF's foreign relations see Brigham, Guerrilla Diplomacy for the early 1960s particularly Chapters 1 and 2.

84 According to a Soviet report the DRV managed to establish a number of bases in South Vietnam due to the use of these aircraft, and they also flew in three complete infantry batallions and a considerable number of officers for 20 batallions. See 'On the situation in South Vietnam', an analysis by Acting Head of the SEAD in MID Nikolai Moljakov, 22 December 1961, AVP RF, f. 079, op. 16, pa. 32, d. 20, p. 107.

85 The Soviet documents do not say anything about the pilots who flew the planes, but in later discussions over the same matter the Vietnamese complain about the lack of educated pilots. It is therefore possible that these planes were equipped with Soviet pilots who could effectively have stopped all attempts to use the planes for purposes other than those approved by Moscow in advance. See Chapter 7 of this book.

86 Although this has yet to be documented, one cannot disregard the possibility that opinions within the Soviet government on whether to support the Vietnamese differed. Until all existing documents on Soviet involvement in Vietnam have been released (intelligence reports, military records, personal papers) it remains impossible to document that incidents of tacit approval that were in opposition to the general Soviet line in Vietnam could have been forced through by individuals or groups within the Soviet leadership positive to the introduction of insurgency in South Vietnam.

6 The fight over Laos, 1961–1962

1 Deng Xiao Ping to Soviet ambassador in Beijing, Stephan Chervonenko, 30 September 1961, AVP RF, f. 0100, op. 54, pa. 466, d. 8, p. 177.

2 Anderson, David L., *Trapped By Success. The Eisenhower Administration and Vietnam, 1953–61*, New York: Colombia University Press, 1991, p. 191.

3 For the period from 1954–60, the Vietnam fund in the AVPRF contains much information on the situation in Laos. This continued also after a separate Laos fund was opened in 1955.

4 Smith, Ralph B., *An International History of the Vietnam War: Vol. I, Revolution versus Containment, 1955–61*, New York: St. Martin's Press, 1983, p. 111; Anderson, *Trapped By Success*, p. 191; Lawrence Freedman, *Kennedy's Wars. Berlin, Cuba, Laos, and Vietnam*, Oxford University Press: New York and Oxford, 2000, p. 294.

5 Record of conversation, Sokolov – Ung Van Khiem, 28 February 1959, AVP RF, f. 079, op. 14, pa. 23, d. 5, pp. 68–73; in late May the same year Pham Van Dong informed the Soviet ambassador in Hanoi that if necessary the DRV was ready to support Laos with arms and other supplies needed for war. See record of conversation, Sokolov – Pham Van Dong, 26 May 1959, AVP RF, f. 079, op. 14, pa. 23, d. 5, pp. 123–126.

6 Record of conversation, Sokolov – Ung Van Khiem, 28 February 1959, AVP RF, f. 079, op. 14, pa. 23, d. 5, pp. 68–73, AVPRF; record of conversation, Sokolov – Ung Van Khiem, 9 March 1959, AVP RF, f. 079, op. 14, pa. 23, d. 5, pp. 74–77.

7 Record of conversation, Soviet Deputy Foreign Minister G.M. Pushkin – Ung Van Khiem, 12 January 1960, AVP RF, f. 079, op. 15, pa. 28, d. 4, p. 1.

8 Ibid., pp. 1–3.

9 'On the situation in South Vietnam', an analysis by Acting Head of the SEAD in MID Nikolai Moljakov, 22 December 1961, AVP RF, f. 079, op. 16, pa. 32, d. 20, p. 107.

10 Anderson, *Trapped By Success*, p. 191.

11 Abramov was originally assigned Soviet ambassador in Cambodia from 1959 to 1962 but was serving as ambassador to Laos simultaneously. That would also explain his swift arrival in Laos.

12 This refers to the International Control Commission set up during the 1954 Geneva conference on Indochina. The commission consisted of representatives from India,

Poland and Canada with India as head of the commission. The commission was set up with these particular members in order to have one representative from the Western side, Canada; one from the Socialist countries, Poland; and finally, a member that was regarded as neutral, India. The changed role and position of India would turn out to be an issue at the Geneva conference on Laos in 1961–62.

13 Captain Kong Le was collaborating with the Pathet Lao forces.

14 Hall, David K., 'The Laos Neutralization Agreement, 1962' in Alexander L. George, Philip J. Farley and Alexander Dallin (eds) *U.S. – Soviet Security Cooperation. Achievements, Failures, Lessons*, Oxford UP: NY, 1988.

15 Paul F. Langer and Joseph J. Zasslov, *North Vietnam and the Pathet Lao. Partners in the Struggle for Laos*, Cambridge, MA: Harvard University Press, 1970, p. 73.

16 Qiang Zhai, *China and the Vietnam Wars, 1950–1975*, Chapel Hill: University of North Carolina Press, 2000, p. 100.

17 Qiang Zhai, *China and the Vietnam Wars*, p. 108.

18 All in all the PRC delegation consisted of some 50 men and women, and according to Arthur Lall who represented India in Geneva, the Chinese delegation made quite an impression when entering the conference room in Geneva. Arthur Lall, *How Communist China Negotiates*, New York: Columbia University Press, 1968, pp. 1–2.

19 Qiang Zhai, *China and the Vietnam Wars*, pp. 99–100.

20 See e.g. Chinese comments on the Soviet need for their support; record of conversation, Gromyko – Chen Yi, 14 May 1961, AVP RF, f. 0445, op. 1, pa. 1, d. 1, pp. 2–3.

21 Marek Thee, *Notes of a Witness. Laos and the Second Indochinese War*, New York: Vintage Books, 1973, pp. 17–18.

22 Record of conversation, Andrei Gromyko – Chen Yi, 14 May 1961, AVP RF, f. 0445, op. 1, pa. 1, d. 1, pp. 2–3. Quote from p. 3.

23 Ibid., pp. 2–3.

24 'On contacts between the Soviet and Chinese delegations at the Geneva conference (May–June)' by MID, 7 December 1961, AVP RF, f. 0445, op. 1, pa. 2, d. 8, p. 33.

25 Such meetings were held on a regular basis throughout the conference. In addition to discussing strategies the main purpose of the meetings was to let the Soviets share information from their meetings with other foreign delegates and, more specifically, from their meetings with the other co-chair, Great Britain.

26 Meeting between the head of delegations from the Soviet Union, PRC, DRV and Poland, 15 May 1961, at 16 h 30 min, AVP RF, f. 0445, op. 1, pa. 1, d. 1, pp. 7–8. Sihanouk did, however, make it to Geneva in time to open the conference on May 16.

27 Ibid., p. 13.

28 Ibid.

29 Roberts, Geoffrey, 'The Soviet Union in World Politics. Coexistence, Revolution and Cold War, 1945–1991', London: Routledge, 1999, pp. 53–54.

30 'On contacts between the Soviet and Chinese delegations at the Geneva conference (May–June)' by MID, 7 December 1961, AVP RF, f. 0445, op. 1, pa. 2, d. 8.

31 Ibid.

32 Meeting between the head of delegations from the Soviet Union, PRC, DRV and Poland, 15 May 1961, at 16 h 30 min, AVP RF, f. 0445, op. 1, pa. 1, d. 1, p. 19.

33 Ibid., pp. 20–21.

34 'On contacts between the Soviet and Chinese delegations at the Geneva conference (May–June)' by MID, 7 December 1961, AVP RF, f. 0445, op. 1, pa. 2, d. 8, p. 31.

35 Record of conversation, G.M. Pushkin – Zhang Hanfu, 15 May 1961, AVP RF, f. 0445, op. 1, pa. 1, d. 2, pp. 1–5. During this conversation Zhang several times referred to the absence of the word independence in references to Laotian neutrality. According to the Chinese it was very important that whenever the word 'neutrality' was mentioned as the future status of Laos, 'independence' should be mentioned as well.

36 This was a question the Chinese raised several times in the early days of the conference.

37 Record of conversation, G.M. Pushkin – Zhang Hanfu, 16 May 1961, AVP RF, f. 0445, op. 1, pa. 1, d. 2, p. 19. The Chinese position on the issue of Chiang Kaishistovs was also emphasized in the overall Soviet analysis on contacts between the Soviet and Chinese delegations at the Geneva conference (May–June), where it was concluded that after the negotiations during summer 1961 the Chinese had stopped insisting on the point about the Chiang Kaishistovs. See also 7 December 1961, AVP RF, f. 0445, op. 1, pa. 2, d. 8, p. 31.

38 'On contacts between the Soviet and Chinese delegations at the Geneva conference (May–June)' by MID, 7 December 1961, AVP RF, f. 0445, op. 1, pa. 2, d. 8, p. 31.

39 Record of conversation, G.M. Pushkin – Zhang Hanfu, 16 May 1961, AVP RF, f. 0445, op. 1, pa. 1, d. 2, p. 20.

40 Apparently, Zhang then went to consult with Chen Yi, whose answer was that he would reconsider once again whether it would be wise for the Chinese to proceed with the issues of Chapter 4 of the agreement. In addition he wanted to hear the Soviet comments on the other Chinese proposals. See, ibid. AVP RF, f. 0445, op. 1, pa. 1, d. 2, pp. 22–23.

41 Ibid., p. 20.

42 Ibid.; AVP RF, f. 0445, op. 1, pa. 1, d. 2.

43 Record of conversation, Chervonenko – Deng Xiao Ping, 30 September 1961, AVP RF, f. 0100, op. 54, pa. 466, d. 8, p. 177.

44 Ang Cheng Guan, Vietnamese Communists' *Relations with China and the Second Indochina Conflict, 1956–1962*, Jefferson, NC: McFarland & Company, Inc., 1997, p. 194.

45 Thee, *Notes of a Witness*, p. 131. A discussion of Marek Thee's account can also be found in Ang Cheng Guan, *Vietnamese Communists'*, pp. 194–196.

46 Record of conversation, G.M. Pushkin – DRV foreign minister Ung Van Khiem, 6 June 1961, AVP RF, f. 0445, op. 1, pa. 1, d. 3.

47 Meeting between the heads of the four Socialist delegations, 7 June 1961, AVP RF, f. 0445, op. 1, pa. 1, d. 6, pp. 30–36.

48 Arguments presented by the heads of the four Socialist delegations concerning the organization of the further work of the Geneva conference on Laos, 1961, AVP RF, f. 0445, op. 1, pa. 1, d. 8, p. 23.

49 Qiang Zhai, *China and the Vietnam Wars*, p. 103.

50 Ibid.

51 In the new government, Souvanna Phouma became prime minister in charge of the Ministry of Defence; Phoumi and Souphanouvong both became deputy prime ministers, each with veto power over cabinet decisions and departmental decisions in defence, interior and foreign affairs. See Qiang Zhai, China and the Vietnam Wars, pp. 104–105.

52 Qiang Zhai, *China and the Vietnam Wars*, p. 106.

53 'On the PRC reaction to the formation of a Lao government', Soviet embassy in Beijing to MID, 18 June 1962, AVP RF, f. 0100, op. 55, pa. 489, d. 67, pp. 223–225. Quotes from p. 225.

54 Record of conversation, Tovmasyan – Pham Van Dong, 19 May 1961, AVP RF, f. 079, op. 16, pa. 31, d. 7, p. 54.

55 Record of conversation, Tovmasyan – Ung Van Khiem, 8 September 1961, AVP RF, f. 079, op. 16, pa. 31, d. 7, pp. 200–201.

56 Record of conversation, Soviet chargé d'affaires in Hanoi P.I. Privalov – Nguyen Zyan, Deputy director of the Asian Department in the DRV foreign ministry and Cham, Head of the department of foreign trade with Socialist countries in the Vietnamese ministry of trade, 9 July 1962, AVP RF, f. 079, op. 17, pa. 34, d. 7, p. 61.

57 Record of conversation, P.I. Privalov – DRV Acting Premier Minister Le Than Ngi, 24 August 1962, AVP RF, f. 079, op. 17, pa. 34, d. 7, p. 89.

58 Ibid.

59 Record of conversation, Tovmasyan – Pham Van Dong, 7 September 1962, AVP RF, f. 079, op. 17, pa. 34, d. 7, pp. 103–104.

60 Record of conversation, Tovmasyan – Pham Van Dong, 24 September 1962, AVP RF, f. 079, op. 17, pa. 34, d. 7, pp. 129–130. The passage on how the Soviet Union was the best choice to assist the DRV in their help to Laos was followed by a personal comment made by Ambassador Tovmasyan saying: 'I personally agree with him.' (l. 130).

61 Ibid. AVP RF, f. 079, op. 17, pa. 34, d. 7, p. 134.

62 The conference on Laos in Geneva was emphasized by Deng Xiao Ping in the end of September 1961 as an example of the fact that Moscow and Beijing were still able to cooperate on the international arena, although they did not agree on everything else. See record of conversation, Chervonenko – Deng Xiao Ping, 30 September 1961, AVP RF, f. 0100, op. 54, pa. 466, d. 8, p. 177.

63 Qiang Zhai, *China and the Vietnam Wars*, p. 106. Quotation marks in the original.

64 Ibid., pp. 106–108.

65 Ibid., p. 111.

7 From disinterest to active support, 1962–1965

1 'On the situation in South Vietnam', 22 December 1961, AVP RF, f. 079, op. 16, pa. 32, d. 20, p. 104.

2 Yang Kuisong, 'Changes in Mao Zedong's Attitude toward the Indochina War, 1949–1973', *CWIHP Working Paper No. 34*, Washington, D.C., February 2002, p. 22.

3 Record of conversation, Tovmasyan – Duong Bac Mai, 18 December 1962, AVP RF, f. 079, op. 17, pa. 34, d. 7, p. 226.

4 In January 1962 Chan Ti Binh, the DRV ambassador in Beijing, told Chervonenko that Ho Chi Minh claimed that he would fight against disagreements within the Communist camp 'until his last drop of blood'. Chan Ti Binh added that without the Soviet Union there would not have been a Communist camp, that disagreements would have to be solved in a friendly way, and that they should be able to find a common course. See, record of conversation, Soviet ambassador to Beijing, Stephan Chervonenko – Chan Ti Binh, 15 January 1962, AVP RF, f. 0100, op. 55, pa. 480, d. 6, p. 11. Chan Ti Binh's attitude was probably rather representative of how the Vietnamese dealt with the widening split in the early part of the 1960s.

5 In January 1962, according to the Soviet embassy, the Vietnamese put much more effort into the celebration of the Chinese recognition of the DRV, than the Soviet recognition. Also, when celebrating the 32nd anniversary of the foundation of the Lao Dong, it was the role of the CCP that was underlined, as well as the role of the Chinese Communists in the Vietnamese revolution. See, memorandum by the Soviet embassy in the DRV – written by L. Kotov, 2nd Secretary, 'Some aspects of the Vietnamese–Chinese relationship', 10 April 1962, AVP RF, f. 079, op. 17, pa. 36, d. 19, pp. 6–8.

6 Ibid. AVP RF, f. 079, op. 17, pa. 36, d. 19, p. 8; see also Chen Jian 2001: 211.

7 Regionally Laos was the main issue that contributed to a closer Sino-Vietnamese relationship. Leaders in Hanoi and Beijing held, to a large degree, similar positions on how to handle, and not least solve, the problems in Laos. Hanoi strongly wanted the air bridge to Laos to continue, mainly because they used it for two vital purposes: first, to bring personnel into South Vietnam and, second, to strengthen the Pathet Lao. These goals coincided with those of the Chinese, who in addition to supporting the Pathet Lao aimed to strengthen a second force in Laos, the group led by Kham Chan in the province of Phong Saly. Ibid. AVP RF, f. 079, op. 17, pa. 36, d. 19, p. 10; sources from the Chinese side also reveal how Beijing already during the Geneva conference in 1961 encouraged Hanoi to keep their forces in Laos in secret. See Yang Kuisong, 'Changes in Mao Zedong's Attitude', p. 21.

8 Economic, trade and cultural relations between the Soviet Union and the Democratic Republic of Vietnam, memorandum by the Southeast Asia Department MID, 3 December 1963, AVP RF, f. 079, op. 18, pa. 39, d. 24, pp. 58–79. However, the Soviets had

several reservations with regard to the quality of this assistance and Vietnamese views on it. According to the SEAD report the Soviet embassy in Hanoi believed that the Vietnamese leadership realized that hoping for a fast economic development in the DRV in the next few years, based on Chinese assistance only, was an illusion. Chinese assistance to the DRV was characterized by overt mistakes, late deliveries and low quality of goods. (67)

9 L. Kotov, 'Some aspects of the Vietnamese–Chinese relationship', 10 April 1962, AVP RF, f. 079, op. 17, pa. 36, d. 19, p. 9.
10 Ibid.
11 Ibid., pp. 9–10. Quotation from p. 10.
12 Qiang Zhai, *China and the Vietnam Wars, 1950–1975*, Chapel Hill: University of North Carolina Press, 2000, p. 113.
13 Record of conversation, Tovmasyan – Ho Chi Minh, 26 May 1962, AVP RF, f. 079, op. 17, pa. 34, d. 7, pp. 18–19. Quotation marks in original text.
14 Record of conversation, Deputy Foreign Minister Pushkin – Ho Chi Minh, 7 June 1962, AVP RF, f. 079, op. 17, pa. 34, d. 4, pp. 11–12.
15 'Soviet–Vietnamese relations', memorandum from the Southeast Asia Department, 2 June 1962, AVP RF, f. 079. op. 17, pa. 35, d. 13, pp. 40–41.
16 L. Kotov, 'Some aspects of the Vietnamese–Chinese relationship', 10 April 1962, AVP RF, f. 079, op. 17, pa. 36, d. 19, pp. 5–6.
17 These suggestions might indicate that there were different views also within the foreign ministry on how to deal with the situation in Vietnam, see AVP RF, memorandum written by A. Skoryokov, Suggestions for the further development of the political, economic and cultural relationship with the DRV and for regulation of international problems', 15 September 1962, AVP RF, f. 079, op. 17, pa. 35, d. 13, pp. 75–76.
18 L. Kotov, 'Some aspects of the Vietnamese–Chinese relationship', 10 April 1962, AVP RF, f. 079, op. 17, pa. 36, d. 19, p. 28.
19 The Soviet embassy in Hanoi and the Southeast Asia Department in the Soviet foreign ministry came up with many ideas on how to increase Soviet influence in Vietnam, ranging from a visit by Nikita Khrushchev to increased economic assistance, but in 1962 none of these were implemented.
20 Zubok, Vladislav and Constantine Pleshakov, *Inside the Kremlin's Cold War. From Stalin to Khrushev*, Cambridge, Mass: Harvard University Press, 1996, pp. 261–262.
21 Kevin Ruane, *War and Revolution in Vietnam*, London: UCL Press, 1998, p. 56.
22 LaFeber, Walter, *America, Russia, and the Cold War, 1945–1996*, New York: McGraw-Hill, 1997, pp. 229–230.
23 The Soviet dependence on other Socialist embassies to obtain information on developments in Vietnam and especially the Sino-Vietnamese relationship coincided with Mao's decision to support the armed struggle in Vietnam. See Yang Kuisong, 'Changes in Mao Zedong's Attitude', p. 22.
24 Record of conversation, Tovmasyan – Findinski and Marek Thee, 8 and 10 September 1962, AVP RF, f. 079, op. 17, pa. 34, d. 7, p. 107.
25 Record of conversation, Tovmasyan – Czechoslovak Ambassador to the DRV, Gerold, 11 September 1962, AVP RF, f. 079, op. 17, pa. 34, d. 7, p. 110. Both quotations from p. 110.
26 Ibid. AVP RF, f. 079, op. 17, pa. 34, d. 7, p. 111. Quotations in the original text.
27 Ibid. AVP RF, f. 079, op. 17, pa. 34, d. 7, p. 111.
28 Ibid.
29 The wording was 'Opiratsa na svoi sily' – 'Depend on one's own forces'.
30 Ibid. AVP RF, f. 079, op. 17, pa. 34, d. 7, p. 111.
31 Record of conversation, Tovmasyan – Findinski, 20 November 1962, AVP RF, f. 079, op. 17, pa. 34, d. 7, p. 201.
32 Memorandum written by A. Skoryokov, 'Suggestions for the further development of the political, economic and cultural relationship with the DRV and for regulation

of international problems', 15 September 1962, AVP RF, f. 079, op. 17, pa. 35, d. 13, pp. 75–77. Quotation from p. 76.

33 Record of conversation, Tovmasyan – leader of the Polish delegation to the ICC Pokhorilts and Findinski, 11 October 1962, AVP RF, f. 079, op. 17, pa. 34, d. 7, p. 164.

34 Ibid., p. 165.

35 Memorandum, 'The PRC delegation to the DRV', L. Kotov, 2nd Secretary of the Soviet embassy in the DRV, 11 November 1962, AVP RF, f. 079, op. 17, pa. 36, d. 19, p. 138.

36 The Soviet embassy placed significance on the fact that Ung Van Khiem had placed a Soviet flag on his car during the visit. See, ibid. 'The PRC delegation to the DRV', AVP RF, f. 079, op. 17, pa. 36, d. 19, p. 140.

37 Ibid., p. 148.

38 Ibid.

39 Ibid., pp. 148–149.

40 Xuan Thuy (DRV foreign minister 1963–65, and DRV representative at the Paris Peace Talks).

41 Record of conversation, Tovmasyan – Duong Bac Mai, 18 December 1962, AVP RF, f. 079, op. 17, pa. 34, d. 7, p. 226.

42 Ibid. AVP RF, f. 079, op. 17, pa. 34, d. 7, p. 228. The last part of the sentence had quotation marks in the original text.

43 In late February 1964, after the visit of Le Duan's delegation to Moscow, Soviet ambassador to the DRV Tovmasyan, in a conversation with the Polish ambassador to the DRV, Shedelevski, provided a clear yes to the Poles' direct question as to whether the DRV now was to be considered pro-Chinese. See record of conversation, Tovmasyan – Shedelevski, 28 February 1964, AVP RF, f. 079, op. 19, pa. 40, d. 6, p. 99.

44 According to a report summarizing two such visits, neither delegation experienced any form of polemic fights, and the participants were in both cases very satisfied with the visits. See Memorandum on 'Political results of the visits to the DRV of delegations from the Supreme Soviet and the Ministry of Defence USSR', 29 January 1963, AVP RF, f. 079, op. 18, pa. 39, d. 17, pp. 1–3.

45 See e.g. record of conversation, Tovmasyan – Duong Bac Mai, 18 December 1962, AVP RF, f. 079, op. 17, pa. 34, d. 7, pp. 225–228; record of conversation, Tovmasyan – Duong Bac Mai, 29 June 1963, AVP RF, f. 079, op. 18, pa. 37, d. 6, pp. 249–256; record of conversation, Privalov – Duong Bac Mai, 21 October 1963, AVP RF, f. 079, op. 18, pa. 37, d. 8, pp. 41–44.

46 Memorandum 'About Novotny's visit to the DRV', written by 3rd Secretary Soviet embassy in Hanoi, L. Boyko, 25 March 1963, AVP RF, f. 079, op. 18, pa. 39, d. 23, pp. 38–47.

47 'Liu Shaoqi's visit to the DRV', Soviet ambassador Tovmasyan to MID, 12 June 1963, AVP RF, f. 079, op. 18, pa. 39, d. 23, p. 70. Quotation marks in the original text; for the Chinese account, see Qiang Zhai 2000: 126.

48 Record of conversation, Tovmasyan – Polish chargé d'affaires Kazimir Hodorek, 9 March 1963, f. 079, op. 18, pa. 37, d. 6, p. 76. Horodek further added that these efforts had made many Vietnamese worry that pro-Chinese groups now had full control over the propaganda machinery of the Lao Dong. They feared that these groups could resort to repression of those who did not share their points of view. However, it seemed as if the Vietnamese believed that as long as Ho Chi Minh remained in power it would probably not come to this, but if these groups were able to restrain Ho's influence within the party this could happen. (78)

49 'Liu Shaoqi's visit to the DRV', Soviet ambassador Tovmasyan to MID, 12 June 1963, AVP RF, f. 079, op. 18, pa. 39, d. 23, p. 70. Quotation marks in the original text.

50 Ibid., pp. 79–80.

51 Ibid., p. 85.

52 SEAD memorandum, G. Zverev, 2nd Secretary, 'The position of the DRV and the USSR in relation to South Vietnam', 26 July 1963, AVP RF, f. 079, op. 18, pa. 39, d. 23, p. 164.

53 Ibid., p. 165.

54 Ibid.

55 In the Soviet foreign ministry files containing records of conversations between the Soviet ambassador and high-ranking North Vietnamese officials for 1963, many documents had been censured and were not available to me while I was working in the reading room. However, later references to individual documents do indicate that the Vietnamese did receive a certain amount of weapons from the Soviets also in 1963, under the condition that it would be impossible to identify that these weapons were delivered by the Soviet Union. However, after the mention of these weapons most of the conversations between the ambassador and the highest-level Vietnamese officials have been restricted from view. See e.g. AVP RF, f. 079, op. 18, pa. 37, dd. 7–8.

56 Record of conversation, Deputy Foreign Minister Sergei Georgevich Lapin – DRV Ambassador to the Soviet Union Nguyen Van Kinh, 30 August 1963, AVP RF, f. 079, op. 18, pa. 37, d. 4, p. 4.

57 Ibid.

58 Record of conversation, Tovmasyan – Ho Chi Minh, 20 December 1963, AVP RF, f. 079, op. 18, pa. 37, d. 8, pp. 159–161.

59 Record of conversation, Tovmasyan – Gerold, 16 November 1963, AVP RF, f. 079, op. 18, p. 37, d. 8, p. 72.

60 Ibid., p. 74.

61 King C. Chen, 'Hanoi's Three Decisions and the Escalation of the Vietnam War', *Political Science Quarterly*, 90 (2), 1975.

62 Qiang Zhai, *China and the Vietnam Wars*, p. 125. Quotation marks from the original text.

63 Record of conversation, Tovmasyan – Dang Kim Xiang, DRV deputy minister of economy, 17 January 1964, AVP RF, f. 079, op. 19, pa. 40, d. 6, p. 16.

64 Ibid., p. 22.

65 Record of conversation, Tovmasyan – Ho Chi Minh, Le Duan, Pham Van Dong and Xuan Thuy, 25 December 1963, AVP RF, f. 079, op. 18, pa. 37, d. 8, pp. 164–165. According to Tovmasyan, Truong Chinh was also supposed to participate during the lunch, but the table was only set for seven people, so there was no seat for him and he had to leave.

66 Duiker, William J., *Ho Chi Minh: A Life*, New York: Hyperion, 2000, p. 537.

67 Duiker's emphasis on the fact that the North Vietnamese were eager not to completely alienate the Soviets, in spite of preference for the Chinese strategy by the majority of the Lao Dong leaders, coincides well with findings in Soviet foreign ministry files. If this is true, it gives increasing credit to the efforts of the local Soviet diplomacy in Hanoi that upheld a working relationship with the North Vietnamese authorities, even at a time when leaders in Moscow displayed less interest for developments in Vietnam. See Duiker, *Ho Chi Minh*, p. 537.

68 The inclusion of To Huu in the delegation was significant as he had made his debut as a political figure during the 9th Plenum when he publicly attacked the Soviet revisionism. See Duiker, *Ho Chi Minh*, p. 538.

69 Qiang Zhai, *China and the Vietnam Wars*, pp. 126–127. Quotation marks in the original text on p. 127.

70 Tovmasyan's diary. 'Le Duan's statements before departure to Moscow'. 26 January 1964, AVP RF, f. 079, op. 19, pa. 40, d. 6, p. 26.

71 Record of conversation, Tovmasyan – Shedelevski, 28 February 1964, AVP RF, f. 079, op. 19, pa. 40, d. 6, p. 98.

72 Ibid.

73 Record of conversation, Tovmasyan – Nguyen Van Vinh, 26 February 1964, AVP RF, f. 079, op. 19, pa. 40, d. 6, pp. 80–90.

74 Qiang Zhai, *China and the Vietnam Wars*, pp. 127–128; and Gaiduk, Ilya V., *The Soviet Union and the Vietnam War*, Chicago: Ivan R. Dee, 1996b, p. 10.

75 Gaiduk, Ilya V., *Confronting Vietnam. Soviet Policy toward the Indochina Conflict, 1954–1963*, Stanford: Stanford University Press, 2003, pp. 203–204.

76 This is based on an analysis of available records of conversations between Soviet embassy officials and Vietnamese leaders during 1963. Some might argue that the Vietnamese assertions of their loyalty to the Soviet Union were pure propaganda. However, the frequency of these assertions and the fact that the Soviet Union, in the end, was the only reliable partner in a war against the Americans support this view. Similar arguments on how Vietnamese leaders were reluctant to cut off all contact with the Soviet Union have been presented in Duiker 2000: 537–538.

77 Comments made by Pham Van Dong to Marek Thee, Polish representative in the ICC Laos, in December 1963. See AVP RF, f. 079, op. 18, pa. 39, d. 24, p. 112; for Pham Van Dong's statement see record of conversation, Tovmasyan – Pham Van Dong, 16 January 1964, AVP RF, f. 079, op. 19, pa. 40, d. 6, p. 14. Quotation marks in the original. After expressing that the conditions were not yet ripe, Pham Van Dong refused to talk more about the subject.

78 Record of conversation, Privalov – Gerold, 11 June 1964, AVP RF, f. 079, op. 19, pa. 40, d. 7, p. 60.

79 Record of conversation, Privalov – Pham Van Dong, 18 June 1964, AVP RF, f. 079, op. 19, pa. 40, d. 7, p. 91.

80 Qiang Zhai, *China and the Vietnam Wars*, p. 132; and Gaiduk, *The Soviet Union and the Vietnam War*, pp. 12–13.

81 Record of conversation, Privalov – Le Duc Tho, 10 August 1964, AVP RF, f. 079, op. 19, pa. 40, d. 7, pp. 202–206; and record of conversation, Privalov – Pham Van Dong, 15 August 1964, AVP RF, f. 079, op. 19, pa. 40, d. 7, p. 216.

82 For hints on improvements in the Soviet–Vietnamese relationship, see record of conversation, Privalov – Bibov, DDR chargé d'affaires in Hanoi, 16 July 1964, AVP RF, f. 079, op. 19, pa. 40, d. 7, pp. 141–142; and record of conversation, Privalov – Pham Van Dong, 9 August 1964, AVP RF, f. 079, op. 19, pa. 40, d. 7, pp. 195–197.

83 Record of conversation, Privalov – Pham Van Dong, 9 August 1964, AVP RF, f. 079, op. 19, pa. 40, d. 7, p. 197.

84 For the exchanges on the U Thanth issue, see record of conversation, Privalov – Pham Van Dong, 21 August 1964, AVP RF, f. 079, op. 19, pa. 40, d. 7, pp. 233–234; and record of conversation, Privalov – Hoang Van Tien, 29 August 1964, AVP RF, f. 079, op. 19, pa. 40, d. 7, p. 242. When delivering the answer to the U Thanth information to Privalov, the exchange was so secret that everyone except Privalov and Tien had to leave the room. Tien also underlined that he had written the answer himself.

85 These Vietnamese concerns were referred to by the DDR ambassador to the DRV, Bergold. See record of conversation, Privalov – Bergold, 17 September 1964, AVP RF, f. 79, op. 19, pa. 40, d. 8, pp. 12–15.

86 Record of conversation, Deputy Foreign Minister Lapin – DRV Ambassador to the Soviet Union Nguyen Van Kinh, 23 December 1964, AVP RF, f. 079, op. 19, pa. 40, d. 4, p. 6.

Conclusion: Changing Alliances

1 Record of conversation, Gromyko – Nguyen Duy Trinh, 11 April 1965, AVP RF, f. 079, op. 20, pa. 45, d. 2, p. 13.

2 Record of conversation, Shcherbakov – Pham Van Dong, 19 February 1965, AVP RF, f. 079, op. 20, pa. 45, d. 4, p. 53.

3 Record of conversation, Shcherbakov – Pham Van Dong, 3 March 1965, AVP RF, f. 079, op. 20, pa. 45, d. 4, pp. 63–64.

4 Record of conversation, Chervonenko – Liu Zhao, 23 March 1965, AVP RF, f. 0100, op. 58, pa. 516, d. 5, p. 46.

5 Ibid., pp. 48–49.

6 Ibid.

7 Record of conversation, Gromyko – Nguyen Duy Trinh, 11 April 1965, AVP RF, f. 079, op. 20, pa. 45, d. 2, pp. 12–13.

8 Qiang Zhai, *China and the Vietnam Wars, 1950–1975*, Chapel Hill: University of North Carolina Press, 2000, p. 17.

9 For the classical interpretations of Moscow's view on the Geneva settlements, see, for example, Randle, Robert F., *Geneva 1954, The Settlement of the Indochinese War*, Princeton, NJ: Princeton University Press, 1969; Nogee, J.L. and Donaldson R.H., *Soviet Foreign Policy since World War II* (3rd edn), New York: Pergamon Press, 1988, pp. 110–111; Cameron, Allan W., 'The Soviet Union and Vietnam: The Origins of Involvement' in W. Raymond Duncan (ed.), *Soviet Policy in Developing Countries*, Waltham: Ginn-Blaisdell, 1970, pp. 189–196; Qiang Zhai, 'China and the Geneva Conference of 1954', *The China Quarterly* (129), 1992, p. 113. See also Olsen, Mari, 'Solidarity and National Revolution. The Soviet Union and the Vietnamese Communists, 1954–1960', *Defence Studies 4/97*, Oslo: Norwegian Institute for Defence Studies, 1997, Chapter 1.

10 According to Nigel Gould-Davies an ideologically driven state would seek to *replicate its domestic system*, while in a similar situation a traditional security-seeking state would attempt to expand their territory. The expansion of ideological states is thus more *geoideological* than geopolitical. Likewise, ideological states define security in terms of the expansion of their own domestic system, and threat in terms of the expansion of their adversary's domestic system. See 'Rethinking the Role of Ideology in International Politics during the Cold War', *Journal of Cold War Studies*, Vol. 1, No. 1 (Winter 1999), pp. 101–104.

11 For a detailed analysis of Soviet perceptions of the change in DRV's Southern strategy, see also Olsen, 'Solidarity', Chapter 5.

12 See e.g. Westad, Odd Arne, Chen Jian, Stein Tønnesson, Nguyen Vu Tung and James G. Hershberg (eds), '77 Conversations between Chinese and Foreign Leaders on the Wars in Indochina, 1964–1977', *CWIHP Working Paper No. 22*, 1998, pp. 142–143. A similar notion can be found in Ilya Gaiduk's latest work, where he talks about Geneva primarily as a way to secure peace in Southeast Asia and prevent American intervention, rather than a way to safeguard the future of a fellow Communist state exemplified by the Soviet view on Vietnamese partition as unproblematic. See Confronting Vietnam. Soviet Policy toward the Indochina Conflict, 1954–1963, Stanford: Stanford University Press, 2003, Chapter 3 and Conclusion.

13 Qiang Zhai, *China and the Vietnam Wars*, p. 111.

14 However, that question cannot be answered satisfactorily until we gain full access to Vietnamese foreign policy archives.

15 According to Marilyn Young, Washington assimilated the war in Vietnam 'in the worldwide fight against Communism in general and its Asian branch in particular'. See *The Vietnam Wars, 1945–1990*, New York: HarperPerennial. 1991, p. 30.

16 Zubok, Vladislav and Constantine Pleshakov, *Inside the Kremlin's Cold War. From Stalin to Khrushev*, Cambridge, Mass: Harvard University Press, 1996, pp. 12–15; Vladislav Zubok, 'Stalin's Plans and Russian Archives', *Diplomatic History*, 21 (Spring 1997), p. 303.

17 Macdonald, Douglas J., 'Formal Ideologies in the Cold War: Toward a Framework for Empirical Analysis', in Odd Arne Westad (ed.), *Reviewing the Cold War: Approaches, Interpretations, Theory*, London: Frank Cass Publishers, 2000, pp. 183–184.

18 Douglas J. Macdonald suggests that in order to explain how and why states act, both ideational and structural analyses are necessary. Ultimately, the study of formal ideology, intersecting with structural considerations, offers an efficient and relatively economical means to do so. See 'Formal Ideologies', p. 194.

Appendix 1: Politburo and Secretariat of the Lao Dong Central Committee

1 Attached list, 11 June 1954, AVP RF, f. 079, op. 9, pa. 6, d. 7.
2 Record of conversation, Zimyanin – Ho Chi Minh, 7 September 1956, AVP RF, f. 079, op. 11, pa. 13, d. 6, p. 93.
3 Record of conversation, A.M. Popov – Ho Chi Minh, June 1957, AVP RF, f. 079, op. 11, pa. 13, d. 8, pp. 93–99.
4 Record of conversation, Zimyanin – Nguyen Duy Trinh, 12–14 June 1957, AVP RF, f. 079, op. 12, pa. 17, d. 5, pp. 220–235.
5 Record of conversation, Sokolov – Le Duc Tho, 6 June 1959, AVP RF, f. 079, op. 14, pa. 23, d. 5, pp. 130–133.
6 Record of conversation, Tovmasyan – Ho Chi Minh, Le Duan, Pham Van Dong and Xuan Thuy, 25 December 1963, AVP RF, f. 079, op. 18, pa. 37, d. 8, pp. 164–165.

Appendix 2: Economic assistance and specialists from the Socialist camp to the DRV, 1955–1962[1]

1 Long-term credits and non-refundable aid from other socialist countries to the Democratic Republic of Vietnam (in million roubles), total sums from 1955 to 1962. Memorandum by the Southeast Asia Department in MID, 3 December 1963, AVP RF, f. 079, op. 18, pa. 39, d. 24, pp. 58–79.

Bibliography

Adelman, Jonathan R. and Deborah A. Palmieri, *The Dynamics of Soviet Foreign Policy*, New York: Harper and Row Publishers, 1989.

Anderson, David L., *Trapped By Success. The Eisenhower Administration and Vietnam, 1953–61*, New York: Colombia University Press, 1991.

Ang Cheng Guan, *Vietnamese Communists' Relations with China and the Second Indochina Conflict, 1956–1962*, Jefferson, NC: McFarland & Company, Inc., 1997.

——, *The Vietnam War from the Other Side. The Vietnamese Communists' Perspective*, London: RoutledgeCurzon, 2002.

Boukharkin, Igor V., 'Moscow and Ho Chi Minh, 1946–1969', paper presented at the *CWIHP conference* 'New Evidence on the Cold War in Asia', Hong Kong, January 1996.

Bradley, Mark Philip, *Imagining Vietnam and America. The Making of Post-Colonial Vietnam, 1919–1950*, Chapel Hill: University of North Carolina Press, 2000.

Brigham, Robert K., *Guerrilla Diplomacy: The NLF's Foreign Relations and the Viet Nam War*, Itacha: Cornell University Press, 1999.

Buttinger, Joseph, *Vietnam. A Political History*, London: Andre Detsch, 1969.

Cameron, Allan W., 'The Soviet Union and Vietnam: The Origins of Involvement' in W. Raymond Duncan (ed.), *Soviet Policy in Developing Countries*, Waltham: Ginn-Blaisdell, 1970.

Chang, Gordon H., *Friends and Enemies. The United States, China, and the Soviet Union, 1948–1972*, Stanford, CA: Stanford University Press, 1990.

Chen Jian, 'China and the First Indo-China War, 1950–54', *The China Quarterly, 1993* (133), 1993.

——, *China's Road to the Korean War*, New York: Columbia University Press, 1994.

——, 'China's Involvement in the Vietnam War, 1964–69', *The China Quarterly, 1995* (142), 1995.

——, *Mao's China and the Cold War*, Chapel Hill: University of North Carolina Press, 2001.

——, 'China and the Indochina Settlement at the Geneva Conference of 1954', paper presented at the Symposium on 'The First Indochina War: Nationalism, Colonialism, and the Cold War', 1–3 November 2002, at the Lyndon B. Johnson Library and Museum, Austin Texas, 2002.

Chen Jian and Yang Kuisong, 'Chinese Politics and the Collapse of the Sino-Soviet Alliance' Westad, Odd Arne (ed.), *Brothers in Arms: The Rise and Fall of the Sino-Soviet Alliance, 1945–1963*, Stanford, 1998.

Cohen, Warren I., *America's Response to China: A History of Sino-American Relations*, New York: Columbia University Press, 1990.

Diplomaticheskii Slovar', Vols I–III, Moskva: Izdatel'stvo 'Nauka', 1986.

Dommen, Arthur J., *Conflict in Laos: The Politics of Neutralization*, New York: Praeger, 1965.
Duiker, William J., *The Communist Road to Power in Vietnam*, Boulder, CO: Westview, 1981.
——, 'Communism and Nationalism' in Robert J. McMahon (ed.) *Major Problems in the History of the Vietnam War*, Lexington, MA: D.C. Heath and Company, 1990.
——, *Sacred War. Nationalism and Revolution in a Divided Vietnam*, New York: McGraw-Hill, 1995.
——, *Ho Chi Minh: A Life*, New York: Hyperion, 2000.
Fall, Bernard B., *The Two Viet-Nams. A Political and Military Analysis*, London and Dunmow: Pall Mall Press, 1963.
——, *Hell in a Very Small Place: the Siege of Dien Bien Phu*. London, 1967.
Fleron, Frederic J. and Eric P. Hoffmann, 'Introduction' in Frederic J. Fleron, Eric Hoffmann and Robbin Laird (eds), *Soviet Foreign Policy: Classic and Contemporary Issues*, New York: Aldine de Gruyter, 1991.
Freedman, Lawrence, *Kennedy's Wars. Berlin, Cuba, Laos, and Vietnam*, New York and Oxford: Oxford University Press, 2000.
Gaddis, John L., *We Now Know. Rethinking Cold War History*, Oxford: Claredon Press, 1997.
Gaiduk, Ilya V., 'The Vietnam War and Soviet–American Relations, 1964–1973: New Russian Evidence', *Cold War International History Project (CWIHP) Bulletin*, Winter 1995/1996 (6–7) Washington, DC: Woodrow Wilson International Center for Scholars, 1996a.
——, *The Soviet Union and the Vietnam War*, Chicago: Ivan R. Dee, 1996b.
——, *Confronting Vietnam. Soviet Policy toward the Indochina Conflict, 1954–1963*, Stanford: Stanford University Press, 2003.
Gittings, John, *Survey of the Sino-Soviet Dispute, 1963–1967*, London, 1968.
Goncharov, Sergei N., John W. Lewis, and Xue Litai, *Uncertain Partners: Stalin, Mao, and the Korean War*, Stanford, 1993.
Goscha, Christopher E., 'Vietnam or Indochina? Contesting Concepts of Space in Vietnamese Nationalism, 1887–1954', *Nias Reports, No. 28*, Nordic Institute for Asian Studies, 1995.
——, *Thailand and the Southeast Asian Networks of the Vietnamese Revolution 1885–1954*, London: Curzon Press, 1999.
——, 'La Survie Diplomatique de la RDVN: Le Doute Sovietique Efface par la Confiance Chinoise (1945–1950)?' *Approches – Asie*, No. 19, 2003.
Gould-Davies, Nigel, 'Rethinking the Role of Ideology in International Politics during the Cold War', *Journal of Cold War Studies*, Vol. 1, No. 1 (Winter 1999).
Hall, David K., 'The Laos Neutralization Agreement, 1962' in Alexander L. George, Philip J. Farley and Alexander Dallin (eds), *U.S. – Soviet Security Cooperation. Achievements, Failures, Lessons*, New York: Oxford University Press, 1988.
Herring, George C., *America's Longest War: The United States and Vietnam, 1950–1975*, New York: John Wiley & Sons, 1979.
Honey, P.J., *Communism in North Vietnam*, Cambridge, MA: MIT Press, 1963.
Huynh Kim Khanh, *Vietnamese Communism: 1925–1945*, Itacha: Cornell University Press, 1982.
Jones, Peter and Sian Kevill (comps.), Alan J. Day (ed.), *China and the Soviet Union 1949–1984*, Harlow: Longman, 1985.
Joyaux, Francois, *La Chine et le règlement du premier conflit d'Indochine (Genève 1954)*, Paris: Publications de la Sorbonne, 1979.
Kahin, George M., *Intervention: How America became Involved in Vietnam*, New York: Knopf, 1986.

Karnow, Stanley, *Vietnam: A History*, London: Pimlico, 1991.

King C. Chen, 'Hanoi's Three Decisions and the Escalation of the Vietnam War', *Political Science Quarterly*, 90 (2), 1975.

Kolko, Gabriel, *Anatomy of a War*, New York: Pantheon Books, 1985.

Kort, Michael, *The Soviet Colossus. A History of the USSR*, London and New York: Routledge, 1990.

Kutler, Stanley I. (ed.), *Encyclopedia of the Vietnam War*, New York: Charles Scribner's Sons, 1996.

Lacouture, Jean, *Ho Chi Minh*, Trondhjem: Tiden, 1968.

LaFeber, Walter, *America, Russia, and the Cold War, 1945–1996*, New York: McGraw-Hill, 1997.

Lall, Arthur, *How Communist China Negotiates*, New York: Columbia University Press, 1968.

Langer, Paul F. and Joseph J. Zasslov, *North Vietnam and the Pathet Lao. Partners in the Struggle for Laos*, Cambridge, MA: Harvard University Press, 1970.

Lankov, A.N., 'Krisis 1956 goda v KNDR', *Vostok. Afro-asiatskie obshchestva: Istoria i sovremennost*, 1995 (4).

Light, Margot (ed.), *Troubled Friendships: Moscow's Third World Ventures*, London: British Academic Press, 1993.

Li Haiwen, *Restoring Peace in Indochina at the Geneva Conference*, paper presented at the The Cold War International History Project conference 'The Cold War in Asia', at Hong Kong University, January 1996.

Lockhart, Greg, *Nation in Arms. The Origins of the People's Army of Vietnam*, Sydney: Allen & Unwin, 1989.

Lundestad, Geir, *The American 'Empire' and Other Studies of U.S. Foreign Policy in a Comparative Perspective*, Oxford: Oxford University Press, 1990.

Luu Van Loi, *50 Years of Vietnamese Diplomacy, 1945–1995, Vol. 1 (1945–1975)*, Hanoi: The Gioi Publishers, 2000.

Macdonald, Douglas J., 'Formal Ideologies in the Cold War: Toward a Framework for Empirical Analysis', in Odd Arne Westad (ed.), *Reviewing the Cold War: Approaches, Interpretations, Theory*, London: Frank Cass Publishers, 2000.

McLane, Charles B., *Soviet Strategies in Southeast Asia. An Exploration of Eastern Policies under Lenin and Stalin*, Princeton, NJ: Princeton University Press, 1966.

McMahon, Robert J. (ed.), *Major Problems in the History of the Vietnam War*, Lexington, MA: D.C. Heath and Company, 1990.

Mansourov, Alexandre Y., 'Stalin, Mao, Kim, and China's Decision to enter the Korean War, September 16–October 15, 150: New Evidence from the Russian Archives', *Cold War International History Project (CWIHP) Bulletin (6–7)*, Washington, DC: Woodrow Wilson International Center for Scholars, Winter 1995/1996.

Marr, David, *Vietnam 1945: The Quest for Power*, Berkeley: University of California Press, 1995.

Mastny, Vojtech, *The Cold War and Soviet Insecurity. The Stalin Years*, New York: Oxford University Press, 1996.

Moise, Edwin E., *Land Reform in China and North Vietnam: Consolidating the Revolution at the Village Level*, Chapel Hill, NC: University of North Carolina Press, 1983.

Morris, Stephen J., 'The Soviet–Chinese–Vietnamese Triangle in the 1970's: The View from Moscow', *CWIHP Working Paper No. 25*, 1999a.

——, *Why Vietnam Invaded Cambodia. Political Culture and the Causes of War*, Stanford, CA: Stanford University Press, 1999b.

Nguyen Vu Tung, 'Coping with the United States: Hanoi's Search for an Effective Strategy' in Peter Lowe (ed.), *The Vietnam War*, London: Macmillan, 1998.

Niu Jun, 'The Origins of the Sino-Soviet Alliance' in O.A. Westad (ed.), *Brothers in Arms. The Rise and Fall of the Sino-Soviet Alliance, 1945–1963*, Washington, DC: Woodrow Wilson Center Press, 1998.

Nogee, J.L. and Donaldson, R.H., *Soviet Foreign Policy since World War II*, (3rd edn), New York: Pergamon Press, 1988.

Olsen, Mari, 'Solidarity and National Revolution. The Soviet Union and the Vietnamese Communists, 1954–1960', *Defence Studies 4/97*, Oslo: Norwegian Institute for Defence Studies, 1997.

Pike, Douglas. 'The USSR and Vietnam' in Robert H. Donaldson (ed.), *The Soviet Union in the Third World: Successes and Failure*, Boulder, CO: Westview, 1981.

——, *Vietnam and the Soviet Union: Anatomy of an Alliance*, Boulder and London: Westview Press, 1987.

Porter, Bruce D., *The USSR in Third World Conflicts. Soviet Arms and Diplomacy in Local Wars 1945–1980*, Cambridge: Cambridge University Press, 1984.

Qiang Zhai, 'China and the Geneva Conference of 1954', *The China Quarterly* (129), 1992.

——, *China and the Vietnam Wars, 1950–1975*, Chapel Hill: University of North Carolina Press, 2000.

Quinn-Judge, Sophie, *Ho Chi Minh: The Missing Years, 1919–1941*, Berkeley: University of California Press, 2003.

Randle, Robert F., *Geneva 1954, The Settlement of the Indochinese War*, Princeton, NJ: Princeton University Press, 1969.

Roberts, Geoffrey, *The Soviet Union in World Politics. Coexistence, Revolution and Cold War, 1945–1991*, London: Routledge, 1999.

Ruane, Kevin, *War and Revolution in Vietnam, 1930–75*, London: UCL Press, 1998.

Smith, Ralph B., *An International History of the Vietnam War: Vol. I, Revolution versus Containment, 1955–61*, New York: St. Martin's Press, 1983.

——, *An International History of the Vietnam War: Vol. II, The Struggle for South-East Asia, 1961–1965*, London: Macmillan, 1985.

Smith, Tony, 'New Bottles for New Wine: A Pericentric Framework for the Study of the Cold War', *Diplomatic History*, Vol. 24, No. 4 (Fall 2000).

Smyser, William R., *The Independent Vietnamese: Vietnamese Communism Between Russia and China, 1956–1969*, Athens, OH: Papers in International Studies, Southeast Asia Series (55), 1980.

Sokolov, Anatolii A., 'From the History of Vietnam Studies in Russia' in *Traditional Vietnam. A Collection of Articles*, Moscow, 1996.

Spence, Jonathan D., *The Search for Modern China*, New York and London: W.W. Norton & Company, 1990.

Thakur, Ramesh and Carlyle A. Thayer, *Soviet Relations with India and Vietnam*, London: MacMillan, 1992.

Thayer, Carlyle A., *War By Other Means. National Liberation and Revolution in Viet-nam 1954–60*, Sydney: Allen and Unwin, 1989.

Thee, Marek, *Notes of a Witness. Laos and the Second Indochinese War*, New York: Vintage Books, 1973.

The Great Vanguard of the Vietnamese People. The History of the Communist Party of Vietnam, Moscow: Polizdat, 1981.

Tønnesson, Stein, *The Outbreak of War in Indochina 1946*, Oslo: PRIO Report 3, 1984.

——, *The Vietnamese Revolution of 1945. Roosevelt, Ho Chi Minh and de Gaulle in a World at War*, London: Sage, 1991.

Tréglodé, Benoît de, 'Premier contacts entre le Viet Nam et l'Union Sovietique (1947–1948). Noveaux documents des archives russes', *Approches – Asie*, No. 19, 1999.

Ulam, Adam B., *Expantion and Coexistence. Soviet Foreign Policy, 1917–1973* (2nd edn) Fort Worth: Holt, Rinehart and Winston, 1974.

Weathersby, Kathryn, 'Soviet Aims in Korea and the Origins of the Korean War, 1945–1950. New Evidence from Russian Archives', *Cold War International History Project Working Paper* 8, Washington, DC: Woodrow Wilson Center for Scholars, 1993.

——, 'New Russian Documents on the Cold War', *CWIHP Bulletin* 6–7, Washington, DC, Winter 1995/1996.

Westad, Odd Arne, 'Secrets of the Second World: The Russian Archives and the Reinterpretation of Cold War History', *Diplomatic History*, Vol. 21, No. 2 (Spring 1997).

—— (ed.), *Brothers in Arms: The Rise and Fall of the Sino-Soviet Alliance, 1945–1963*, Stanford, 1998.

——, 'The New International History of the Cold War: Three (Possible) Paradigms', *Diplomatic History*, Vol. 24, No. 4 (Fall 2000), 2000a.

—— (ed.), *Reviewing the Cold War: Approaches, Interpretations, Theory*, London: Frank Cass Publishers, 2000b.

Westad, Odd Arne, Chen Jian, Stein Tønnesson, Nguyen Vu Tung and James G. Hershberg (eds), '77 Conversations between Chinese and Foreign Leaders on the Wars in Indochina, 1964–1977', *CWIHP Working Paper No. 22*, 1998.

Wohlforth, William C., 'A Certain Idea of Science. How International Relations Theory Avoids the New Cold War History', *Journal of Cold War Studies*, Vol. 1, No. 2 (Spring 1999).

Yang Kuisong, 'Changes in Mao Zedong's Attitude toward the Indochina War, 1949–1973', *CWIHP Working Paper No. 34*, Washington, DC, February 2002.

Young, Marilyn B., *The Vietnam Wars, 1945–1990*, New York: HarperPerennial, 1991.

Zagoria, Donald S., *The Sino-Soviet Conflict, 1956–1961*, Princeton, NJ: Princeton University Press, 1962.

——, *Vietnam Triangle: Moscow, Peking, Hanoi*, New York: Pegasus, 1967.

Zubok, Vladislav, 'Soviet Intelligence and the Cold War: The 'Small' Committee of Information, 1952–53', *CWIHP Working Paper No. 4*, 1992.

——, 'Stalin's Plans and Russian Archives', *Diplomatic History*, 21 (Spring 1997).

Zubok, Vladislav and Constantine Pleshakov, *Inside the Kremlin's Cold War. From Stalin to Khrushev*, Cambridge, MA: Harvard University Press, 1996.

Index

August Revolution   1–3
Autumn border campaign (1950)   22–3

Bangkok
   'Representational Office of the
      Democratic Republic of
      Vietnam'   2, 12
   Vietnamese diplomatic initiatives in
      Moscow and   5–11
Berlin conference   29–30
Brothers in Arms: The Rise and Fall of the
   Sino-Soviet Alliance, 1945–63
   [Westad (ed.)]   xvi

Calcutta Conference (1948)   4, 7–8
Central Office for South Vietnam
   (COSVN)   90
China
   Dien Bien Phu campaign   36–8
   military assistance to DRV
      22–6
   Moscow and Communist victory
      in   14–16
   preparations for the Geneva
      conference   30–1
   readiness to assist DRV   17
   representation in DRV and Soviet
      18–19
   responsibility for colonial liberation
      struggles in Asia   19–20
China and the Vietnam Wars, 1950–75
   (Qiang Zhai)   xvi
Chinese Military Advisory Group
   (CMAG)   22–4, 37, 54
Chinese Political Advisory Group
   (CPAG)   23–4
Cold War International History Project
   (CWIHP)   xvi
Cominform   5–6

Democratic Republic of Vietnam
   approaches to America and Soviet
      Union   3
   China versus Soviet representation
      in   18–19
   Chinese aid   11
   Chinese military assistance   22–6
   Chinese recognition   16–17
   Dien Bien Phu campaign   36–8
   discussions and misunderstandings
      over exchange of
      representatives   18–21
   establishment, 1
   focus of Soviet foreign ministry   50
   Ho Chi Minh as President   1, 2–3
   importance of recognition from China
      and Soviet   20
   land reform   62–6
   recognition and new challenges   26–7
   recognition as a legitimate
      government   15–21
   recognition from the Communist
      world   15
   recognition of DRV as the legitimate
      government   16–21
   renewed Soviet interest in   11–12
   role of Bangkok   2–3
   search for allies   1–4
   Sino-Soviet assistance   77
   Sino-Soviet skepticism towards use of
      foreign specialists   77–8
   Soviet economic and military
      assistance   50, 52
   Soviet military cooperation   53–4
   Soviet recognition   17–18
   transport assistance from Soviet
      51–2
   withdrawal of Chinese military
      assistance   54–5

Franco-Vietnamese War　4, 21–6
French Communist Party (PCF)　6

Gaiduk, Ilya V.　xiv–xv, 131
Geneva agreement and Sino-Soviet
　　relations　55–8
Geneva conference (1954)
　　and future Soviet–Vietnamese
　　　　relations　44–7
　　Geneva agreements (July 20, 1954)　29
　　Indochina phase (May 8, 1954)　29
　　negotiating in the　38–44
　　outcome of　44–7
　　preparation for the conference　29–35
　　settlement in Indochina
　　　　problem　44
　　Soviet's promotion and support to
　　　　China　29–30
　　the Final Declaration　44
Geneva conference on Laos
　　(1961–62)　97–100

Ho Chi Minh
　　active member of PCF　11
　　as president of DRV　1
　　communication between Stalin and　25
　　links with the communist world　3
　　meetings with Mao and Stalin
　　　　14–15
　　search for allies　1–3
　　secret trip to the Nineteenth Congress of
　　　　CPSU　25
　　trip to Soviet　14–15

Inside the Kremlin's Cold (Zubok and
　　Pleshakov)　xvi
International Control Commission
　　(ICC)　33

Laos
　　assistance to　108–11
　　civil war in　95–7
　　DRV, China and Soviet's interest on　94
　　Geneva conference to discuss
　　　　97–100
　　negotiations in Geneva　100–5
　　temporary setback　105–8
Liu Shaoqi
　　discussion with Stalin about future
　　　　relationship between Moscow and
　　　　Beijing　xiii
Luo Guibo
　　China's representative to Vietnam　18
　　role in CPAG　23–4

Mao Zedong　13, 14–15
　　first official visit abroad　14
　　meeting with Stalin (October 1,
　　　　1949)　13
　　meetings with Ho and Stalin　14–15
　　recognition of DRV　16–17
Mao's China and the Cold War (Chen
　　Jian)　xvi
'maximum plan'　57–8
Mendès-France, Pierre　40–1
'minimum plan'　57–8
Molotov, Vyacheslav　20, 30, 32, 38–9,
　　41, 43, 51, 142

National Liberation Army　22
Nguyen Long Bang　19, 24–5

'peace offensive'　29
People's Army of Vietnam (PAVN)　23, 53
'rectification of errors campaign'　64–5
'regroupees'　81

Sino-Soviet Treaty of Friendship, Alliance
　　and Mutual Assistance　14, 16, 17
Southeast Asia Treaty Organization
　　(SEATO)　49
Southeast Asian Youth Conference see
　　Calcutta Conference (1948)
Soviet Strategies in Southeast Asia
　　(Charles B. Mclane)
　　shift of focus from Europe to Asia　4
　　views on colonial strategies of Soviet
　　　　Union (1947–50)　4
Soviet Union
　　approaches from DRV　3–4
　　attempts to improve Soviet–Vietnamese
　　　　relations　121–5
　　Chinese representation in　18–19
　　colonial strategies　4
　　cooperation and coordination　141–5
　　establishing relationship with
　　　　Vietnam　139–41
　　from disinterest to active support　133–5
　　impact on the French because of
　　　　recognition of DRV　20–1
　　information on internal developments in
　　　　Vietnam　22
　　information on the developments of the
　　　　Franco-Vietnamese War　22
　　leverage and ideology　145–9
　　passive role in relations with DRV　4
　　perceptions of China in Vietnam　114–18
　　preparations for the Geneva
　　　　conference　32–5

promotion of China in Geneva
conference 29–30
relations with Europe and United
States 4–5
renewed interest in Asia 11–12
strategies in Southeast Asia 4–5
success in the Geneva conference 45
and the Communist victory in
China 14–16
and the result of the 9th Plenum of Lao
Dong 129–32
tougher frontlines within the communist
camp 118–21
Vietnam's changing alliances 136–9
Vietnam's turn to China 125–9
see also Stalin, Joseph
Stalin, Joseph
discussion with Liu Shaoqi about future
relationship between Moscow and
Beijing xiii
meeting with Ho Chi Minh 15
meeting with Mao 13
meeting with Mao Zedong
(October 1, 1949) 13
meetings with Ho and Mao 14–15
recognition of DRV 16–17
support to CCP 14
State of Vietnam 29

Thach, Dr Pham Ngoc 6–7
American support initiatives 2–3
meeting with Kulazhenkov (1947) 6

Tran Van Giau 3–4, 5
Tréglodé, Benoit de
formative years of Soviet–Vietnamese
relationship xv–xvi
'two-camp' thesis 5, 7

*Vietnamese Communists' Relations with
China and the Second Indochina
Conflict, 1956–62* (Ang Cheng
Guan) xvi
Vietnamese reunification plans
(1957–61)
end of diplomacy 92–3
Lao Dong – policy on
reunification 79–84
meditiating emerging Sino-Soviet
conflict 88–90
Moscow and new Southern
strategy 90–2
new Southern strategy 84–8
North Vietnam and South
Vietnam 73–5
renewed interest in the Geneva
Agreement 76–7
Sino-Soviet cooperation 77–9
Vietnamese Workers Party (VWP)
23, 37

Zhdanov, Andrei
speech at founding of Cominform 5
'two-camp' thesis 5, 7, 8
Zhou Enlai 14, 24, 30–1